Frommer's

San &
Austin
day BY day™

1st Edition

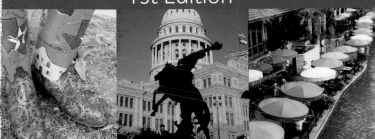

by Janis Turk

WILEY

John Wiley & Sons Canada, Ltd.

Contents

Published by:

John Wiley & Sons Canada, Ltd.

6045 Freemont Blvd.

Mississauga, ON L5R 4J3

ISBN 978-0-470-67780-3
Editor: Gene Shannon
Production Editor: Pamela Vokey
Project Coordinator: Lynsey Stanford
Editorial Assistant: Katie Wolsley
Photo Editor: Photo Affairs, Inc.
Cartographer: Lohnes + Wright
Vice President, Publishing Services: Karen Bryan
Production by Wiley Indianapolis Composition Services

For information on our other products and services or to obtain technical support, please contact our Customer Care Department within the U.S. at 877/762-2974, outside the U.S. at 317/572-3993 or fax 317/572-4002.

Wiley also publishes its books in a variety of electronic formats. Some content that appears in print may not be available in electronic formats.

Manufactured in China

5   4   3   2   1

A Note from the Editorial Director

Organizing your time. That's what this guide is all about.

Other guides give you long lists of things to see and do and then expect you to fit the pieces together. The Day by Day guides are different. These guides tell you the best of everything, and then they show you how to see it *in the smartest, most time-efficient way*. Our authors have designed detailed itineraries organized by time, neighborhood, or special interest. And each tour comes with a bulleted map that takes you from stop to stop.

Hoping to while away an afternoon on San Antonio's River Walk, or catch some of Austin's legendary live music? Planning to dine at some of Austin's famous barbeque joints, or tour the historic Alamo? Whatever your interest or schedule, the Day by Days give you the smartest routes to follow. Not only do we take you to the top attractions, hotels, and restaurants, but we also help you access those special moments that locals get to experience— those "finds" that turn tourists into travelers.

The Day by Days are also your top choice if you're looking for one complete guide for all your travel needs. The best hotels and restaurants for every budget, the greatest shopping values, the wildest nightlife—it's all here.

Why should you trust our judgment? Because our authors personally visit each place they write about. They're an independent lot who say what they think and would never include places they wouldn't recommend to their best friends. They're also open to suggestions from readers. If you'd like to contact them, please send your comments our way at feedback@frommers.com, and we'll pass them on.

Enjoy your Day by Day guide—the most helpful travel companion you can buy. And have the trip of a lifetime.

Warm regards,

Kelly Regan

Kelly Regan, Editorial Director
Frommer's Travel Guides

About the Author

Janis Turk is an award-winning travel writer, photographer, and editor whose writing and photography have appeared in the *Chicago Tribune*, *Dallas Morning News*, and *San Antonio Express-News*, as well as United Airlines' *Hemispheres*, *Luxx Living*, and more. Ms. Turk also writes for Frommers.com and GoNomad.com. She is the co-author of *The Groom's Guidebook* (Skyhorse 2007), her prose appears in the anthology *Louisiana in Words* (Pelican 2007), and she has written travel guides on New Orleans and San Antonio. She is also a guest travel consultant appearing on the NBC-affiliate *San Antonio Living* show. Ms. Turk divides her time between Texas and the New Orleans French Quarter. She won the GoNomad award for Best Travel Writing 2009.

Acknowledgments

Special thanks to my editor, Gene Shannon, who was ever patient and instrumental in shaping this book. Many thanks to Marc Nadeau for being my best travel compadre, constant mentor, and supportive shoulder. Thanks to Danny Meldung and Katie Wolsley for help with photography and maps; Jacqueline Thayer for her immeasurable help; Robert French and Lynn Glenewinkel for their fine photography; and my mother Carolyn Turk and sister Carrie Schnoor, who always had great Austin answers. Big thanks to Michael Gaffney, Beverly Purcell Guerra, and Gerald Lair for advice on San Antonio. Thanks also to Gigi and Harry Benson for their encouragement. Most of all, I thank my patient family, Dan, Reid, Carrie, and Landin. This book is for Danny, who is infinitely understanding, supportive, and proud of me. I love him most of all for encouraging my wanderlust, for he knows his "softest whisper's louder than the highway's call to me."

An Additional Note

Please be advised that travel information is subject to change at any time—and this is especially true of prices. We therefore suggest that you write or call ahead for confirmation when making your travel plans. The authors, editors, and publisher cannot be held responsible for the experiences of readers while traveling. Your safety is important to us, however, so we encourage you to stay alert and be aware of your surroundings.

Star Ratings, Icons & Abbreviations

Every hotel, restaurant, and attraction listing in this guide has been ranked for quality, value, service, amenities, and special features using a **star-rating system.** Hotels, restaurants, attractions, shopping, and nightlife are rated on a scale of zero stars (recommended) to three stars (exceptional). In addition to the star-rating system, we also use a **kids** icon to point out the best bets for families. Within each tour, we recommend cafes, bars or restaurants where you can take a break. Each of these stops appears in a shaded box marked with a coffee cup–shaped bullet ☕ .

The following **abbreviations** are used for credit cards:

AE	American Express	DISC	Discover	V	Visa
DC	Diners Club	MC	MasterCard		

Frommers.com

Now that you have this guidebook to help you plan a great trip, visit our website at **www.frommers.com** for additional travel information on more than 4,000 destinations. We update features regularly to give you instant access to the most current trip-planning information available. At Frommers.com, you'll find scoops on the best airfares, lodging rates, and car rental bargains. You can even book your travel online through our reliable travel booking partners. Other popular features include:

- Online updates of our most popular guidebooks
- Vacation sweepstakes and contest giveaways
- Newsletters highlighting the hottest travel trends
- Podcasts, interactive maps, and up-to-the-minute events listings
- Opinionated blog entries by Arthur Frommer himself
- Online travel message boards with featured travel discussions

A Note on Prices

In the "Take a Break" and "Best Bets" sections of this book, we have used a system of dollar signs to show a range of costs for 1 night in a hotel (the price of a double-occupancy room) or the cost of an entree at a restaurant. Use the following table to decipher the dollar signs:

Cost	Hotels	Restaurants
$	under $100	under $10
$$	$100–$200	$10–$20
$$$	$200–$300	$20–$30
$$$$	$300–$400	$30–$40
$$$$$	over $400	over $40

An Invitation to the Reader

In researching this book, we discovered many wonderful places—hotels, restaurants, shops, and more. We're sure you'll find others. Please tell us about them, so we can share the information with your fellow travelers in upcoming editions. If you were disappointed with a recommendation, we'd love to know that, too. Please write to:

Frommer's San Antonio & Austin Day By Day, 1st Edition
John Wiley & Sons Canada, Ltd. • 6045 Freemont Blvd. • Mississauga, ON L5R 4J3

19 Favorite
Moments

19 Favorite **Moments**

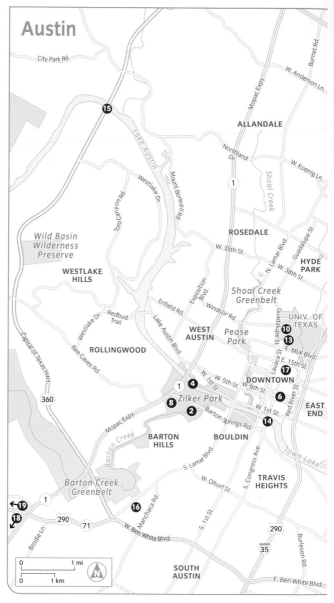

Austin

City Park Rd.

ALLANDALE

Lake Austin

Northland Dr.

W. Anderson Ln.

Burnet Rd.

W. Koenig Ln.

Shoal Creek

1

Mopac Expy.

Westlake Dr.

Mount Bonnell Rd.

15

ROSEDALE

W. 35th St.

Guadalupe St.

HYDE PARK

W. 38th St.

N. Lamar Blvd.

Wild Basin Wilderness Preserve

Tom Carlton Rd.

WESTLAKE HILLS

Shoal Creek Greenbelt

Westlake Dr.

Redbud Trail

Enfield Rd.

Exposition Blvd.

Windsor Rd.

WEST AUSTIN

Pease Park

UNIV. OF TEXAS

Guadalupe St.

10

ROLLINGWOOD

Bee Caves Rd.

Lake Austin Blvd.

E. MLK Blvd.

13

Lavaca St.

E. 15th St.

Capital of Texas Hwy.

360

1

4

W. 5th St.

W. 6th St.

17

DOWNTOWN

6

Red River St.

EAST END

8

Zilker Park

2

Barton Springs Rd.

W. 1st St.

14

Mopac Expy.

Barton Creek

BARTON HILLS

BOULDIN

Town Lake

S. Lamar Blvd.

W. Oltorf St.

S. Congress Ave.

S. 1st St.

TRAVIS HEIGHTS

Barton Creek Greenbelt

1

19

16

W. Manchaca Rd.

290

71

290

35

18

Brodie Ln.

W. Ben White Blvd.

Burleson Rd.

0   1 mi

0   1 km

SOUTH AUSTIN

E. Ben White Blvd.

Previous page: A cowboy rides in the Alamo.

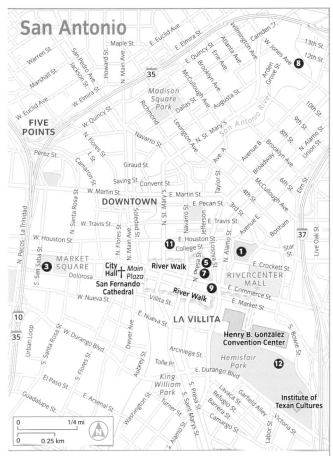

1 The Alamo
2 Barton Springs
3 Mi Tierra Café y Panadería
4 Lady Bird Lake
5 The Landing
6 6th Street
7 San Antonio River Walk
8 Zilker Tree
9 San Antonio River
10 University of Texas at Austin Tower
11 Majestic Theatre
12 Tower of the Americas
13 Harry Ransom Center
14 Ann W. Richards
   Congress Avenue Bridge
15 Pennybacker Bridge
16 Broken Spoke
17 Texas State Capitol
18 Salt Lick Bar-B-Que
19 Luckenbach, Texas (Hill Country)

The he Capital City of Austin and the Alamo City of San Antonio couldn't be more different, even though they're only a short drive (75 miles/121km) from one another. With the diverse cultures, traditions, and styles of each, it's hard to say which place I like best. But a song by Texas songwriter Gary P. Nunn called "You Ask Me What I Like about Texas" lists many things that locals love best about the Lone Star State, and most of them made my cut.

❶ Stroll past the Alamo. A shrine to Texas's fight for independence from Mexico, this 18th-century Spanish mission remains one of the most-treasured monuments in Texas. Visitors are often surprised by how small it is and how it sits engulfed by downtown San Antonio buildings. Its famous facade is lovely when lit at night. *See p 99.*

❷ Swim in the sacred waters of Barton Springs. The heart of Austin is a 1,000-foot-long (305m) natural spring-fed swimming pool in Zilker Park. Its main spring pumps about 27 million gallons a day and seems to pulsate like a heartbeat. Chilly waters don't deter devoted fans of the springs, which American Indians believed to have healing powers. *See p 69.*

❸ Enjoy a midnight mariachi serenade at Mi Tierra's. San Antonio has an Old Mexico flavor best enjoyed late at night over a plate of steaming enchiladas and icy salt-rimmed margaritas. The iconic all-night Mi Tierra Café y Panadería at El Mercado (Market Square) drips with

colorful lights, and strolling mariachis serenade guests. *See p 103.*

❹ Kayak Lady Bird Lake. Austin is a vibrant city, and a river runs through it—even though the part of the Colorado River flowing though town is called Lady Bird Lake. Locals still call it by its former name, Town Lake. Explore hike-and-bike trails, rent a kayak or canoe, or enjoy a paddlewheel dinner cruise. *See p 70.*

❺ Jazz things up on the San Antonio River Walk. For over 40 years, Jim Cullum's Jazz Band played at the Landing, San Antonio's premier address for traditional jazz. Today, music is still in the air—and *on* the air—with a live radio broadcast of *River Walk Jazz* heard nationwide on 150-plus radio stations and the Internet (see www.riverwalkjazz. org). *See p 100.*

❻ Hit 6th Street after dark. You don't have to be in your 20s to enjoy all that Austin's famous party-hard boulevard has to offer—but it helps. Sixth Street's 7-block section, from I-35 to Congress Avenue, is the

Swimming in the refreshing Barton Springs.

Traditional jazz can be heard on the San Antonio River Walk.

entertainment epicenter of Texas, with live music venues, rockin' dance spots, cool comedy clubs, and much more. *See p 10.*

⑦ Light up the night at Fiesta de Las Luminarias. More than 6,000 white paper bags filled with sand and burning candles line the San Antonio River Walk and its arched bridges on weekends in December during this holiday season festival. At the same time, 122,000 twinkling lights cascade from trees along the river, creating a romantic canopy of color. *See p 189.*

⑧ Spin under the Zilker Tree. It's not really a tree as much as it is a beloved Austin holiday tradition. Standing 155 feet (47m) tall, this tower is encircled by 3,309 lights. Families gather under the tree on December nights to look up as they twirl under the lights, creating a thrilling dizzy sensation. *See p 189.*

⑨ Float down the San Antonio River. During a 35-minute narrated open-air boat tour along the slender green San Antonio River, you can glide past shops, restaurants, hotels, and cafes. Kiss your sweetheart as you pass under the bridges—a tradition as romantic as San Antonio itself. *See p 101.*

⑩ See the University of Texas at Austin Tower glow burnt orange. Austin loves college football, and what better way to celebrate victory than to light its 307-foot-tall (94m) UT Tower in school colors. As the UT Longhorn team fans say, "Hook 'em horns!" *See p 56.*

⑪ Take in a show at the Majestic. Whether you hear Tony Bennett (1926–) croon, see a symphony, or catch a performance of *The Lion King*, there's no place more magical than the Majestic Theatre in San Antonio. An ornate Spanish-village scene built into the walls of the theater steals the show every time. *See p 170.*

⑫ Take in the view from the Tower of the Americas. The sights are spectacular from the observation deck of San Antonio's 750-foot (229m) lookout at Hemisphere Plaza. With glass elevators, a revolving restaurant, and 3-D motion-sensory theater, it's worth the vertigo. *See p 105.*

⑬ Touch a piece of history at the Harry Ransom Center in Austin. See hand-written short stories by Hemingway (1899–1961), a Guttenberg Bible from 1455, and J.D. Salinger's (1919–2010) private letters, or investigate Woodward (1943–) and Bernstein's (1944–)

The University of Texas at Austin Tower lit up at night.

Watergate notes. It's all there (and more) in the University of Texas archives. *See p 55.*

⓮ Hang out with the bats on the Ann W. Richards Congress Avenue Bridge.

You won't believe what a big deal this is in Austin. March through October, hundreds of locals and tourists flock to the bridge at sundown to see the largest urban bat colony in North America come out to play. *See p 13.*

⓯ Cross the Pennybacker Bridge.

This 1,150-foot-long (351m) arched, weathered steel bridge, on the Capital of Texas Highway over Lake Austin, leads to the lake country northwest of town. Ranch Road 2222 wends through even more stunning lake-luscious scenery on the way to the Texas Hills. *See p 71.*

⓰ Two-step at the Broken Spoke.

Willie Nelson (1933–), Dolly Parton (1946–), and George Strait (1952–) have all played here, but when Texas legend Jerry Jeff Walker (1942–) sings the unofficial national anthem of Texas, "I Want to Go Home to The Armadillo" (aka "London Homesick Blues") the roof nearly comes off as everyone dances and sings—or shouts—along. The good

The regal Texas State Capitol building.

guy in the white hat, owner James White, can give you a tour of the "tourist trap" museum room between sets. There, you'll find photos and memorabilia from all the legendary country-western stars who've ever stood on the Broken Spoke stage. Check out the bus in front of the building, too. *See p 24.*

⓱ Look up at the Capitol rotunda.

The regal pink granite Texas State Capitol building in Austin is the largest state capitol in the U.S., and the sight of the ceiling of the capitol dome is a wonder to behold. *See p 9.*

⓲ Let barbecue sauce run down your wrists at the Salt Lick.

On a country road south of Austin, you'll find some of the best barbecue in the state. You may spend over an hour drinking longnecks outside while waiting for a table indoors, but the BBQ brisket, ribs, chicken, and sausage are worth it. *See p 80.*

⓳ Go to Luckenbach, Texas.

No, Willie, Waylon, and the boys don't hang out here much any more, but lots of folks do. This legendary Hill Country ghost town west of Austin is home to the quintessential Texas beer joint, dance hall, outhouse, post office, and general store, and remains relatively untouched by time. Popular contemporary bands like Cross Canadian Ragweed and Pat Green (1972–) sometimes play here, so it's not just a place for old men who chew tobacco and pitch washers out back. There's no finer way to spend a cold winter afternoon than to sit inside with strangers in a circle around the glowing cast-iron stove as if it were a campfire. Someone always picks up a guitar, and soon you'll be singing like it's summer camp and you're a little kid again. *See p 175.* ●

The Best **in One Day**

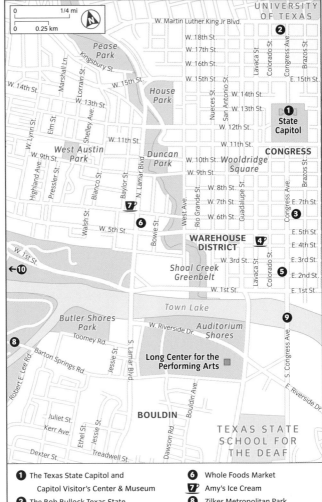

UNIVERSITY OF TEXAS

W. Martin Luther King Jr Blvd.

CONGRESS

State Capitol

Pease Park

House Park

West Austin Park

Duncan Park

Wooldridge Square

WAREHOUSE DISTRICT

Shoal Creek Greenbelt

Town Lake

Butler Shores Park

Auditorium Shores

Long Center for the Performing Arts

BOULDIN

TEXAS STATE SCHOOL FOR THE DEAF

1. The Texas State Capitol and Capitol Visitor's Center & Museum
2. The Bob Bullock Texas State History Museum & IMAX Theater
3. 6th Street
4. Halcyon Coffee House Bar & Lounge
5. Downtown's West Side (Warehouse District & Beyond)
6. Whole Foods Market
7. Amy's Ice Cream
8. Zilker Metropolitan Park
9. The Ann W. Richards Congress Avenue Bridge
10. The Oasis

Previous page: A statue honoring Austin native, guitar-god, and songwriter Stevie Ray Vaughan.

The city's slogan is "Keep Austin Weird," but this self-proclaimed Music Capital of the World is not nearly as weird as it is wonderful. Lakes and hills to the west roll into town, creating a green urban scene. Hike-and-bike trails, gardens, greenbelts, and parks abound. But it's the capital city's progressive mindset that makes it a creative cultural oasis. With a smokin' music scene, a world-class university, and its old-hippie reputation, Austin is as exciting as it is, well, weird. Tour starts in the center of town at the State Capitol. START: **At the Texas State Capitol at 11th and Congress Ave.**

❶ ★★ kids The Texas State Capitol and Capitol Visitor's Center & Museum. This largest state capitol in the nation, second in size only to the U.S. Capitol in Washington, features a 667,000-square-foot (61,966-sq.-m) four-level underground extension and a Renaissance Revival–style main building with an impressive rotunda built in 1888 after a fire destroyed the original 1852 limestone structure. The Capitol's sunset red granite exterior glows pink at sunset, like the colors of the sky in a luminous Maxfield Parrish painting. Free guided tours and self-guided walks with pamphlets are available. The Visitor's Center on the grounds features interactive exhibits and films about Texas history. As you enter the building from the front, note the imposing marble statues of Texas heroes Stephen F. Austin (1793–1836) and Sam Houston (1793–1863) by celebrated sculptress Elisabet Ney (1833–1907), and then make a mental note to visit her former studio and museum while you're in town (see p 17). ⏱ *1 hr. 112 E. 11th St. (at Congress Ave.).* ☎ *512/463-0063. www.tspb.state. tx.us. Free admission. Mon–Fri 7am–10pm, Sat & Sun 9am–8pm; hours extended during regular legislative sessions (held in odd-numbered years, starting the second Tues in Jan, for 140 straight calendar days). Closed major holidays. Free guided tours Mon–Fri 8:30am–4:30pm, Sat*

9:30am–3:30pm, Sun noon–3:30pm. Bus: 1L, 1M, 9 & 450.

❷ ★★★ kids The Bob Bullock Texas State History Museum & IMAX Theatre. The story of Texas comes to life with three floors of interactive exhibits and the Star of Destiny special-effects multimedia show at the museum's Texas Spirit Theater. Revolving exhibits (no permanent collections) mean next time you visit, you'll see something new. My kids love this museum because it's also home to Austin's only IMAX theater. Children 15 and under must be accompanied by an adult. ⏱ *2 hr. 1800 N. Congress Ave. (at MLK, Jr. Blvd.)* ☎ *512/936-8746. www.thestoryoftexas.com. Exhibits $7 adults, $6 seniors 65 & over, $4*

The Bob Bullock Texas State History Museum.

The flamboyant Ester's Follies on 6th Street.

children 5–18, free admission children 4 & under; IMAX theater $7 adults, $6 seniors, $5 children; Texas Spirit Theater $5 adults, $4 seniors and children. Mon–Sat 9am–6pm, Sun noon–6pm. Closed major holidays. Parking $8 ($2 rebate w/ticket to museum or theater, or w/gift shop purchase of $5 or more). Bus: 100, 103, 110 & 142.

❸ ★★ 6th Street. It's said that Austin is "Austintatious"—no, not ostentatious, pretentious, or materialistic, but rather fun and flamboyant, cool, and "in community." And no other place embodies Austin's upbeat attitude more than its most famous boulevard—6th Street. With its celebrated string of restaurants, bars, boutiques, tattoo parlors, vintage clothing and vinyl shops, comedy clubs, and the historic Driskill Hotel, this club-infested strip, once called Pecan Street, practically pulsates at night. Sure, it can be crowded, rowdy, and full of frat

boys, but you can also find a quiet corner in a chic eatery like **Chez Nous** (510 Neches St. ☎ **512/473-2413),** or duck into a dark jazz club. Though it's no stranger to the night, 6th Street doesn't sleep in late or nap all day. On any afternoon, you might stumble upon a film crew setting up a shot or spot a celebrity trying on vintage cowboy boots in a shop. For all its bad boy fame, 6th Street isn't sinister or seedy. It's brilliant, not bawdy, and most of all, it's "Austintatious." 🕐 1½ hr. Bus: 100-Inbound & 4-Westbound.

❹ ★ **Halcyon Coffee House Bar & Lounge.** The ex-hippie vibe is alive and well on West 4th Street at this quirky coffee house. I go here more for the atmosphere and Wi-Fi than anything else, but it's fun to slouch on a couch with a cup of coffee or grab gourmet panini for a quick pick-me-up before I walk some more. 218 W. 4th St. ☎ 512/472-9637. $.

❺ **Take a walk on the West Side.** The West Side, known as the Warehouse District, is where you'll find the heart of Austin nightlife, but even during the day, it's worth touring around to spot the highlights. Walk along Congress Avenue to West 2nd Street—the fastest-growing area for fashionable Austin restaurants and clubs. Then hit West 4th Street, home to popular music venues like **La Zona Rosa** (612 W 4th St.) (p 96). On West 5th Street, pass an Austin favorite for blues lovers at **Antone's** (213 W 5th St.) (see p 32). But then be sure to check out the new **Austin Music Hall** (208 Nueces St.) at 3rd and Nueces streets. Fashionable "thirty-somethings" frequent clubs and restaurants in this Warehouse District,

Apples at the Whole Foods Market.

(7,432-sq.-m) two-story flagship store is the pride of Austin. Located just blocks away from where it all began in 1980 with a small neighborhood grocery (they now have 270-plus stores nationwide), this impressive market features an intimate village-style layout, natural and organic foods, "green" products, restaurants, cafes, music venues, and a sincere commitment to sustainable agriculture. In addition to the produce and fine wines, flowers, and household products, Whole Foods has numerous in-store dining venues, and I highly recommend having lunch here. With seating areas indoors and out—and the freshest seafood, pizza, salads, pasta, barbecue, and more—there's something wholly fabulous here for everyone. If there's time, drop by Austin's biggest independent bookstore, **BookPeople** (603 North Lamar Blvd.) (see p 62), next door. 🕐 *1 hr. 525 N. Lamar Blvd. (at 5th St.).* ☎ *512/476-1206. www.whole foodsmarket.com. Daily 8am–10pm. Free parking in front & in covered garage below store. Bus: 4-Westbound & 21.*

while the younger tend to stick close to 6th Street. Congress Avenue seems to draw a vague demarcation line between age groups, and that's fine by me. 🕐 *30 min. Bus: 1L, 1M, 6 & 7.*

6 ★★ **Whole Foods Market.** Every local I spoke to insisted I include this stop. This 80,000-square-foot

The Philosopher's Rock, a bronze statue commemorating naturalist Roy Bedichek, humorist J. Frank Doble, and historian Walter Prescott Webb, at Zilker Memorial Park.

7 ★★ kids **Amy's Ice Cream.** Look for the neon cows on the sign, and you'll find Austin's original Amy's homemade "super premium" ice cream—a local tradition for 20-plus years. As the staff mixes and makes your favorite individual frozen concoction, watch them toss scoops of ice cream high into the air. Kids squeal with glee, and adults like it, too. While you're there, pop into Waterloo Records (see p 28) next door to see their impressive vintage vinyl collection. *600 N. Lamar Blvd.* ☎ *512/480-0673. $.*

8 ★★★ kids **Zilker Metropolitan Park.** More than just another pretty park, Zilker is home to Austin's most beloved spot—a natural spring-fed swimming pool, **Barton Springs.** It's also home to the **Zilker Botanical Garden** and **Umlauf Sculpture Garden & Museum** (see p 41). This 351-acre

The Mexican free-tailed bat in mid-flight.

(142-hectare) park features a 46-acre (19-hectare) "great lawn," as well as the **Zilker Zephyr,** a miniature train kids adore. With sand volleyball courts, a disc-golf course, an outdoor theater, the kids "Splash" environmental exhibit, miles of hike-and-bike trails, and canoe rentals on **Lady Bird Lake,** Zilker is also home to the **Austin Nature and Science Center.** In summer, be sure to catch a free evening musical at the **Zilker Hillside Theatre** (see p 93). My favorite spot in the park is Philosopher's Rock, with its big bronze depictions of beloved Austin writers, forward-thinkers, and old friends naturalist Roy Bedichek, humorist J. Frank Dobie, and historian Walter Prescott Webb. The statues seem to be engaged in an animated discussion of life's most important questions while real-life little kids climb into their laps—I'm sure nothing would honor those men more. If I could visit only one place in Austin, Zilker would be

Amy's "super premium" homemade ice cream has been a local tradition for more than 20 years.

A breathtaking view of Austin at The Oasis.

it. ⏱ *2 hr. 2201 Barton Springs Rd. Zilker Zephyr* ☎ *512/478-8286; Austin Parks & Recreation* ☎ *512/974-6700. www.ci.austin.tx.us. Free admission. Bus: 30-Northbound.*

⑨ ★ kids The Ann W. Richards Congress Avenue Bridge. Home to about 1½ million Mexican free-tailed bats, who hang out under this bridge spanning Lady Bird Lake (the Colorado River), the bridge is just steps from downtown. It's quite a show when the bats take flight before sundown. From July to mid-August is said to be peak bat-watching season, but they generally hang around from March through November, so you can see them even if you don't make it to Austin during the summer. View it from the grassy knoll on the *Austin American-Statesman* newspaper building property on Riverside Drive and South Congress Avenue, or just stand on the bridge and wait every evening at that same bat time, same bat channel. ⏱ *30 min.*

Congress Ave. at Riverside Dr. ☎ *512/416-5700, ext 3636 (the Austin American-Statesman's Bat Hotline). Bus: 1L, 1M, 5, 7 & 9.*

⑩ ★★ The Oasis. It's an Austin tradition to applaud as the sun sets over Lake Travis. The best place to watch it dip its toe into the water is from the many decks of this beautiful casual dining spot cantilevered over a cliff. The food is just okay, but the view and the long scenic drive through the hills west of Austin are not to be missed. The last visitor I brought there said he had no idea Austin was this beautiful. ⏱ *1½ hr. 6550 Comanche Trail* ☎ *512/266-2442. www.oasis-austin. com. Summer hours: Mar–Oct Mon–Thurs 11.30am–10pm, Fri 11:30am–11pm, Sat 11am–11pm, Sun 11am–10pm; winter hours: Oct–Mar Mon–Thurs 11:30am–9pm, Fri 11:30am–10pm, Sat 11am–10pm, Sun 11am–9pm. No city bus service available.*

The Best **in Two Days**

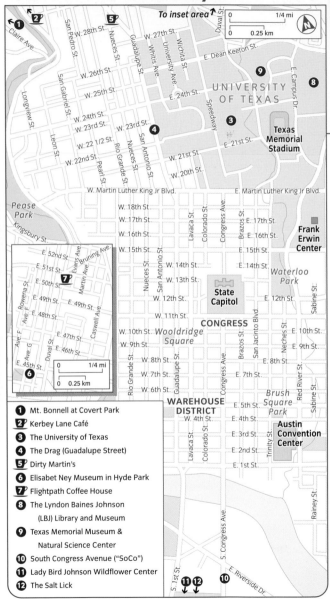

1 Mt. Bonnell at Covert Park
2 Kerbey Lane Café
3 The University of Texas
4 The Drag (Guadalupe Street)
5 Dirty Martin's
6 Elisabet Ney Museum in Hyde Park
7 Flightpath Coffee House
8 The Lyndon Baines Johnson
  (LBJ) Library and Museum
9 Texas Memorial Museum &
  Natural Science Center
10 South Congress Avenue ("SoCo")
11 Lady Bird Johnson Wildflower Center
12 The Salt Lick

Austin is known for its exciting outdoor recreational offerings, but it's also a Mecca for shoppers who like quirky vintage outfits, wild Howdy-Doody cowboy boots, eclectic coffee shops, and musty used book and vinyl record stores. Shopping is an adventure in areas like "The Drag" and Austin's beloved "SoCo," while museums, like those at the University of Texas, offer a low-key way to enjoy and learn about the city without spending a lot of money. For your second day in town, I've given you a taste of all of that, with time to shop, explore, and take your tour of Austin to new, often breathtaking, heights. START: 1 mile (1.6km) past the west end of 35th St. (Bus 9-Northbound).

❶ ★ kids Mt. Bonnell at Covert Park. Start your day with a sunrise climb to the highest point in Austin—the 775-foot (263m) summit of Mt. Bonnell—called "the oldest tourist attraction in town." The peak was named for George W. Bonnell (unknown–1842), Sam Houston's commissioner of Indian affairs in 1836. Getting to the top doesn't involve hiking as much as it does climbing: Take the outdoor stairway up 106 steps for a view from the top. Once there, short trails and a pavilion provide spectacular views of the Texas Hill Country to the west. It's a moderate to slightly difficult climb and is not accessible to the disabled or those with mobility challenges. Dogs are allowed; bikes aren't. Go early; it can get crowded. 🕐 45 min. 3800 Mt. Bonnell Rd. (about 1mile /1.6km past the west end of 38th St.). No phone. Free admission (free parking below at Covert Park). Daily 5am–10pm. Bus: 9-Northbound.

❷ ★★ Kerbey Lane Café. I spent the better part of the '80s in this cozy wooden cottage and 24-hour pancake place. For years, *Austin Chronicle* readers have voted Kerbey Lane "the best breakfast in town," and now four locations are scattered across Austin. But this central location, just a few miles from Mt. Bonnell, is still my favorite place to get a taste of authentic Austin flavor—not to mention fabulous pancakes, sandwiches, soups, salads, "Kerbey Queso," and more. Kerbey Lane is committed to using as many fresh, local farm-to-table foods and "green" products as possible; it's also a great place to read the paper, and wake up and smell the coffee. *3704 Kerbey Lane.* ☎ 512/451-1436. $.

A look atop Mt. Bonnell.

A fountain at the University of Texas.

❸ ★★ The University of Texas. One of the largest public universities in the U.S., the University of Texas at Austin was founded in 1883. This 350-acre (142-hectare) campus, home to nearly 50,000 students, is like a "city within a city" in the heart of Austin. I could spend all day in the **Harry Ransom Humanities Research Center** (see p 55, ❶), enjoying the exhibits and digging through the treasures of its archives, and that's just one of many museums and special event centers connected to the University, including the **Lyndon Baines Johnson Presidential Library and Museum** (see p 58, ⓮) and the **Jack S. Blanton Museum of Art** (see p 59, ⓱). Check out which films are playing in the student center and take a **UT Tower tour** (see p 56, ❺). Tours of the **Austin City Limits KLRU soundstage** (see p 27, ❶) take place on Friday mornings in the **Jesse H. Jones Communication Building B** (see p 58, ⓫) —but be sure to note that "ACL" will soon move to a new home adjacent to **The W Hotel– ACL** (see p 89) downtown. Locals claim that more people with PhDs live in Austin than any other Texas city; when students finish grad school here, they never want to

leave. Campus info is available from 7am until 3am (weekdays only) at The Texas Union Information Center at the corner of 24th and Guadalupe streets. 🕐 *1 hr. Corner of MLK, Jr. Blvd. & Guadalupe St. UT main switchboard* ☎ *512/471-3434; Texas Union Information Center* ☎ *512/475-6636. www.utexas.edu. Bus: 1L, 1M, 5, 101 & 410.*

❹ ★ The Drag (Guadalupe Street). The long section of Guadalupe Street, from about Martin Luther King, Jr. Boulevard to 29th Street, is a strip locals long ago dubbed "The Drag." There, you'll find bookstores, coffee shops, and eclectic fashion and collectibles shops—along with the old hippie-style outdoor 23rd Street Renaissance Artist's Market. There, Birkenstock-types sell tie-dyed T-shirts, candles, hammocks, and earrings and beads, and a mural celebrates the local color and characters who helped create Austin's freethinking creative culture. Get a real feel for campus life on this eclectic strip stretched out in the shadow of UT's famed tower. 🕐 *30 min. Start at the corner of MLK, Jr. Blvd. & Guadalupe St.* ☎ *512/471-3434. www.utexas.edu. Bus: 1L, 1M, 5, 101, 410-Northbound, 481 & 982.*

5 ★ **Dirty Martin's.** An Austin tradition since the 1920s, Dirty's thick malts and shakes, hand-battered onion rings and fries, homemade chili, and juicy drip-down-your-wrists hamburgers make for a great pick-me-up stop. *2808 Guadalupe St. (just south of 29th St.).* ☎ *512/477-3173. $.*

6 ★★★ **Elisabet Ney Museum in Hyde Park.** Quite possibly Austin's best-kept secret, this little museum lies hidden in a wooded area along a creek in the old Hyde Park neighborhood north of the UT campus. This enchanting neoclassical-style structure built in 1892 is the former studio of celebrated European sculptress, Elizabet Ney (1833–1907), who became prominent in Texas as the founder of the UT Austin Art Department, the Texas Commission on the Arts, and various museums and art schools. The spirit of the artist seems to linger here still, with hauntingly beautiful life-sized statues in every room. My favorite place to be on a quiet rainy morning. ◷ *1 hr. 304 E. 44th St.* ☎ *512/458-2255. www.elisabet ney.org. Free admission. Wed–Sun noon–5pm. Bus: 338.*

7 **Flightpath Coffee House.** One of the oldest—and quietest—coffeehouses in Austin, Flightpath doesn't have live music, poetry slams, open-mikes, and the like—just good coffee, beer, and bakery items. It once sat in the noisy flight path of the old airport, until the Austin Bergstrom Airport was built south of town in 1999. *5011 Duval St. (at 51st St.).* ☎ *512/458-4472. $.*

8 **The LBJ Library and Museum.** The Lyndon Baines Johnson Library and Museum, located on the northeast edge of the UT campus, is home to permanent historical and cultural exhibits, including LBJ's (1908–1973) '68 stretch limousine, a room replicating his White House Oval Office, 45 million pages of historical documents, and more. ◷ *1 hr. 2313 Red River St.* ☎ *512/ 721-0200. www.lbjlib.utexas.edu. Free admission & parking. Daily 9am–5pm; closed Christmas Day. Bus: 18, 142, 464, 986 & 990; a UT Shuttle Bus also serves this area.*

9 ★★ **kids** **Texas Memorial Museum & Natural Science Center.** Named one of the best museums in Texas for children, the

Beautiful life-sized busts and statues at the Elisabet Ney Museum.

A replica of Lyndon Baines Johnson's Oval Office at the LBJ Library and Museum.

Texas Memorial Museum is the exhibit hall of the Texas Natural Science Center on the UT campus. With a huge pterosaur skeleton suspended above the great hall and floors full of fossils, dioramas, and more, kids and adults are both going to have fun. ⏱ 1½ hr. 2400 Trinity St. ☎ 512/471-1604. www.utexas.edu/tmm. Free admission. Mon–Fri 9am–5pm, Sat 10am–5pm, Sun 1–5pm. Bus: 640, 651, 653 & 684.

⑩ ★ South Congress Avenue ("SoCo"). Think New York's SoHo meets Texas. A favorite stop is the

Lucy in Disguise's colorful façade.

gigantic costume shop, **Lucy in Disguise** (see p 49, **③**)—even the building's facade is entertaining. Shops, chic boutique hotels, nightclubs, and food-vendor trailers line the section between Riverside Drive and Oltorf Street, making this one of the most popular parts of town. Shops stay open late for "First Thursday" madness every month. ⏱ 1½ hr. S. Congress Ave. at Academy Dr. Bus: 1M.

⑪ ★★★ Lady Bird Johnson Wildflower Center. Founded in 1982 by actress Helen Hayes (1900–1993) and former First Lady "Lady Bird" Johnson (1912–2007) as part of a national wildflower research organization, this 279-acre (109-hectare) botanical garden is home to thousands of native North American plants, including spectacular early spring displays of Texas wildflowers. It is also an Organized Research Unit of the University of Texas at Austin. Explore the public gardens, woodlands, and meadows, and wander along short scenic walking trails. Austin considers the Wildflower Center its own backyard garden, and locals come here often. Visitors should, too. A gift shop and cafe are on site. ⏱ 1½ hr. 4801 La Crosse Ave. (just south of Slaughter Lane). ☎ 512/292-4100. www.wild flower.org. $8 adults; $7 seniors 60 & older, students 13 & older w/

Drinks in Dry Texas

Of Texas' 254 counties, 30 are completely dry, 42 are completely "wet," and the rest are, well, "damp." By damp, I mean "dry-ish"—you can *sometimes* get *some* drinks in *some* places, under *some* circumstances, as long as you take care to note some really odd restrictions. For instance, only beer that is 5% alcohol by volume and wine that is 14% alcohol by volume are legal in some areas. Throughout the state, a person "may not consume or possess with the intent to consume" beverages in a public place before noon on Sundays—but if food is served with it (even a bag of pretzels at a bar) you can indulge at 10am. Even in some so-called "dry" areas, you can buy a mixed drink—but only if you join a "private club" (which may mean simply writing your name on a tablet). Rules about how late Texas bars can sell drinks are equally confusing. Most bars can serve alcohol only until midnight on Fridays, and until Saturdays at 1am, but others are able to sell alcohol until 2am every day of the week. Liquor stores have to stop selling by 9pm Mondays through Saturdays, and they can't sell on Sundays at all. Seems screwy? Well, when you consider that Texans couldn't legally buy mixed drinks anywhere in the state until 1971, you'll see they're making progress.

student ID; $3 children 5–12; free for children under 5 & members Open Mon–Sat 9am–5:30pm, Sun noon–5:30pm; closed Mondays June 1–Mar 14. Closed July 4th, Thanksgiving, and mid/late Dec–Jan 1. No bus service to this location.

⓬ ★★ **The Salt Lick.** Don't tell me you've never heard of the Salt Lick if you've heard of Austin and you eat red meat. Rarely has so much ink been printed about such an out-of-the-way rustic barbecue joint. Hollywood celebrities supposedly go here a lot—but then so does everyone else. Locals and visitors alike love it and don't mind the 30-minute, two-lane drive southwest of Austin along a winding cedar, cypress, and pecan tree–lined country road. It's in a "dry" area, so bring your own beer. Located in the tiny Texas community of Driftwood, the Salt Lick is definitely worth the trip. Go early to avoid a long wait. Bring a fan or ice chest because you may have to wait for a table outside, and it can be killer hot here in summer. Drift toward Driftwood, taking US-290W, then turn left on Camp Ben McCullough Road (aka R.R./FM 1826 S.) and head south for 11 miles (18km). When you spy the split-rail fence and smell the smoke, you've found the Salt Lick. ⏱ 1½ hr. *18301 FM 1826, Driftwood.* ☎ *512/858-4959. www.saltlickbbq.com. Daily 11am–10pm.*

The Salt Lick, a haven for red-meat dining in Austin.

The Best **in Three Days**

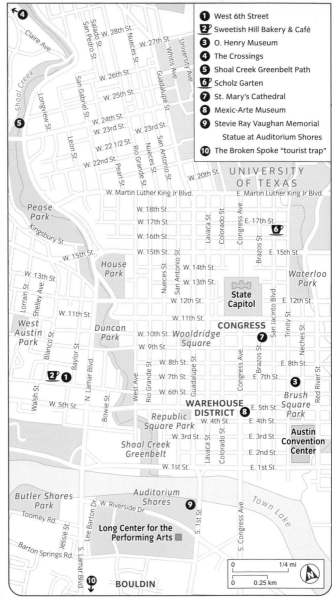

1 West 6th Street
2 Sweetish Hill Bakery & Café
3 O. Henry Museum
4 The Crossings
5 Shoal Creek Greenbelt Path
6 Scholz Garten
7 St. Mary's Cathedral
8 Mexic-Arte Museum
9 Stevie Ray Vaughan Memorial
   Statue at Auditorium Shores
10 The Broken Spoke "tourist trap"

After a couple of days in Austin, you may feel you've seen it all—but, actually, you're just getting started. Today, you'll wander northwest toward the place where the Highland Lakes meet the Texas Hill Country after exploring a bit more in the center of town. Don't worry—you'll relax along the way. Austin is green and glorious. You'll see more of the creeks, greenbelts, lakes, and river that ramble through it all, and then end up back in town to enjoy some of the classic cowboy fun for which Austin is known. **START: Take Bus 4 or Bus 21-Westbound from Congress Ave. to W. 6th St.**

① ★ **West 6th Street.** Explore antiques shops, coffee shops, bookstores, and eclectic boutiques along West 6th Street, from Lamar Boulevard to Loop 1 (MoPac). Several restaurants and clubs are tucked away in this area, too, and there are antiques shops like **Whit Hanks** (1009 W. 6th St.) and great taco spots like **El Arroyo** (1616 W. 5th St.) to try. While you're there, check out a place just across the street called **Mean-Eyed Cat** (see p 95). It sits next to a sushi restaurant, but this charming but scruffy, Johnny Cash–themed bar with billiards, beer, and an outdoor patio is a great place to hear live music. Parking can be problematic along West 6th Street, so take a bus, or park and walk a bit. ⏱ *1 hr. Bus: 4 & 21.*

② ★ **Sweetish Hill Bakery & Café.** Grab a cup of coffee and a pastry, or sit out and have brunch in the sun. Sweetish Hill has been baking up sweet somethings in Austin for over 30 years. If you can find a spot, park in front and then pop into some of the shops next door while you're there. *1120 W. 6th St.* ☎ *512/472-1347. $.*

③ ★ **O. Henry Museum.** William Sidney Porter (whose pseudonym was "O. Henry") is perhaps best known as the man who penned the famous short story "The Gift of the

Sweetish Hill has been serving Austin baked goods for over 30 years.

Magi." This little house, where he lived from 1893 to 1895, was relocated from just 1 block away to its current location on East 5th Street. Today, it is a small museum containing authentic items such as Porter's writing desk and bed. Next door sits the newly-opened **Joseph and Susanna Dickinson Hannig Museum** (see p 47, **⑦**). Dickinson (1814–1883) and her daughter Angelina (1834–1871) were two of only a few survivors of the Battle of the Alamo, and Dickinson and her fourth husband Joseph Hannig lived in this house from 1870 to 1873. Both the Dickinson Museum and the O. Henry Museum are owned by the City of Austin Parks and Recreation Department. ⏱ *1 hr. 409 E. 5th St. (near Trinity St.).* ☎ *512/472-1903. www.ohenrymuseum.org. Free admission; metered parking. Wed–Sun noon–5pm. Bus: 9.*

The O. Henry Museum, home of William Sidney Porter.

④ ★★ The Crossings. This progressive 32-acre (13-hectare) "green" resort, learning center, and wellness spa, located 21 miles (34km) from downtown, may seem an interesting choice for a day tour, but it offers so much of what epitomizes the Austin experience. Set on the lush 200-acre (81-hectare) Balcones Reserve overlooking Lake Travis, the Crossings is a tranquil place with an emphasis on spiritual and physical rejuvenation. A day pass that includes a fresh, healthful lunch in the newly renovated restaurant enables visitors to enjoy the grounds, a junior-sized Olympic pool with an infinity edge overlooking the lake, a hot tub, steam room, and 2 miles (3.2km) of hiking trails; or attend special classes, demonstrations, lectures, and workshops—all inclusive. Sit in on a yoga class or see a tai-chi demonstration, meditate in the chapel, or just lounge by the pool to watch the sunset. Austin doesn't get much more "Zen" than this. The property recently reopened following a full renovation, making it lovelier than ever. Reservations are required for day pass visitors or overnight stays. ⏱ 3 hr. 13500 FM 2769. ☎ 512/225-1075. www.thecrossings austin.com. Day passes (including lunch & use of all facilities) Mon–Thurs $65, Fri–Sun $75. Spa Day packages

(including lunch, full use of the facilities & a 50-minute spa treatment) $195. Daily 7:30am–9pm. No bus service available.

⑤ kids Shoal Creek Greenbelt Path. From the neighborhoods of central Austin, near 38th Street, all the way south to Lady Bird (Town) Lake, this multi-use greenbelt trail along Shoal Creek cuts a 4.4-mile (7.1km) path through the heart of Austin. Ride a bicycle, run with your dog, or walk at a leisurely pace, enjoying parks and neighborhoods along the way, like Pease Park with its playground equipment and Duncan Park with its wild Bicycle Motocross (BMX) track. Or stop and visit the Austin Recreation Center. A good place to begin the trail is at

The decorated steins of Scholz Garten.

Water, Water, Everywhere

No visit to Austin would be complete without spending time on one of the six Highland lakes: **Lake Buchanan, Inks Lake, Lake LBJ, Lake Marble Falls, Lake Travis,** or **Lake Austin.** Even land-lubbers find water sports a breeze when they rent a small water-craft or a party barge. **Just for Fun Watercraft Rental** (☎ 512/266-9710), at Emerald Point Marina on Lake Travis, empha-sizes safety and affordability, and they provide careful instructions before you hit the waves. Rent pontoon boats, party barges, ski boats, wave runners, or even large luxury houseboats and other water sport accessories. Boats are equipped with plenty of gas, water skis, ropes, and life vests. For a small additional charge, knee boards, inner tubes, and kids' water skis are available. Bring bin-oculars for bird watching, or take along snorkel or scuba equip-ment and fishing gear. Views are stunning, and the scenic 30-minute drive from downtown Austin is worth taking. Get discounted rates Monday through Thursday. Depart by 8:30am, and get 4-hour rent-als for the price of 3 hours. Rates begin at $55 per hour for pontoon boats and $70 an hour for personal watercraft, but rates get better the more hours you're out enjoying the water.

35th Street and Lamar Boulevard, heading south. 🕐 *2 hr. www. ci.austin.tx.us/parks/traildirectory. htm. Free admission & parking. Bus: 151 & 338.*

6 ★ **Scholz Garten.** Sit in the shade of giant oak trees in Austin's oldest *biergarten* and enjoy a Texas beer, like Shiner Bock. There are burgers and German fare, ball-games on big-screen televisions, and sometimes even live music out back. This is a popular spot to watch the UT football games if you want to avoid the crowds just up the street at UT's Texas Memorial Stadium. Garages near Scholz' have free parking after 5pm. *1607 San Jacinto Blvd. at 17th St.* ☎ *512/474-1958. $.*

7 **St. Mary's Cathedral.** Squeezed in tightly between down-town buildings, this pretty Gothic-Revival–style cathedral, built in 1884, is the oldest Catholic church in Austin and was designed by Texas architect Nicholas J. Clayton (1840–1916). Stained-glass windows were added in the1890s, and reno-vations were done in the 1940s. Recent restoration efforts have made this cathedral lovelier than ever. There are no organized tours, but visitors are welcome to quietly step inside. It offers daily services. 🕐 *15 min. 203 E. 10th (at San Jacinto Blvd.).* ☎ *512/476-6182. www.smcaustin.org. Free admission. East entrance Mon–Fri 11:30am–4:30pm; main entrance daily 11:30am–1pm; Ave Maria Gift Shop Thurs & Fri 11am–2pm. Bus: 2, 10, 18, 37 & 137.*

The beautiful stained-glass windows and interior of St. Mary's Cathedral.

8 ★ **kids** **Mexic-Arte Museum.**
I love the strange and wonderful Dia de Los Muertos (Day of the Dead) displays here each early November, but this fine arts museum, focusing on the work of Mexican and Mexican-American artists, is a thrill year-round. Located in an old storefront building, it looks from the street more like a colorful Mexican exports shop than a museum, but it's not. It's a fun place to browse for a bit and enjoy eclectic art exhibits and exciting educational programs.

The Mexic-Arte Museum features the work of Mexican and Mexican-American artists.

Here, you get a sense of the city's colorful infusion of Mexican culture. 🕐 *1 hr. 419 Congress Ave.(at 5th)* ☎ *512/480-9373. www.mexic-arte museum.org. Mon–Thurs 10am–6pm, Fri & Sat 10am–5pm, Sun noon–5pm. Adults $5; seniors & students with ID, $4; children 12 and under, $1. Free admission for museum members. Bus: 1M, L, 5 & 9.*

9 **Stevie Ray Vaughan Memorial Statue at Auditorium Shores.** Austin guitar-god and songwriter Stevie Ray Vaughan's (1954–1990) name is almost synonymous with the Austin music scene, so it's only fitting that his life-sized bronze statue stands on Auditorium Shores at Lady Bird Lake. The City of Austin erected the statue in 1991 honoring Texas's beloved native son. 🕐 *10 min. 920 W. Riverside Dr.* ☎ *512/974-6700. Bus: 110 & 10.*

10 ★★ **The Broken Spoke "tourist trap."** You know you've been to Texas if you've been to the Broken Spoke. This authentic Texas dancehall, restaurant, and country music "museum," set under an enormous oak tree on Lamar Boulevard in South Austin, is not to be missed. Whether you two-step to a live country band on a Saturday night, or just grab a burger and play shuffle-board on a lazy weekday afternoon, be sure to boot-scoot on over to the back room of "The Spoke" to see its hokey, but interesting, little country music museum—a shrine to all the country-western stars who've ever played here, including Willie Nelson (1933–), Dolly Parton (1946–), George Strait (1952–), and even Bob Wills (1905–1975) and the Texas Playboys, just to name a few. Long-time Owner James White, who dons a white cowboy hat, calls this room "the tourist trap" and takes pride in giving impromptu tours. Go in the afternoon, spin some George Jones on the jukebox, drink a longneck or a Coke, and play shuffle-board with friends; or slide into a booth and order a chicken fried steak with cream gravy—a tasty, traditional, and yes, artery-clogging Texas-sized meal. ⏱ 45 min. 3201 South Lamar Blvd. ☎ 512/442-6189.

The Broken Spoke features country music and a museum dedicated to country stars that have graced their stage.

www.brokenspokeaustintx.com. Free admission to restaurant, bar & museum; cover charge for dancehall in back. Restaurant & museum 11am–11pm. Bus: 331, 338 & 484.

Star Struck

Texas is called the Lone Star State, and Austin is where you're most likely to see the biggest stars—celebrities who've fallen in love with the area. Those who call Austin home, or who have lived here in recent years, include Matthew McConaughey, Lance Armstrong, Sandra Bullock, Andy Roddick, Drew Brees, Natalie Maines, Renee Zellwiger, Jessica Simpson, Dennis Quaid, Michael Dell, and many others. Hollywood types like Jake Gyllenhaal, Ashton Kutcher, and Quentin Tarantino have been spotted here recently, too. And during the South by Southwest festival, hundreds of musicians, directors, and movie stars descend on the Music Capital. Oscar winning actress Sandra Bullock is said to often frequent two Austin eateries she owns: Bess Bistro (500 W 6th St. ☎ 512/477-2377) and Walton's Fancy and Staple, a combination bakery and floral shop (609 W Sixth St. ☎ 512/ 417-6454). Tour de France champion Lance Armstrong opened Mellow Johnny's bicycle shop and its adjacent Juan Pelota Café downtown (see p 62), and music superstar Willie Nelson and basketball legend Magic Johnson are partners in the new Austin City Limits Studio at the new W Austin Hotel & Residences on 2nd St. (see p 89).

Austin for **Music Fans**

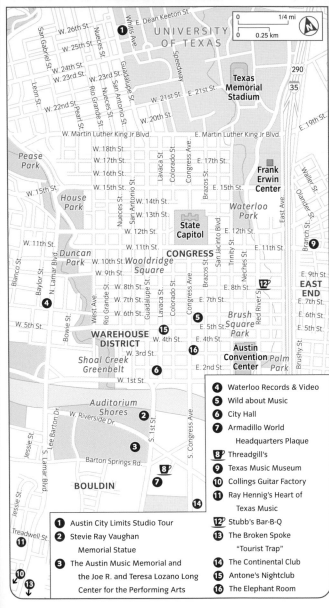

0	1/4 mi
0	0.25 km

UNIVERSITY OF TEXAS

Texas Memorial Stadium

Pease Park

House Park

State Capitol

CONGRESS

Frank Erwin Center

Waterloo Park

Duncan Park

Wooldridge Square

WAREHOUSE DISTRICT

EAST END

Brush Square Park

Shoal Creek Greenbelt

Austin Convention Center

Palm Park

Auditorium Shores

BOULDIN

- **4** Waterloo Records & Video
- **5** Wild about Music
- **6** City Hall
- **7** Armadillo World Headquarters Plaque
- **8** Threadgill's
- **9** Texas Music Museum
- **10** Collings Guitar Factory
- **11** Ray Hennig's Heart of Texas Music
- **12** Stubb's Bar-B-Q
- **13** The Broken Spoke "Tourist Trap"
- **14** The Continental Club
- **15** Antone's Nightclub
- **16** The Elephant Room

- **1** Austin City Limits Studio Tour
- **2** Stevie Ray Vaughan Memorial Statue
- **3** The Austin Music Memorial and the Joe R. and Teresa Lozano Long Center for the Performing Arts

Austin calls itself the "music capital of the world," and that's not a stretch, considering the enormous popularity of the Austin City Limits Festival, the South by Southwest music and film festival, the city's rockin' 6th Street venues, sizzling SoCo clubs, and local musicians like Willie Nelson and the late Stevie Ray Vaughan, who helped put Austin on the music map. A plunge into the Austin music scene may mean venturing out after dark, but even during the day, music is in the air. If you can arrange it, take this tour on a Friday so you won't miss some of the special Friday-only fun music stops Austin has to offer. START: **Take FA UT Shuttle bus to Guadalupe & Dean Keaton sts., at the UT Campus.**

① ★ Austin City Limits Studio Tour. The longest-running music television series in American history, Austin City Limits is a popular PBS show that first premiered with a pilot starring Willie Nelson in 1974. Although it appears to be set on a hill overlooking Austin, it's actually taped in front of a live audience on KLRU-TV station soundstage on the UT campus. Shows usually tape in the spring and summer, and free tickets are available through the blog of the ACL website. A 30-minute studio tour is held each Friday at 10:30am. Cameras allowed. *Note:* The studio is scheduled to move to a new location ("Block 21") in the new ACL Music Hall, which will stand on West 5th Street at Nueces Street, near the new W Hotel–ACL (see p 89), sometime in either late 2010 or in 2011. *⏱ 30 min. UT Communications Building "B," corner of Dean Keaton & Guadalupe sts.* ☎ *512/475-9077. www.austincitylimits.org. Free admission. Fri 10:30am. Buses: 1L, 1M, 410-Northbound & FA UT Shuttle Bus north on Guadalupe St.*

② ★ Stevie Ray Vaughan Memorial Statue. The spirit of famed guitar-god Stevie Ray Vaughan stands guard over the Austin music scene near Auditorium Shores on Lady Bird Lake, where so

Austin City Limits *is the longest-running music television series in American history.*

A life-sized bronze statue of Stevie Ray Vaughn.

many musicians have played over the years—and still do. See p 24, **9**.

❸ The Austin Music Memorial and the Long Center for the Performing Arts. The Austin Music Memorial, located at the Long Center's City Terrace, overlooks Lady Bird Lake and pays tribute to individuals who have made important contributions to the development of music and the Austin music community. The Long Center, located on the site of the former Palmer Auditorium, underwent a $77-million construction project and opened in March of 2008 to become one of Austin's most celebrated venues for performing arts. Free public tours are held noon Wednesdays in the Rollins Studio Theatre Lobby. ⏱ *30 min. 701 West Riverside Dr. (at S. 1st St.).* ☎ *512/457-5100. www.thelong center.org. Free admission & tours. Mon–Fri 10am–6pm, Sat 10am–4pm. Parking $7 in the Palmer Events Center garage, accessible via Riverside Dr. Buses: 5, 10, 29 & 110.*

❹ ★ Waterloo Records & Video. The *Austin Chronicle* once named this Austin's best record store, and I agree. Perhaps it's because I always come across hard-to-find classic vinyl LPs in their bins, or maybe it's their new CDs and videos I adore. I also love the live music events Waterloo hosts. Part of the community since the 1980s, Waterloo (now with its 1,200-sq.-ft./111-sq.-m store) has a knowledgeable, helpful staff. The name "Waterloo"

The memorial plaque for Austin's music Mecca, the Armadillo World Headquarters.

Outside Threadgill's, next to the former site of the Armadillo.

comes from a community that pre-dated the current capital city in this area, so you'll see that word a lot around town. 🕒 *30 min. 600A N. Lamar Blvd.* ☎ *512/474-2500. www. waterloorecords.com. Mon–Sat 10am–11pm, Sun 11am–11pm. Bus: 4, 21, 22 & 122.*

⑤ Wild about Music. This art and music gallery on Austin's famous club scene row, 6th Street, is dedicated entirely to all things musical. With instruments and music-themed jewelry, apparel, art, posters, home decor, gifts, T-shirts, bags—you name it—it's not a typical gift or music shop. 🕒 *15 min. 115 E. 6th St.* ☎ *877/370-1700 or 512/708-1700. www.wildaboutmusic. com. Mon–Thurs 10am–7pm, Fri & Sat 10am–9pm, Sun 10am–6pm; During SXSW Music Festival, the shop stays open as late as midnight, and on Christmas Eve as late as 10pm. Bus: 1L, 1M, 5, 6, 7 & 9.*

⑥ ★ City Hall. No wonder they call Austin the music capital; even its City Hall becomes a music venue during lunch hour on Fridays. "Live from the Plaza" is a free concert series hosted by the City of Austin at the Plaza of City Hall, Fridays from noon to 1pm. Bring a sack lunch or

try a local vendor's weekly special. Check the city calendar online for concert season dates. While there, tour the People's Gallery art exhibit inside City Hall—you can pick up a self-guided tour packet in the lobby. *Tip:* Free parking in the City Hall garage between 11:30am and 1:30pm. 🕒 *1 hr. 301 W. 2nd St.* ☎ *512/974-2000. www.ci.austin. tx.us. Free admission. Noon–1pm. Bus: 10, 29 & 110.*

⑦ Armadillo World Head-quarters Plaque. Okay, this is *not* the most impressive memorial you'll ever see. In fact, it's just a paper-like plaque placed, almost as an afterthought, on a stick-like stand at the edge of a parking lot. So why stop here at all? Well, Austinites consider this "holy ground"—the site of the Armadillo World Head-quarters (aka "The Armadillo"), the most venerated music venue in Austin's history. This popular 1970s music Mecca, set in an abandoned armory building, achieved legendary status when Texas "Outlaws" Willie Nelson and Waylon Jennings (1937–2002) played here, as did Ray Charles (1930–2004), Count Basie (1904–1984), Johnny Cash (1932–2003), AC/DC, Van Morrison

The Texas Music Museum is dedicated to preserving Texas' diverse musical traditions.

(1945–), Jerry Jeff Walker (1942–), Frank Zappa (1940–1993), and hundreds of others. That freewheeling "Progressive Country" music scene was part long-haired gonzo/hippie/folk music, part blues, part soul, a little bit country, and a little bit rock-n-roll—and it gave Austin a heart, an anthem, a hangover, and a place to call home. But as Willie Nelson sings, "Time changes everything," and to the community's horror, the

building was demolished in 1991 to put up an office building. In 2006, the City of Austin dedicated this commemorative plaque, but I'm completely underwhelmed. Either way, locals and visitors still make pilgrimages here. ⏱ *10 min. 1 Texas Center (corner of Barton Springs Rd. & S. 1st St.). www.armadilloworld headquarters.com. Bus: 5.*

🍵 ★★ **Threadgill's.** If you hoped for a better memorial to "The Armadillo," you're in luck. Park your car by the plaque and step inside Threadgill's. "Feel-good food for 75 years and counting" is the motto of this Austin-themed eatery that's been a local institution on North Lamar Boulevard since the 1930s. (Be sure to try Threadgill's "famous" Texas-sized chicken fried steak.) But music lovers will want to visit this Riverside Drive location next to the former site of the Armadillo. Here, "The Armadillo" rocks on in memory with authentic 'dillo memorabilia, including a huge photo of the hall, original posters, and pictures. The jukebox holds 100 CDs by musicians

Guitars line the walls of Ray Hennig's.

Country music memorabilia at the Broken Spoke.

who played "The Armadillo" in its 1970s hippie heyday. *301 W. Riverside Dr.* ☎ *512/472-9304. $–$$.*

⑨ ★ Texas Music Museum. Two galleries in the Marvin C. Griffin building in East Austin are the current home of the Texas Music Museum, a non-profit organization dedicated to the celebration, and preservation, of Texas's diverse music traditions through its interesting exhibits, educational programs, and performances. Call ahead for a guided tour or just linger in the galleries alone as you learn more about and listen to Texas music. 🕐 *30 min. 1009 E. 11th St.* ☎ *512/472-8891. www.texasmusicmuseum.org. Free admission. Mon–Fri 9am–5pm. Bus: 2.*

⑩ Collings Guitar Factory. Want to see how a guitar—or even a mandolin—is made? Visit the Collings Guitar Factory store, just west of the Oak Hill area, and take their factory tour on scheduled Friday afternoons. The 1- to 2-hour tour will walk you through all the intricate steps involved in the process—from the selection of the wood to the final polished product. Call ahead for tour schedules. 🕐 *1½*

hr. 11210 W. Hwy. 290. ☎ *512/288-7776. www.collingsguitars.com. Free admission. For safety reasons, children under 12 not admitted. Fri 3:30pm (if scheduled). No bus service available to this location.*

⑪ ★ Ray Hennig's Heart of Texas Music. You're more likely to run into a famous musician in this store than just about any place you'll go in Austin—or so that's been my experience. One review called this place "slack and homely," and maybe they're right. Still, it's a comfortable store with guitars, amps, other musical instruments, electronics, and a laid-back attitude. They won't mind if you take a guitar off the wall and strum a bit. The staff is knowledgeable and ready to share stories of the Austin music scene. Ask iconic owner Ray about guitars he loaned Stevie Ray Vaughan. Hennig is such an Austin treasure, he could be a music tour stop all by himself. 🕐 *30 min. 1002 S Lamar Blvd.* ☎ *512/444-9750. www.heartoftexasmusic.com. Bus: 3 & 338.*

⑫ ★★ Stubb's Bar-B-Q. Hard to say whether the barbecue or the music venue is the biggest draw at

The Continental Club, rockin' Texas since 1957.

Stubbs, but I'm pretty discriminating about my barbecue, so I'd vote "music." Still, the down-home cooking and Texas barbecue are consistently good, if not great, and side dishes (like spicy onion rings) are super. Top bands keep the joint jamming, indoors and out, which may mean a long wait by the bar and lots of standing around. Drinks can be pricey, but you're going to want to go here anyway. A big "Hallelujah" for the heavenly Gospel Brunch on Sundays—make a reservation for that. *801 Red River St.* ☎ *512/480-8341. $–$$.*

⓭ ★★★ **The Broken Spoke "tourist trap" museum, restaurant, and dancehall.** One of Austin's most beloved honky-tonks—with a back room full of fabulous country music memorabilia and photos of America's biggest country music stars. ⏲ *30 min. See p 24, ⓾.*

⓮ ★★★ **The Continental Club.** When asked to name the quintessential Austin music club, most locals are evenly split between The Continental Club and Antone's. Located in the popular SoCo area,

the Continental Club is a small venue that's been home to live music since 1957. It first opened as a swank supper club featuring touring orchestras such as those of Tommy Dorsey (1905–1956) and Glenn Miller (1904–1944). In the '60s, it was a burlesque joint. The '70s brought changes, along with performers like Stevie Ray Vaughan. In 1987, the club's look was "retro-fitted" to reflect its 1950s roots. Today, this cool dive-like club continues to rock on. ⏲ *30 min. 1315 S. Congress Ave.* ☎ *512/441-2444. www.continentalclub.com. Cover charge $5–$25. Mon–Fri 4pm–2am, Sat 2pm–2am, Sun 8pm–2am. Bus: 1L, 1M, 9, 450 & 486.*

⓯ ★★★ **Antone's Nightclub.** Austin's best bet for the blues, Antone's was founded in the 1970s by music promoter Clifford Antone, who booked music moguls such as Muddy Waters (1915–1983) and B.B. King (1925–) on his stage. Bono (1960–), Eric Clapton (1945–), and Elvis Costello (1954–) have played Antone's, too, though it's primarily known as a blues club. Still, you never know who you might find playing here tonight. ⏲ *30 min. 213 W. 5th St.* ☎ *512/320-8424.*

South by Southwest

There is no such direction as "north by northwest"—the name of the classic Alfred Hitchcock film starring Cary Grant; likewise, there's no one direction to take to get to Austin's popular South by Southwest Festival (SXSW)—the four-day interactive music and media fest spreads all over town each March. By night, music, musicians, celebrities, and fans spill into the streets, clubs, bars, courtyards, beer joints, theaters, and dance halls of Austin, with more than 2,000 performers from around the globe featured on more than 90 stages and new indie films screened all over town. By day, conference attendees do business at the SXSW Trade Show and attend panel discussions with hotshots from the music and film industry. Buy a single pass to all events, or get individual tickets to specific venues, but rush to book your trip now—the festival books up fast, and is said to have surpassed even the Sundance Film Festival in popularity.

www.antones.net. Daily 8:30pm–2am. Tickets $15–$25. Bus: 4, 22 & 451.

⓰ ★★★ **The Elephant Room.** Music goes underground here on Congress Avenue as, somewhere below street level, jazz burns up the night. Look for the club's small neon sign in a window low to the ground near 3rd Street and Congress Avenue, and follow a narrow stairwell down to this dark cave-like club, where a burnt saxophone can burrow deep into your soul. It's my favorite Austin club, and Wynton Marsalis (1961–) named it one of his top 10 favorite jazz venues in the U.S. He should know. ⏱ *1 hr. 315 Congress Ave.* ☎ *512/473-2279. www.elephantroom.com. No cover Sun–Thurs; $5 cover Fri & Sat. Mon–Fri 4pm–2am, Sat & Sun 8pm–2am. Bus: 1L, 1M, 5, 7 & 9.*

Soulful jazz plays at the Elephant Room.

Austin **with Kids**

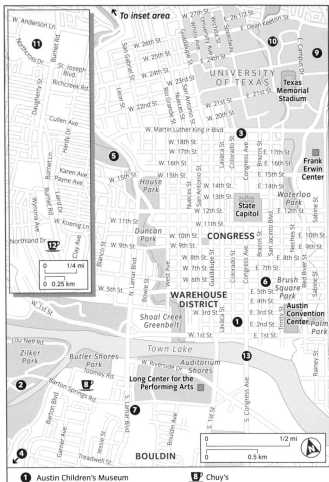

1. Austin Children's Museum
2. Zilker Metropolitan Park, The Zilker Zephyr & Barton Springs Pool
3. The Bob Bullock Texas State History Museum & IMAX theater
4. Austin Zoo and Animal Sanctuary
5. Pease Park
6. Austin Duck Adventures
7. Peter Pan Mini Golf
8. Chuy's
9. The Lyndon Baines Johnson Presidential Library & Museum
10. Texas Memorial Museum & Natural Science Center
11. Chaparral Ice Northcross
12. Phil's Ice House
13. Ann W. Richards Congress Avenue Bridge

Because Austin is such a casual place, you may find it to be more kid- and family-friendly than many other cities its size. Parents tend to strap babies on their backs, load toddlers into jogger-compatible strollers, and bring kids along to outdoor concerts, restaurants, stores—even yoga classes. In summer, some local bookstores, museums, and libraries host educational day-camps for kids. Parks are full of Frisbees, swimming pools, and kiddie-trains. Austin isn't fussy—it's all about family. This tour takes advantage of the mild south-central Texas weather and gets the kids out of doors and into Austin. Worried your children might get bored on this trip? Not possible. START: Take Bus 9 to Colorado & W. 2nd sts.

❶ ★ kids Austin Children's Museum. Curious kids of all ages love the colorful educational exhibits, fun play-scapes, art project areas, and story and music times here. It's not a huge space and parking can be a problem at the Dell Discovery Center where it's located, but it's still worth a visit. What better way to spend a summer afternoon when summer temperatures reach triple digits or rain threatens your plans? The museum allows parents and kids to play and learn together, with crafts, activities, and interactive exhibits for all ages. It may lack a "wow-factor" compared to other museums, but kids don't seem to notice. The Museum will soon relocate to an events complex at the site of the former Robert Mueller Airport; a moving date has yet to be announced, so check the

website for updates. Children must be accompanied by an adult, and the museum is free to the public every Sunday from 4 to 5pm, or at other times upon request by calling to inquire about the museum's "Open Door Policy." It's generally less crowded on weekday afternoons and on the first Tuesday of every month—"No Tour Tuesdays." ⏱ 2 hr. 201 Colorado St. ☎ 512/472-2499. www.austinkids.org. $6.50 adults & children 2 & up, $4.50 children 1–2, free for children under 1. Tues–Sat 10am–5pm, Wed "Community Night" 5–8pm, Sun noon–5pm. Closed most major holidays. Bus: 1L, 1M, 5, 7 & 9.

❷ ★★★ Zilker Metropolitan Park, The Zilker Zephyr & Barton Springs Pool. After taking a dip in the Barton Springs Pool or

Kids love learning at the Austin Children's Museum.

The Zilker Zephyr pulls into the station.

climbing on a playground jungle gym, be sure to ride the Zilker Zephyr, a miniature light rail train that makes slow, scenic, 25-minute tours of Zilker Park along Baron Creek and Lady Bird Lake. There's plenty of room for moms, dads, grandparents, and lots of kids—and your pets can ride, too. A whistle and a loud "All aboard!" from the conductor signal the train is about to leave the little station across from the Barton Springs Pool. Clean public restrooms nearby and a well-stocked concession stand come in handy. While there, visit the permanent **"SPLASH! Into the Edwards Aquifer"** interactive exhibit for kids located in the old Barton Springs Pool bathhouse, now the Beverly S. Sheffield Education Center, and check out the big bronze Philosopher's Rock statue nearby. ⏱ *1½ hr. See p 12,* ⑧.

③ ★★★ **The Bob Bullock Texas State History Museum & IMAX theater.** This museum is geared toward kids and families, and makes learning about Texas history a lot of fun. My son loved a Davy Crockett memorabilia exhibit and an IMAX show we saw there once that brought the story of the Lewis & Clark expedition to life. ⏱ *2 hr. See p 9,* ②. *Bus: 100, 103, 110 & 142.*

④ **Austin Zoo and Animal Sanctuary.** Austin isn't your typical town, and this isn't your typical zoo. For starters, it's smaller than most big-city zoos, and there isn't a regular concession stand (except on weekends), so they don't mind if you bring your own snacks and beverages—making any outing with kids a lot more affordable. But bring $1 to buy a bag of feed that your kids can give goats, sheep, and deer in the petting zoo area. One of the nicest things about this zoo is that it's also a non-profit animal sanctuary, assisting creatures large and small in need of rescue and rehabilitation. Because the focus here isn't on fancy habitat exhibits, kids can get a closer look at the 300-plus animals who've found a safe home here. Located about 15 miles (24km) southwest of downtown, near Oak Hill, it first began as a goat ranch and grew into the nice little zoo it is today. ⏱ *1½ hr. 10807 Rawhide Trail.* ☎ *512/288-1490. www.austin zoo.org. $8 adults; $6 seniors, students & military w/ID; $5 children 2–12 and guests of members; free to members and to children under 2.. Feb–Oct daily 10am–6pm (no entry after 5pm); Nov–Jan daily 10am–5:30pm (no entry after 4:30pm). Closed Thanksgiving & Christmas Day. No city bus service available.*

5 Pease Park. Who wouldn't love a park that throws an annual birthday party for Eeyore, the malcontent A.A. Milne (1882–1956) character from *Winnie-the-Pooh?* This large, rather bohemian festival for families, children, students, and singles takes place one Saturday each spring and features costumed revelers, drum circles, live music, food booths, and family-friendly games and events. But even if you miss the party, Pease Park is a nice spot year-round, located along the Shoal Creek Greenbelt, just blocks from downtown. Go on a fossil hunt with your kids along the creek or hike the whole greenbelt one morning (see p 22, **5**). With picnic tables; barbecue pits; a playground and a "sprayground" (water feature) for youngsters; as well as a disc golf course, and basketball and volleyball courts for bigger kids, Pease is sure to please the whole family—and Eeyore, too. A "Trees for Pease" campaign has pledged to plant 200 new trees in the park to replace trees felled during recent storms. ⏱ *30 min. 1100 Kingsbury St. (at Enfield Rd. where it becomes NW Pkwy.).* ☎ *512/974-6700. Daily 5am–10pm. www.ci.austin.tx.us/parks. Bus: 338.*

A tour at the Bob Bullock Texas State History Museum.

6 ★ Austin Duck Adventures. This is one of those things your kids will beg you to do, and you really should give in this time. Take an amphibious 75-minute sightseeing tour of downtown and Lake Austin while aboard a U.S. Coast Guard–inspected land- and water-friendly Hydra Terra vehicle. The tour will duck down 6th Street, then pass the Texas State Capitol building, the Bob Bullock Texas State History Museum, and the Governor's Mansion, before rolling into Lake Austin. Be at the departure site 30 minutes before the scheduled tour. Make reservations online or by telephone, or purchase tickets at the Visitor's Center. ⏱ *1½ hr. Visitor's Center 209 E. 6th St.; departure spot 2 blocks away at 301 W. 2nd St.* ☎ *512/4-SPLASH. www.austinducks.com. $26 adults, $24 seniors, $16 children 3–12. Visitor's Center daily 9am–4pm. Tours Mon & Tues noon; Wed–Fri 11am & 2pm; Sat & Sun 11am, 2 & 4pm. Bus: 10, 29, 110 & 486.*

7 ★ Peter Pan Mini Golf. An affordable, enjoyable way for a family to spend a summer evening in Austin is to play all 36 whimsical holes of this old-fashioned miniature golf course. An Austin landmark since 1948, Peter Pan Mini Golf is known for its giant fiberglass statue of Peter Pan, resting on bended knee, keeping a look-out for pirates, Tinker Bells, and Lost Boys along Barton Springs Road. With an enormous dinosaur, a bow-tie-wearing pig, a giant-sized rabbit, and a huge whale, characters along the course have nothing to do with the Peter Pan tale but everything to do with kids' rich imaginations. A charming, if rather unusual, thing about this kiddie land is that, for adults, it is BYOB-friendly—as long as you don't bring glass bottles. This authentic "vintage" putt-putt place might be

Peter Pan Mini Golf.

considered slightly well-worn, or even tatty—but, hey, that's part of its charm. It stays open till midnight on weekends, making it a novel, cheap date night, too. It features two 18-hole courses—one side designed to be a bit easier. Friday and Saturday night tend to be crowded, so go early or try it on a weekday. ⏱ *1 hr. 1207 Barton Springs Rd.* ☎ *512/472-1033. For 18 holes: $5 adults & children over 5, $3 children 5 & under; for an additional 18 holes $2 more for adults and children over 5, $1 more for children 5 & under. Bus: 3 & 338.*

8 ★ **Chuy's.** Maybe it's the bust of Elvis by the front door, the kitschy black-velvet paintings inside, or the colored Christmas lights on the roof; or perhaps it's just the consistently good Tex-Mex fare—nachos, tacos, and the like—that kids love. But Chuy's always seems like the perfect place for an impromptu celebration. Adults go

for the margaritas. It's more kid-friendly during the daytime, but crazy-busy crowded most nights, weekends, and even Saturday mornings. Seating indoors and out. Just down the street from Peter Pan Mini Golf. *1728 Barton Springs Rd.* ☎ *512/474-4452. $–$$.*

9 **The Lyndon Baines Johnson Presidential Library and Museum.** School-aged kids may find it fascinating to see the detailed ⅞-scale replica of President Lyndon Baines Johnson's Oval Office in the White House or to see his old Model T. Spend a little time here before going next door to the Texas Memorial Museum & Natural Science Center. ⏱ *45 min.* See p 58, **14**.

10 ★ **Texas Memorial Museum & Natural Science Center.** This museum was voted one of Austin's best for kids in the Nickelodeon's Parents' Picks Awards. My son loves to check out the dinosaur skeletons, fossils, and meteorites in the Hall of

Geology and Paleontology that takes up the entire 5,200-square-foot (483-sq.-m) first floor. ⏱ 1½ hr. See p 17, ➒.

⓫ ★★ Chaparral Ice Northcross.

I can't remember a time when this ice skating rink didn't sit at the center of the small Northcross Plaza in north-central Austin. The shopping mall hit hard times, but after all these years, the rink remains as wonderful as it has always been. In fact, it's even better after its recent full-scale renovation. The place is clean and kid-friendly, so on hot summer days when you want to get out of the sun, or in winter when it's hard to find that holiday feeling while wearing shorts, head to the rink. Their slogan is "Everything is cooler on ice," and I have to agree. To avoid crowds, skate Mondays and Tuesdays. ⏱ 1 hr. Northcross Mall, 2525 West Anderson Lane. ☎ 512/252-8500. www. chaparralice.com. Admission $6 adults & children over 5 ($4 skate rental), $5 children 5 & under (admission & skate rental combined). Sun, Mon & Wed noon–5pm, Tues noon–5:30pm, Thurs 11am–7pm, Fri noon–5pm & 7–10pm, Sat noon–4pm & 7–10pm. Bus: 3, 5, 19 & 325.

⓬ ★★ Phil's Ice House.

This converted gas station turned kid-friendly hamburger joint is a dream-come-true for parents seeking an inexpensive meal for their energetic—or even rowdy—fun-loving kids. Phil's serves up juicy hamburgers, regular and sweet potato fries, and great shakes, but moms and dads like being able to see their kids on the on-site playground from most indoor and outdoor tables. Phil's veggie burgers are egg-free and vegan-friendly. Meat lovers, try the 78704—a zip-code-named burger that regulars rave about, especially when it comes to the bun. Not that your kids will let you forget it, but remember Austin's own Amy's Ice Cream is right next door (see p 12, ➐). Phil's is not quite as kid-crazy/wild on weekdays. 5620 Burnet Rd. ☎ 512/524-1212. $.

⓭ ★★★ Hang out with the bats on the Congress Avenue Bridge.

Most little kids will think there's no better way to end their day in Austin. Squeamish types may think it's icky, but in a cool way, too. ⏱ 30 min. See p 13, ➒.

Mexican free-tail bats swarm the sky, at the Congress Avenue Bridge.

Romantic Austin

1. Austin Carriage Service
2. Capital Cruises
3. Umlauf Sculpture Garden and Museum
4. Mt. Bonnell
5. Fonda San Miguel
6. One World Theatre
7. The Driskill Hotel
8. The Paramount Theatre
9. The Mansion at Judge's Hill

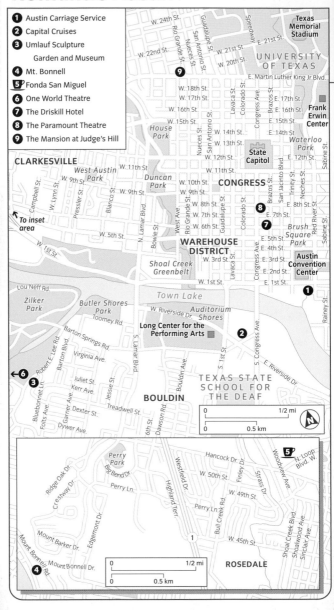

There's no shortage of romance in a city surrounded by lakes and in love with music. Enjoy a walk along a lush greenbelt, a canoe ride for two on a lake, or a dizzy dose of jazz in a loud late-night club. Here, romance is defined by the moments that take your breath away—whether that means a brisk climb up Mt. Bonnell or an intimate dinner for two. START: **Take Bus 1L or 1M to Congress Ave. & 11th St.**

❶ Austin Carriage Service. It's a bit cliché, but I love it anyway—a romantic carriage ride downtown after dark. Your carriage awaits you at most downtown hotels, and beautiful Percheron horses will pull you in style to restaurants, entertainment venues, and downtown attractions. For a ride with fewer interruptions from the driver, request a tour past old homes in West Austin. Reservations are required. A discount coupon is available on the website. At night, you can often find a carriage near the gates of the State Capitol, too. ⏲ *30-, 40-, 60- & 75-min tours available. 96 Red River St.* ☎ *512/243-0044. www.austincarriage.com. Sat & Sun 11am–6pm, Sun–Thurs dusk–11pm, Fri & Sat dusk–midnight. $50 30-min tour, $75 45-min tour, $100 1-hr tour, $125 75-min (downtown area) tour. Bus: 17 & 22.*

❷ ★ Capital Cruises. A boat cruise on Lady Bird Lake can take any size or shape you want: a lunch or dinner cruise on the 70-foot (21m) double-deck boat; a ride in a small electric boat with a canopy; or just a trip on a kayak, paddle boat (this is fun for two!), or—my favorite way—by a quiet canoe. Public sightseeing cruises and bat-watching excursions are a great value for your travel dollar, though not quite as romantic as a private outing. Call for reservations and departure times for public cruises and rental info. ⏲ *1½ hr. 208 Barton Springs Rd.* ☎ *512/480-9264. www.capital cruises.com. Public sightseeing cruise $8 adults, $6 seniors, $5 children 4–12 (prices vary for dinner cruise meal choices); canoe, kayak & paddle boat rentals $10/hr. Public tours Sat & Sun 1pm, daily 30 min. before sunset; call for specific cruise times. Bus: 5- & 30-Southbound.*

❸ ★★ Umlauf Sculpture Garden and Museum. It's no wonder so many couples get married here. This lush garden offers a quiet romantic retreat just across Lady

Capital Cruises offers a range of ways to see Lady Bird Lake.

The quiet Umlauf Sculpture Garden.

Bird Lake and the rest of the Zilker Park area. Art and nature cohabit in tranquil balance here, where the work of artist Charles Umlauf is displayed in a small wooded park. With sculpture pieces scattered throughout the garden, it seems as though faeries appear and dance between the trees. The museum is small and austere, and the grounds dream-like and calming. ⏱ *1 hr. See p 41,* ❸.

❹ **Mt. Bonnell.** The view of the city from the top of Mt. Bonnell will make you swoon—and so will climbing the steps leading there. ⏱ *1 hr. See p 15,* ❶.

5 ★★★ **Fonda San Miguel.** Because it's tucked away in north-central Austin, this place gets missed by most tourists, though it's one of the city's most romantic date-night spots. True to its authentic Mexican Interior roots, the restaurant serves cuisines native to seven different regions in Mexico and fine wines from all over the world. Sip drinks in the dimly lit patio area or enjoy a delectable, if rather expensive, dinner; this place has the cure if you crave romance. Former president George W. Bush (1946–) is said to have proposed to wife Laura (1946–) here. Rich warm, colorful glazed walls, a flowing fountain, and old Spanish-style furnishings give it a soft, surreal glow. Known for its eclectic Sunday brunch. *2330 W. North Loop Blvd.* ☎ *512/459-4121. $$$–$$$$.*

❻ ★★★ **One World Theatre.** A local poll named this Spanish Mission–style theater complex as one of the best places to get married in Austin, but I'd vote it one of the best concert venues in the city. Performers like Shawn Colvin (1956–), Dave Mason (1946–), The Manhattan Transfer, Duncan Sheik (1969–),

Authentic Mexican cuisine is served at Fonda San Miguel.

A packed night at the Paramount Theatre.

and more have played this small "green-built" theater on a hill in West Austin. Seating just 300, the venue offers that "feels like they're playing in your living room" sense that makes this concert experience unique—and so romantic. With terra cotta-colored walls and a silhouette vaguely reminiscent of the Alamo, One World is wildly romantic and other-worldly after dark. *See p 93.*

⑦ ★★ The Driskill Hotel. Dark, cozy, romantic—the piano bar of this historic hotel offers a quiet escape from the din of boisterous 6th Street. Its laid-back look is part polo-club lounge, part longhorn-steer-style cowboy bar. My husband and I went here on our first date. The adjacent Driskill Grill is crystal-wine-glass-and-white-tablecloth lovely. Honeymooners, the Renaissance Bridal Suite has a private balcony overlooking downtown Austin. ⏱ *1 hr. 604 Brazos St. (at 6th St.).* ☎ *800/252-9367. www.driskillhotel. com. Sun–Thurs noon–midnight, Fri & Sat noon–2am; happy hours Mon–Sat 5–7pm, Sun all-day-&-night specials on domestic beers & Brasilian Caipirinha. Bus: 4, 210 & 451. See p 46,* **④**.

⑧ ★★★ The Paramount Theatre. Since 1915, this part classical, Revival, and Baroque–Revival style theater has brought both culture and romance to Congress Avenue. Its stage has seen the likes of famous vaudeville acts like the Marx Brothers and crooners like Tony Bennett (1926–) and even island-cowboy Jimmy Buffett (1946–). Catch a live stage show or concert, or view a classic film like *Casablanca* during one of the Paramount's many movie nights and matinees offered throughout the year. *1714 Congress Ave.* ☎ *512/472-5470. www.austin theatre.org. Tickets $35–$150 concerts/Broadway shows, $10–$50 films & local artists' concerts. Bus: 1L, 1M, 5, 6, 7 & 9.*

⑨ ★★★ The Mansion at Judge's Hill. The epitome of elegance, this luxury boutique hotel, in the Goodall Wooten Mansion built in 1900, features the fine dining and superior wines of Judge's Hill Restaurant & Bar—just the right touch of romance to make you fall in love with Austin. Spend the night and sip morning coffee on a broad verandah with views of the Capitol dome. *1900 Rio Grande St. (at the corner of MLK, Jr. Blvd. & Rio Grande St., just west of the UT campus).* ☎ *800/311-1619. Bus 410 southbound & 624. $$$. See p 89.*

Downtown Austin

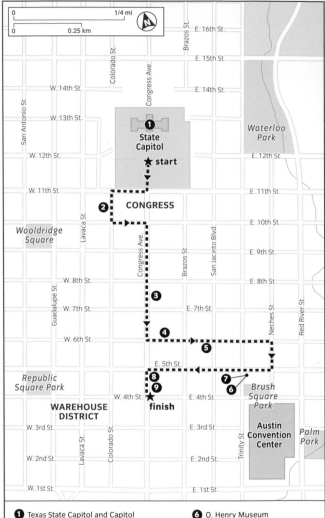

1. **Texas State Capitol and Capitol Visitor's Center & Museum**
2. **The Governor's Mansion**
3. **The State Theatre & The Paramount Theatre**
4. **The Driskill Hotel**
5. **6th Street Entertainment District**
6. **O. Henry Museum**
7. **Joseph and Susanna Dickinson Hannig Museum**
8. **Mexic-Arte Museum**
9. **Frost Bank Tower**

The heart of any bustling city can be found downtown, and in Austin, that area includes impressive sites such as the Texas State Capitol, the Governor's Mansion, and the sassy 6th Street entertainment district. Stroll along Congress Avenue and get a feel for Austin's exciting urban scene. The most impressive structures are those that have been standing a while—buildings from the 1800s featuring high arched windows and limestone facades. Sure, Austin leans toward all things bohemian, but it still wears a suit when it works downtown. START: **Take bus 1L or 1M to Congress Ave. & 11th St.**

---

① ★★★ kids The Texas State Capitol and Capitol Visitor's Center & Museum. I love to tour the impressive State Capitol complex and stroll its 22-acre (8.9-hectare) grounds, especially on a spring day when its gardens are in bloom. The Capitol rotunda is tall and stunning, and the building is accessible and visitor-friendly, staying open to the public whenever the State Legislature is in session. Sometimes, the lawmakers meet late into the night—so a midnight stroll through the historic building isn't entirely out of the question on some occasions. On the lawn, see the foundation of the original statehouse used while the current Capitol was being

Inside the Capitol's stunning rotunda.

built. Free guided tours of the Capitol Complex and self-guided walks with pamphlets are available. The Visitor's Center, located in the old General Land Office, built in 1857, features interactive exhibits and films about Texas history. *See p 9, ①.*

② The Governor's Mansion. You can't go inside, but stop and admire the Governor's Mansion. On June 8, 2008, it was damaged by arson, engulfing in fire the Greek Revival residence of Texas governors since June 1856. One of the oldest structures of the Capitol Complex, the Governor's Mansion is a registered National Historic Landmark and the oldest executive residence west of the Mississippi. Fortunately, furnishings and contents of the mansion were in storage at the time of the fire. *1010 Colorado St.* ☎ *800/843-5789 or 512/463-5516. www.txfgm.org. Closed for structural restoration until 2012.*

③ ★★ The State Theatre & the Paramount Theatre. Sleek Art Deco decor and ornate gilded glam stand side by side in these two historic theaters. Now part of the Austin Theatre Alliance, the State (1935) and the Paramount (1915) have served as movie, vaudeville, and performing arts theaters. Listed on the National Register of Historic Places, the Paramount housed offices of the War Department in 1939, and the Adjunct General of the Republic of Texas occupied this site. Texas hero Sam Houston once had an office here. The State Theatre, which is currently closed except for acting classes, stands on the site of the old Avenue Hotel, next door to the still quite popular Paramount. A 1990s restoration revived the now 320-seat venue at the State, but a break in a water main flooded the building and now another restoration is underway. Tours are sometimes given of the Paramount, but not the State (call to schedule); however, tickets to Paramount stage performances and films are available at the box office and on the Web. *713 Congress Ave. (Paramount Theatre) & 719 Congress Ave. (State Theatre).* ☎ *512/472-5470. www.austintheatre.org.*

④ ★★★ The Driskill Hotel. There's something so intrinsically Texan about this old hotel. Completed in 1886, this limestone-and-brick landmark sits on land purchased by cattle baron and honorary Confederate army colonel Jesse Lincoln Driskill (1824–1890), who spent $7,500 for the city block and $400,000 to build and furnish the hotel. Originally a 60-room inn, the hotel now features 189 guest rooms and suites. In October 1898, the first long-distance telephone call from Austin was placed from the lobby. President Lyndon Johnson is said to have spent the night of the 1964 presidential election here waiting for returns. Today, the hotel offers a retreat from crowds on 6th Street. The dark piano bar is a favorite of Austin businessmen after work and a nice date-night spot. *See p 43,* **⑦**.

⑤ 6th Street Entertainment District (East 6th Street). Once called "Pecan Street", 6th Street's 7-block section from Congress Avenue to the I-35 is known for music and comedy clubs, bars, restaurants, and shops. This area is a madhouse on Halloween and New Year's Eve, and during special events such as the South by Southwest music and film festival. *See p 10,* **❸**.

⑥ ★ The O. Henry Museum. This quaint museum housed in a small Queen Anne–style cottage was once the home of famed American author William Sidney Porter, who penned short stories under the pseudonym "O. Henry." Porter first

The luxurious Driskill Hotel.

came to Austin in 1884 and, 10 years later, began publishing a satirical weekly newspaper *The Rolling Stone* (not related to today's music magazine). Porter is perhaps best known for "The Gift of the Magi," a tale with a twist about a poor couple who sell the best they have to buy gifts for one another. Today, the house where Porter lived from 1893 to 1895 sits at 409 E. 5th St. as a museum featuring artifacts and memorabilia from his life in Austin. *See p 21,* ❸.

❼ The Joseph and Susanna Dickinson Hannig Museum. Battle of the Alamo survivor Susanna Dickinson and her fourth husband Joseph Hannig lived in this house from 1870 to 1873. Today, the 1,600-sq.-ft (149-sq.-m), six-room stone structure is a museum dedicated to Dickinson who, with her 15-month old daughter Angelina, were two of only a few survivors of The Alamo. Hannig, 20 years Dickinson's junior, was a city alderman, cabinet and furniture maker/distributor, and coffin maker, and he built this house for her. Featuring artifacts from Dickinson's descendants and an original bedroom set from the Joseph Hannig Company. On Thursday afternoons, the museum hosts a Pioneer Quilting Bee, and family programs are offered most weekends. *See p 21,* ❸.

❽ ★ Mexic-Arte Museum. The "Official Mexican and Mexican-American Fine Art Museum of Texas," this space features colorful collections and exciting exhibits.

The Frost Bank Tower pierces Austin's skyline.

The gift shop offers handmade Mexican imports, books, and art. *See p 24,* ❽.

❾ Frost Bank Tower. At 515 feet (157m), this attractive 33-story skyscraper, built in 2003, is now one of the most recognizable features of the Austin skyline. Designed by Duda/Paine Architects, I like to think of this silver-blue glass skyscraper as Austin's answer to the Chrysler Building. Local newspaper columnist John Kelso writes it has a "huge glass design at the top that looks like a nose-hair trimmer." Weird, but true. *401 Congress Ave.* ☎ *512/536-8400.* www.tpgaustin.com.

South Congress ("SoCo")

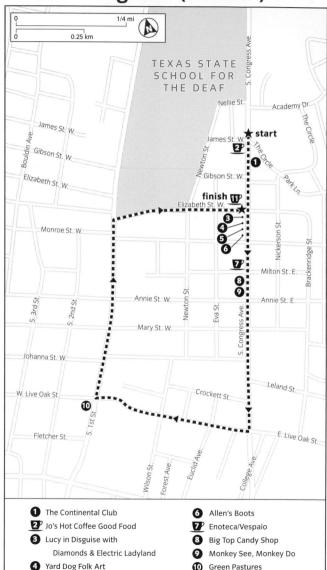

1. The Continental Club
2. Jo's Hot Coffee Good Food
3. Lucy in Disguise with Diamonds & Electric Ladyland
4. Yard Dog Folk Art
5. Uncommon Objects
6. Allen's Boots
7. Enoteca/Vespaio
8. Big Top Candy Shop
9. Monkey See, Monkey Do
10. Green Pastures
11. Guero's Taco Bar

Austin is often called the "Third Coast," and here, you'll see why. If New York has SoHo, Austin has SoCo, an *avant garde* area of eclectic shops, music venues, and young, trendy hotels. Vintage cowboy boots, Airstream food trailers, oddball accessories, costumes, and jewelry—all on one eccentric strip boldly intent on keeping Austin interesting. On the first Thursday of each month, shops stay open late. Bohemian? You bet. **START: Take 1M-Southbound to 1315 South Congress Ave.**

❶ ★ The Continental Club. It's a little loud, a little shabby, and *so* Austin—so I love it. The Continental Club has long been one of Austin's most-venerated clubs, and there's no telling what band you might see here (or who you might run into) late at night. Hit "Hippie Hour" on Tuesday nights for folk music and blues. *See p 32,* **⓮**.

❷ Jo's Hot Coffee Good Food. Free Wi-Fi, good strong coffee, outdoor tables, and a shared parking lot with the Hotel San Jose make this a nice, simple place to start, or stop, on your stroll along SoCo. The food ain't bad, either—they make a mean Frito pie. *1300 S. Congress Ave.* ☎ *512/444-3800. $.*

❸ ★★ Lucy in Disguise with Diamonds & Electric Ladyland. Two stores opened their doors on April Fool's Day in 1984 and soon merged into one mega-fun 8,000-square-foot (743-sq.-m) space for costumes, masks, wigs, shoes, vintage clothing, cheap-jewelry, kooky hats, and stuff so weird and wonderful it'd make Elton John, Elvis, and Liberace proud. If Austin is weird, this is why.

❹ Yard Dog Folk Art. This self-proclaimed "maximalist, colorful, edgy" gallery features folk and "outsider" art, with a particular fondness for pieces found in the Deep South. With wood carvings, paintings, sculpture, and unusual pieces by noted Americana artists, you're sure

Vintage lunchboxes and other curiosities can be found in Uncommon Objects.

"Party at the Moontower!"

If you saw the cult-classic 1993 indie film Dazed and Confused, set in Austin, you may remember the line "Party at the moon-tower!" and the scene filmmaker Richard Linkletter set under one of Austin's Moonlight Towers. So what's a "moontower"? Standing 165-feet (50m) above their 15-foot (4.6m) base, these old fashioned towers illuminate Austin with bright lights, creating a bright moon-light-like glow. Popular in the late 1800s across the U.S. and Europe, the original moonlight towers were established in Austin between 1884 and 1885. Today, Austin is the only city in the world still utilizing moontower lighting, though only 17 of the original 31 towers remain. Each tower originally contained six carbon arc lamps, illuminating a 1,500-ft-radius (457m) circle, which is said to have burned "brightly enough to read a watch from as far away as 1,500 feet." Originally, the towers were connected to generators on the Colorado River. In the '20s, those were changed to incandescent lamps, and in the 1930s, mercury vapor lamps were lit by a switch at each tower's base. During World War II, a central switch controlled the lights, allowing city-wide blackouts in case of air raids. As a part of a $1.3-million project in 1993, the City of Austin dismantled and meticulously restored each piece of the 17 towers. The towers were officially recognized as state archeological landmarks in 1970 and were later collectively listed in the National Register of Historic Places in 1976. Austin's towers are scattered all over town, with greatest concentration being near the Capitol; however, the city's most popular tower may be the one standing in Zilker Park which is used to create the Zilker tree each December. For a while a replica moonlight tower stood on this spot where the Dazed and Confused scene was set; however, today an authentic moontower stands on the spot.

to find something unusual to make your own.

⑤ ★★★ Uncommon Objects. Even those who disdain shopping don't mind poking in this "antiques shop" full of curious odd items and kitschy nostalgic junk. Quirky and interesting, here you can find the perfect pair of vintage early–Dale Evan's cowboy boots, a Partridge Family lunchbox, a Formica kitchen table, and retro salt and pepper shakers to match. Look for the

cowboy riding a giant jackrabbit on the sign. See p 63.

⑥ ★★ Allen's Boots. Not just for cowboys anymore, boots are more important to an Austin wardrobe than a dark suit or a little black dress. And with nearly 5,000 pairs to pick from, Allen's Boots is the place to get your Texas footwear fix. Ostrich, eel, alligator—there are a bazillion kinds to try on. With a huge selection of vintage boots for cowboys—wildly colorful ones for cowgirls, too—and enough western wear to make you holler "Yippee kay yay!"—you'll spend a lot more time and money in this store than you intend. See p 62.

7 ★★ **Enoteca/Vespaio.** Italian was never so inviting as at Enoteca, an "unfussy" little bistro on the avenue, with Vespaio its adjacent nighttime dinner date counterpart. With a few tiny tables scattered around the small space before a brick oven and open kitchen, and a deli-case of delight near the front door, this little eatery is so appealing—though this bright space can be awfully loud at times, and the wait for a table can seem endless. Pass the time perusing the choice wine list and seeing their fresh herb garden out back. *1610 S. Congress Ave. Enoteca* ☎ *512/441-7672; Vespaio* ☎ *512/ 441-6100. $–$$ Enoteca; $$–$$$ Vespaio.*

8 ★ **Big Top Candy Shop.** The Good Ship Lollipop must have dropped anchor here and propped up a circus tent of treats at this SoCo soda fountain and sugar shack. With enough candy to make your sweet tooth ache, here you'll

Novelty and nostalgia define the merchandise at Monkey See, Monkey Do.

find saltwater taffy, jawbreakers, candy necklaces, malts, and everything else your mom said not to eat between meals. It often stays open late when the store is busy. *1706 S. Congress Ave.* ☎ *512/462-2220. No website. Sun–Fri 11am–7pm, Sat 10am–7pm.*

9 ★ **Monkey See, Monkey Do.** It's a toy shop for adults—but not the sexy kind. No, this quirky shop features nostalgic novelty finds: toys, clocks, posters, bags, gum, candy, patches, buttons, and more. Where else can you find candy cigarettes, Magic Eight Balls, meat-themed toys, rubber chickens, sock monkeys, and talking George

Big Top Candy Shop's collection of sweets.

Meals on Wheels—South Congress Food Trailer Park Row

Food concession trailers are all the rage across the U.S. these days, especially in late-night entertainment areas like SoCo. Here, "meals-on-wheels" has taken on a whole new meaning with a centrally located strip of Airstream and RV eateries on the Avenue. In laid-back Austin, no one is in a hurry to eat on the run, so here tables are set up and little lights hang above the gravel parking lot, making this food trailer court a place to gather with friends, grab good food, and stay a while. *The Wall Street Journal* called SoCo's Mighty Cone one of "The Top-10 Trailers in America." Currently located in the gravel parking lot next to Congress Avenue Baptist Church (1511 S. Congress Ave.), the trailers may soon find a new location on South Congress when a new boutique hotel is built on this spot. For more info, visit www.austinfoodcarts.com.
Here's a list of a few fun trailers to try:

- **The Mighty Cone:** Known for hot and crunchy fried wraps (or "cones") made with chicken, shrimp, or avocado and served with mango aioli and slaw. It's no wonder this place gets such raves—its haute cuisine counterpart is the elegant, highly acclaimed Hudson's on the Bend (see p 77) restaurant on Lake Travis, whose chefs helped launch this hot trailer stop.
- **Flip Happy Crepes:** Featuring tasty tarragon-mushroom crepes with goat cheese, caramelized onions, spinach, and tomatoes.
- **Love Puppies Brownies:** Homemade brownies made by people who love puppies. Voted Austin's Best Kept Secret in the 2009 Best of Austin readers' poll in *The Austin Chronicle*.
- **Torchy's Tacos:** Go for the green chili pork tacos topped with queso fresco, cilantro, onions, and lime.
- **Hey Cupcake!:** Among their quirky cupcakes is "The Michael Jackson"—chocolate on the inside with cream cheese icing.
- **Vaquero Cocina:** Yummy smoked brisket and sweet plantain chips.
- **The Holy Cacao:** Ooooh, I love their sweet S'mores on a Stick and chocolate mint Grasshopper cake-balls.
- **Izzoz's Tacos:** Said to be the largest food trailer in Austin. Pronounced "ee-zoes," it's located at 1207 S. 1st St. (☎ 512/326-4996).
- **Lucky J's Chicken and Waffles:** Best known for their waffle tacos served with hot sauce and syrup. www.luckyjs.com

The Mighty Cone is known for its hot and crunchy fried wraps.

W. Bush dolls? An hour in here will surely bring out the little rascal in you.

⑩ ★★ **Green Pastures.** Just a few blocks from the hurly-burly bohemian business of SoCo, Green Pastures is a gentle giant hidden under a canopy of trees at the edge of a quiet neighborhood. This historic Victorian mansion, with its attractive 5-acre (2-hectare) grounds, is a favorite for wedding receptions, birthday and anniversary celebrations, and Sunday brunch. A sprawling Victorian country house built in 1884 and 1885, it's the Grand Dame of South Austin and a favorite with visitors who just knew there had to be more to South Austin than the fey urban fuss and retro-ruckus of South Congress Avenue. *811 W. Live Oak St.* ☎ *512/444-4747. wwwgreenpasturesrestaurant. com. Daily 11am–2pm & 6–10pm.*

⑪ ★★ **Guero's Taco Bar.** This place is wildly popular—although, with all the great Tex-Mex spots around, I've never completely understood why. Sure, it was always the place to go for breakfast on weekends when it was located on East Oltorf Street, and I always enjoyed their breakfast tacos and migas in the morning—but since Guero's moved to SoCo in 1995, its popularity has jettisoned off the charts. Maybe it's their smart central SoCo location or the laid-back patio dining scene that everyone likes. Perhaps it's the dangerously delicious hand-squeezed lime margaritas they make. Whatever it is, it works, and I get that. Busy, cheap, and fun, with hot salsa and cold beer. *1412 S. Congress Ave.* ☎ *512/477-7688. $–$$.*

The University of Texas

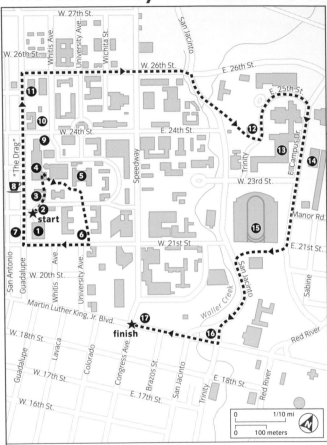

1. Harry Ransom Center
2. Sutton Hall
3. Goldsmith Hall
4. Texas Union Building
5. Main Building and Tower
6. Littlefield Memorial Fountain
7. The Drag
8. Caffé Medici
9. Battle Oaks
10. Littlefield Home
11. Jesse H. Jones B Communication Center
12. Texas Memorial Museum & Natural Science Center
13. Performing Arts Center
14. LBJ Library and Museum
15. Darrell K. Royal/Texas Memorial Stadium
16. Santa Rita No. 1
17. Blanton Museum of Art

A towering testament to the spirit of The Lone Star State, the University of Texas at Austin stands with its feet proudly planted in its rugged cowboy past and with the eyes of Texas locked on the horizon of a bright future. Here, ancient oak trees, stately buildings, world-class museums, and the latest in cutting-edge technology come together to create one of the largest public universities in the United States. Founded in 1853, the school currently has an enrollment of more than 50,000 students. Fewer than 2 miles (3.2km) from the State Capitol, the UT Campus is the young heart of Texas's favorite city. START: **Bus 1M or 1L to the Harry Ransom Humanities Research Center.**

Travel Tip

Because the campus sits on 350,000 acres (141,640 hectares), a comprehensive campus tour on foot may not be feasible for all visitors. Even the following tour, highlighting some of the campus's most interesting sites, might be better divided into two parts: walking stops 1 through 11—which can be done in less than an hour—and driving between stops 11 and 17, returning later to visit museums and buildings you'd further like to explore. However, for those in good health and with sturdy walking shoes, walking the entire tour is doable, although somewhat difficult.

❶ ★★★ **Harry Ransom Center.** This is the research library, museum, and historic archive collection of the Humanities Research Center of the University of Texas. A.S. Byatt's (1936–) best-selling novel *Possession* is ostensibly based on this place. On the first floor, view just one of five complete Gutenberg Bibles in the U.S., along with one of the world's first photographs, created by Joseph Nicèphore Nièpce (1765–1833) in 1826. Upstairs, treasured documents such as love letters by ee cummings (1894–1964) and original manuscripts by Ernest

Hemingway (1899–1961) are archived, along with original notes on Watergate donated by Bob Woodward (1943–) and Carl Bernstein (1944–). *300 W. 21st St.* ☎ *512/471-8944. Free admission. Ransom Center Galleries: Tues, Wed & Fri 10am–5pm; Thurs 10am–7pm; Sat & Sun noon–5pm. Closed Mon. Library reading/viewing rooms: Mon–Fri 9am–5pm, Sat 9am–noon. Closed Sun. Docent-led tours of the Ransom Center Galleries Tues noon & Sat 2pm.*

❷ **Sutton Hall.** Designed by Cass Gilbert (1859–1934) in 1918, Sutton Hall is part of the School of Architecture. Mediterranean in style with terra cotta-colored moldings, a red-tile roof, and Palladian windows, the building is architecturally arresting.

Across the sidewalk, facing northwest, see . . .

❸ **Goldsmith Hall.** Architectural design classes are held in this building designed by Paul Cret (1876–1945), featuring beautiful dark slate floors. Outside, a central courtyard is shaded by tall palm trees.

❹ ★★ **Texas Union Building.** UT's student union building was also designed by Paul Cret. With everything from shops to food courts to a bowling alley and a formal ballroom, here in the shade of the UT Tower, the Texas Union is always a popular

The Mediterranean-styled architecture of Sutton Hall.

gathering place for students. *SW corner of 24th & Guadalupe sts. Free admission. Mon–Fri 7–3am, Sat 10–3am, Sun noon–3am.*

❺ ★★ **Main building and tower.** This famous postcard-shot spot features a 307-foot-high (94m) tower that glows an impressive burnt orange color when lit to celebrate a Longhorn sports victory. Designed by Paul Cret in 1937 in the Beaux Arts style, the clock tower is Austin's most famous edifice, with the possible exception of the Texas State Capitol. Cret called the tower "the image carried in our memory when we think of the place." However, the beauty of Cret's tower may always be overshadowed by the memory of a fateful day in August 1966 when sniper Charles Whitman (1941–1966) shot and killed 17 people and wounded 31 more from the tower before he, too, was killed. Closed to the public in 1975 after a series of suicide leaps from its observation deck, the tower reopened for supervised visits in 1999. One of the loveliest features of the tower is its classical temple on top and its 56-bell carillon, the largest in Texas. Make reservations (either by phone or in person at the Hospitality Desk located in the Texas Union Building), as tours are often booked as much as a week in advance. *Guided UT tower tours 45 min.* ☎ *512/475-6633 (reservations) Sat & Sun 2–6pm.*

❻ ★★ **Littlefield Memorial Fountain.** This three-tiered fountain at the foot of the **South Mall** was built in 1933 as a memorial to students who died in World War I

The 307-foot-high University of Texas Tower was built in 1937 in the Beaux Arts style.

The Littlefield Memorial Fountain, dedicated to students who died in World War I.

and stands at the entrance to what was the University's original 40-acre (16-hectare) campus. In the distance behind it stands the Texas State Capitol. The fountain features an artistic allegorical depiction of a battleship sailing across the ocean to aid World War I Allies. Major General George W. Littlefield's (1842–1920) $250,000 donation funded the fountain and six sculpture figures.

7 The Drag. Dubbed "The Drag" by students, the section of Guadalupe Street that runs along the west side of campus from Martin Luther King, Jr. Boulevard up to about 26th Street is Austin's most popular pedestrian strip. (Some would argue "The Drag" stretches as far as 45th Street, but most people think of it as being the section that edges the UT Campus.) Home to bookstores, fast-food restaurants, coffee shops, co-ops, trendy shops, and the bohemian 23rd Street Renaissance Market, this main artery keeps UT student life lively. *Guadalupe St., from MLK, Jr. Blvd. to 29th St.*

8 Caffé Medici. For a hit of espresso, latte, or some chai tea, visit this little student-filled cafe, firmly committed to a sustainable model of business, including green products, recycling, careful product selection, and (of course) good coffee. *2222B Guadalupe St.* ☎ *512/524-5049. $.*

9 ★ Battle Oaks. These three ancient oak trees stood on the original 40-acre (16-hectare) UT campus when it opened in September of 1893, and the oldest of these is said to pre-date the Civil War. Named for Dr. W.J. Battle, a professor of classics and an acting president of the University from 1914 to 1916, who is said to have camped under the trees with a shotgun to save them from "the administration axe" that threatened to chop them down to erect a biology building on the site in 1923. Thanks to Dr. Battle, students still study in the shade of the trees' massive branches.

⏺ ★ **Littlefield Home.** This ornate Victorian home was built in 1893 at a cost of $50,000 by Confederate Civil War veteran Major George W. Littlefield, a wealthy developer, cattle rancher, and banker who lived in this house with his wife Alice. The home was donated to the University upon Alice's death in 1935. The house is said to be haunted by Alice, who according to legend, may be heard banging on a piano late at night. Note in front the impressive 35-foot-high (11m) deodar cedar tree imported from the Himalayas. The building currently houses some of the University Development offices. *24th & Whitis sts.*

⏺ **Jesse H. Jones B Communication Center.** As home to KLRU-TV (Channel 18), KUT Radio (90.5 FM), and the nationally syndicated Latino USA radio program, this three-building center (completed in 1973) was named for a Houston politician, entrepreneur, and publisher of *The Houston Chronicle*. Building B is probably best-known as the place where the PBS television show *Austin City Limits* (see p 27, ⏺) has long filmed on a soundstage; however, *Austin City Limits* will soon move tapings to a new theater to be located downtown, adjacent to the W Hotel–ACL (see p 89).

Walk 1 block east to UT shuttle bus stop K2 at Dean Keaton St. & University Ave. Take bus 21-Eastbound to Robert Dedman Dr.

⏺ ★★ **Texas Memorial Museum & Natural Science Center.** The Texas Memorial Museum is the exhibit hall of the Texas Natural Science Center, which is also home to the **Vertebrate Paleontology Laboratory,** the **Non-Vertebrate Paleontology Laboratory,** and the **Texas Natural History Collections.** This museum is free and open to the

Outside the Texas Memorial Museum & Natural Science Center.

public, and is popular with school-aged children. *2400 Trinity St.* ☎ *512/471-1604. Free admission. Mon–Fri 9am–5pm, Sat 10am–5pm, Sun 1–5pm.*

⏺ ★ **Performing Arts Center.** This center is home to the 3,000-seat **Bass Concert Hall,** the 700-seat **Bates Recital Hall,** and other College of the Fine Arts auditoriums, which present music, theater, dance, and lecture events throughout the year, including popular touring Broadway productions and concert attractions. The Bates Recital Hall is home to the largest tracker organ in the country. *2350 Robert Dedman Dr. Performing Arts Center:* ☎ *512/471-2787; Mon–Fri 9am–5pm. Ticket office:* ☎ *512/471-1444; Mon–Fri 10am–6pm.*

⏺ ★ **LBJ Library and Museum.** The 30-acre (12-hectare) site of the Lyndon Baines Johnson Library and Museum building complex sits on a plaza adjoining Sid Richardson Hall and the LBJ School of Public Affairs. It is the first presidential library to be built on a university campus. Among the museum's exhibits is a ⅞-scale replica of the Oval Office as it looked when the Johnsons occupied the White House. *2313 Red River St.* ☎ *512/721-0200. www.lbjlib.utexas.edu. Free admission. Daily 9am–5pm.*

⓯ ★★ Darrell K. Royal/Texas Memorial Stadium. Home to the UT Longhorn football team since 1924, the first of the annual UT–Texas A&M Thanksgiving Day games was played in this stadium. The upper deck was added in 1972. Legend maintains that, to fund the original stadium, female students sold their hair and male students sold their blood, and wealthy timber-family heir, UT alum, and longtime Board of Regents member H.J. Lutcher Stark (1887–1965) matched every $10,000 they raised with $1,000 of his own funds. The stadium's name was changed in 1996 to honor legendary Longhorn football coach Darrell K. Royal (1924–). Today, with its current seating capacity of 100,119, the stadium is home to one of the largest high-definition video-screen scoreboards in the world, nicknamed "Godzillatron" by fans. *2100 San Jacinto Blvd. Ticket office* ☎ *512/471-3333; tour reservations* ☎ *512/708-0505. www.texassports.com. Free 30–40 min tours Tues, Wed, Thurs 11am & 12:30pm. Call on the Sun prior to the tour you wish to schedule.*

⓰ Santa Rita No. 1. This West Texas oil rig came in big on May 28, 1923, spraying oil over the top of the derrick and covering a 750-foot (229m) area around the site on land belonging to the University of Texas System. The money gained was distributed among UT system campuses, including UT Austin and Texas A&M University, though UT Austin received more—two-thirds. In 1940, under the leadership of the **Texas State Historical Association,** Santa Rita was moved from its original site to the UT Austin campus. *Corner of San Jacinto & MLK, Jr. blvds.*

⓱ Blanton Museum of Art. The Blanton Museum of Art features a permanent collection of more than 18,000 works, including European paintings, prints, and drawings, and modern contemporary American and Latin American art. It is located across the street from the Bob Bullock Texas State History Museum (see p 9, ❷). *200 E. MLK, Jr. Blvd.* ☎ *512/471-7324. www.blanton museum.org. $5 adults, $4 seniors 65 & older, $3 youth 13–25, free children 12 & younger; free admission on Thurs. Tues, Wed & Fri 10am–5pm, Thurs 10am–8pm, Sat 11am–5pm, Sun 1–5pm. Parking $3 w/ validation. Bus: 100, 103, 110 & 142.*

Santa Rita No. 1 moved from its original location to the UT Austin campus.

Best of **Austin Shopping**

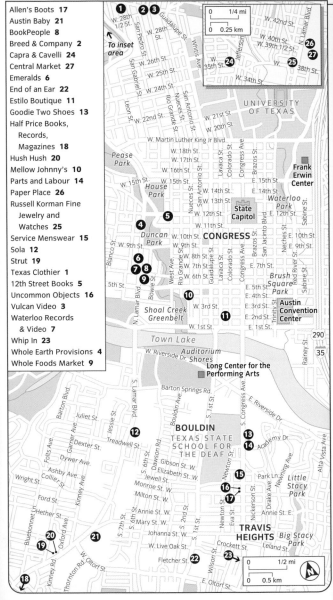

Shopping Best Bets

Best **Bike Shop**
★★★ Mellow Johnny's Bike Shop,
400 Nueces St. (p 62)

Best **Bookstore**
★★★ BookPeople, *603 N. Lamar
Blvd. (p 62)*

Best **Clothing**
★★ Sola, *2003 S. Congress Ave.
(p 64)*

Best **Collectibles/Antiques**
★★★ Uncommon Objects, *1512 S.
Congress Ave. (p 63)*

Best **Convenience Store**
★ Whip In, *1950 S. I-35 (p 63)*

Best **Cowboy Boots**
★★ Allen's Boots, *1522 S. Congress
Ave. (p 62)*

Best **Factory Outlet Mall**
★★ Tanger Outlet Center/Prime
Outlets, *IH-35 S. 900, San Marcos
(p 67)*

Best **Food Market**
★★★ Whole Foods, *525 N. Lamar
Blvd. (p 65)*

Best **Local Hardware & More
Store**
★★★ Breed & Co., *718 W. 29th St.
(p 65)*

Best **Outdoor Gear**
★★ Whole Earth Provision, *1014 N.
Lamar Blvd. (p 67)*

*Antiques and collectibles on display at
Uncommon Objects.*

Best **Record/CD Store**
★★★ Waterloo Records & Video,
600A N. Lamar Blvd. (p 66)

★★ End of an Ear, *2209 S. 1st St.
(p 66)*

Best **Stationery**
★★★ Paper Place, *4001 N. Lamar
Blvd. (p 64)*

Best **Shoes**
★ Goodie Two Shoes, *1111 S. Congress Ave. (p 67)*

Austin Shopping A to Z

Bikes

★★★ Mellow Johnny's Bike Shop WAREHOUSE DISTRICT Native son Lance Armstrong (1971–) opened this cycle shop that he calls "a temple to two-wheeled living." With bike sales and rentals ($20 for 4 hours), cool gear and stylish apparel, and even showers and lockers for commuters, Lance is on a roll here. The adjacent Juan Pelota Café features smoothies and organic coffee. The staff is happy to help map out your next scenic Austin ride. *400 Nueces St.* ☎ *512/473-0222. www. mellowjohnnys.com. AE, DISC, MC, V.*

Books

★ 12th Street Books LAMAR BLVD I can think of few better ways to spend a Saturday than with a good book in the corner of this classy little store brimming with out-of-print, used, and hard-to-find books. *827 W. 12th St. at Rio Grande St.* ☎ *512/499-8828. www.12thstreetbooks.com. AE, MC, V.*

★★★ kids BookPeople MARKET DISTRICT With over 200,000 titles, it's the largest independent book store in town and just a stone's throw from Whole Foods. Owner Steve Bercu is a co-founder of the "Keep Austin Weird" campaign, but the store is fairly mainstream— think Barnes & Noble, but with a distinct Austin vibe. *603 N. Lamar Blvd.* ☎ *512/472-5050. www.bookpeople. com. AE, DISC, MC, V.*

★★ kids Half Price Books, Records, Magazines SOUTH AUSTIN I like to get my holiday cards and shopping done here. Prices are great, and they have books, calendars, music, gifts, and more. It's part of a chain—but it sure doesn't look like one. *2929 S. Lamar Blvd.* ☎ *512/443-3138; 5555 N. Lamar Blvd.* ☎ *512/451-4463. www.halfpricebooks.com. AE, DISC, MC, V.*

Boots

★★ Allen's Boots SOCO Whether you go for a Howdy-Doody vintage vanguard or prefer a classic cattle-rancher Lucchese look, this store has the quintessential Texas cowboy boot for you, with Stetson hats, jeans, western wear, handbags, stuffed-animal armadillos, and more deep in the heart of SoCo. *1522 S.*

Rare and out-of-print books fill the shelves of 12th Street Books.

SoCo's Allen's Boots.

Congress Ave. ☎ *512/447-1413. www.allensboots.com. AE, DISC, MC, V.*

Collectibles
★★★ Uncommon Objects
SOCO I could spend all afternoon in this eclectic antique and collectibles shop, with its vintage and offbeat items, from Partridge Family lunchboxes to pillbox hats. (*See p 50.*) *1512 S. Congress Ave.* ☎ *512/442-4000. www.uncommon objects.com. AE, DISC, MC, V.*

Convenience Store
★ Whip In SOUTHEAST AUSTIN
More like an old hippie college coffeehouse than convenience store,

this quirky shop offers aisles of ales and specialty beers, wine, smokes, gourmand foods, and even a lunch counter offering Indian cuisine and microbrews. *1950 S. I-35.* ☎ *512/442-5337. www.whipin.com. AE, DISC, MC, V.*

Fashion (Men's)
★★ Service Menswear SOCO
GQ Magazine named this small shop one of the top 100 men's stores in the U.S. With high-end brands and affordable standbys like Levis, too, they've got the right stuff to make guys look great. Ladies, run next door for your own fashion fun at By George!. *1400 S. Congress Ave.* ☎ *512/447-7600. www.service menswear.com. AE, DISC, MC, V.*

★ Texas Clothier WEST CAM-
PUS An Austin business for over 25 years, this men's fashion Mecca is old-money expensive but caters to a savvy, young, and decidedly upscale clientele. *2905 San Gabriel St.* ☎ *512/478-4956. www.texas clothier.com. AE, DISC, MC, V.*

Fashion (Men's & Women's)
★ Capra & Cavelli BRYKER
WOODS With 4,600 square feet (427 sq. m) of fashions for men and women here, you're sure everyone will find something to like. While they also have a new shop downtown in the Hilton, the main store on Jefferson is their best and largest

Shopping Around the Clock

It's good to know when shops will be open before you head out. Specialty shops in Austin usually open Monday through Saturday around 9 or 10am and close at about 5:30 or 6pm; many have Sunday hours from noon to 6pm. Malls tend to keep the same Sunday schedule, but Monday through Saturday, they don't close their doors until 9pm. Sales tax in Austin is 8.25%.

Estilo Boutique offers stylish, original designer wear.

location. I'd let the staff here dress my husband anytime. *3500 Jefferson St. ☎ 512/450-1919. www.capra cavelli.com. AE, MC, V.*

★★ **Estilo Boutique** WAREHOUSE DISTRICT   Estilo offers swank apparel by designers Black Halo, Sherri Bodell, SKY, and Nicole Miller. The owner is hands-on, and the staff is as attentive as they should be in a place where you're sure to shell out a lot of cash. *234 W. 2nd St. ☎ 512/236-0488. www.estiloaustin.com. AE, DISC, MC, V.*

Fashion (Women's)
★★ **Parts & Labour** SOCO
Locals have been raving about this hip boutique since they enlarged their space, making room for more Texas and Austin-area designers' merchandise. A fab outlet for the work of local artisans, the shop features everything from witty off-beat T-shirts (for guys, too) to ladies bags, shoes, and clothing. *1117 S. Congress Ave. ☎ 512/326-1648. www.partsandlabour.com. MC, V.*

★★ **Sola** SOUTH AUSTIN   This is the place to pop in and find that perfect thing to perk up your spirits. A cocktail dress? Cute shoes? A scarf? Sure. Why not? *2005 S. Lamar Blvd. ☎ 512/441-7370; 815 W. 47th St. ☎ 512/467-7370. www.solastyle. com. MC, V.*

★ **Strut** SOCO   Strut topped the list of favorite women's boutiques in a local poll last year, and they've opened a popular clearance shop called **Hush Hush** (see p 67), where prices are even better. *3100 S. Congress Ave. ☎ 512/707-1523; 3500 Guadalupe St. ☎ 512/374-1667; 2208 S. Lamar Blvd. ☎ 512/326-2303. www.shopstrut.com. AE, DISC, MC, V.*

Fashion (Children's)
★★ **kids Austin Baby!** SOUTH AUSTIN   Cloth diapers, organic baby bedding, strollers, layette items, nursery furnishings, breast-feeding advice, diaper-service contacts—it's all here. Austin Baby! has everything an expectant mother with green leanings needs for her sweet baby-to-be. *701 S. Lamar Blvd. ☎ 512/448-0118. AE, DISC, MC, V.*

Gifts & Stationery
★★ **Emeralds** MARKET DISTRICT
Unique home accents, jewelry, snappy shoes, clothing, bags, cards, candles—everything fashion-forward females crave. *624 N. Lamar Blvd. ☎ 512/476-4496. www.hello emeralds.com. AE, MC, V.*

★★★ **Paper Place** TRIANGLE STATE/CENTRAL PARK   With fine stationery, engraved invitations, leather-bound journals and day planners, and pretty picture frames—I adore this store. Located near the **Central Market** (see p 65), Paper Place features gifts and stationery, and with the other shops, makes a delightful shopping

Austin Baby! specializes in eco-friendly baby gear.

excursion. *4001 N. Lamar Blvd.* ☎ *512/451-6531. www.paperplace austin.com. AE, DISC, MC, V.*

Gourmet Food, Wine & Kitchen Products

★★★ **Breed & Company** WEST CAMPUS & WESTLAKE   Part gourmet kitchen gadget shop, part hardware store, part garden and patio place, part china shop—this is the local answer to Restoration Hardware, only better. For over 35 years, Breed has been all Austin needs in the way of gourmet foods, housewares, gifts, bridal registry items, nuts and bolts, cookware, and dinnerware. *718 W. 29th St.* ☎ *888/269-6679 or 512/474-6679; 3663 Bee Cave Rd.* ☎ *512/328-3960. www. breedandco.com. AE, DISC, MC, V.*

★★★ **kids** **Central Market** TRI-ANGLE SQUARE/CENTRAL PARK & WESTGATE   Like **Whole Foods** (see p 11), Central Market supports fresh, organic foods and "green" products. A great place to taste samples, catch live music and dine outside, grab a cup of coffee, pick up fresh flowers, or buy groceries for that special meal you want to make tonight. Free valet parking and cooking classes, too. But be warned: Even two paper bags full of groceries will cost you a bundle.

4001 N Lamar Blvd. ☎ *512/206-1000; Westgate, 4477 S Lamar Blvd.* ☎ *512/899-4300. www.central market.com. AE, DISC, MC, V.*

★★★ **kids** **Whole Foods Market** MARKET DISTRICT   Whole Foods's fabulous flagship store is one of Austin's top tourist attractions. It's fun to look but pricey to buy here. I enjoy having a scoop of gelato and a cup of hot coffee while ogling everything in this huge store. A large, well-lit underground parking garage sits below the building. *See p 11. 525 N. Lamar Blvd.* ☎ *512/477-4455. AE, DISC, MC, V.*

Some of the stylish footwear available at Emerald's.

End of an Ear was voted the best vinyl store in town by the locals.

Jewelry & Precious Stones

★★ Russell Korman Fine Jewelry and Watches TRIANGLE STATE   My diamond and platinum ring came from this store, and I've also found reasonably priced gifts here—silver earrings, gold chain necklaces, watches, and the like. I like to stop here after visiting **Central Market** (see p 65) across the street. *3806 N. Lamar Blvd.* ☎ *512/451-9295. www.russellkormanjewelry.com. AE, DISC, MC, V.*

Music & Video

★★ End of an Ear SOUTH AUSTIN   This laid-back little musty music shop on South 1st Street has been voted the best vinyl shop in town in local polls and carries the best in indie pop, experimental, obscure, jazz, soul, funk, punk, lounge, reggae, techno music, hip-hop, and more. The staff is so crazy-knowledgeable about music that it's kind of freaky. They host in-store concerts, release parties, and even co-sponsor Alamo Music Mondays at the Ritz theater downtown, featuring music-related films for a song ($2 adults; $1 students, seniors, and members). *2209 S. 1st St.*

☎ *512/462-6008. www.endofanear.com. AE, DISC, MC, V.*

★★★ Vulcan Video WEST CAMPUS   My mom is in her 70s, but she pops into Vulcan Video more often than I do to find old movies. This offbeat little family-owned video store (with two locations in Austin) has a cult following of loyal locals who love classic, cult, foreign, oldie, and indie films, along with new releases. If I can't find a certain DVD anywhere else, I can always find it at Vulcan. *609 W. 29th St.* ☎ *512/478-5325; 112 W. Elizabeth St.* ☎ *512/326-2629. www.vulcanvideo.com. AE, DISC, MC, V.*

★★★ Waterloo Records & Video MARKET DISTRICT   New and used CDs, LPs, and DVDs are all available at this popular Austin music lovers' Mecca. They also buy and trade music, so bring in your old CDs and vintage vinyl. Parking can be problematic, so while here, step around the corner to have a scoop of **Amy's Ice Cream** (see p 12) to make the stop even sweeter and the parking headache bearable. *See p 28. 600A N. Lamar Blvd.* ☎ *512/474-2500. www.waterloorecords.com. AE, DISC, MC, V.*

Outlet Malls
★★★ Tanger Outlet Center/ Prime Outlets SAN MARCOS
Voted the "Third-Best Place to Shop in the World" by ABC's *The View*, this San Marcos shopping center, just 30 miles south of Austin, is home to fashionable brands like Lacoste, Ralph Lauren, Brooks Brothers, and more. *3939 S. IH-35 (Exit 200), San Marcos.* ☎ *800/628-9465 or 512/396-2200. www.tangeroutlet.com.*

Resale Shop
★★★ Hush Hush SOUTH AUSTIN Here, in the clearance shop for **Strut** (p 64), clothing leans toward cute and trendy, though quality sometimes gets lost in the bargain bin of it all. Still, you may just find the snappy sandals and tiny tank you've been wanting. A monthly "Everything $10" sale makes dropping by worthwhile. Check their website for "secret sales," too. *2200 S. Lamar Blvd.* ☎ *512/383-9010. AE, DISC, MC, V.*

Shoes
★ Goodie Two Shoes SOCO High-heel green ostrich Mary Janes? Purple suede ankle boots? Gilded gladiator sandals? Carrie Bradshaw would be so jealous! One-of-a-kind shoes, bargain boutique clothing, and cute accessories in SoCo? I'm so there. *1111 S. Congress Ave.* ☎ *512/443-2468. AE, DISC, MC, V.*

Sports, Outdoor Recreation & Camping Gear
★★ Backwoods BEE CAVE A big outfitter for adventure travelers and hip vagabonds, Backwoods has all the smart travel gear, equipment, clothing, footwear, and accessories that intrepid adventurers want before charting their next thrilling expedition. *12921 Hill Country Blvd.* ☎ *512/263-3610. www.backwoods. com. AE, DISC, MC, V.*

★★ kids Whole Earth Provision MARKET DISTRICT The very "in community" Whole Earth began in Austin in 1970 and now, with six more stores in Texas, is outfitting outdoor types with the best in gear, clothing, shoes, books, maps, tents, and other equipment. There's even a great selection of quality toys for kids. *1014 N. Lamar Blvd.* ☎ *512/476-1414; 2410 San Antonio (Northface Store)* ☎ *512/478-1577; 4477 S. Lamar (Westgate Shopping Center)* ☎ *512/899-0992. www.wholeearth provision.com. MC, V.*

Toys
★★ kids Terra Toys ALLANDALE With colorful, durable, quality toys, educational offerings—and fun nonsense stuff, too—this splendid toy store will bring out the mischievous, curious little kid in you. Their "Dragonsnaps" section has soft cotton baby and kids' clothing, too. *2438 W. Anderson Lane.* ☎ *512/445-4489. www.terratoys.com. AE, DISC, MC, V.*

Trendy and affordable selections from Hush Hush.

Austin's **Great Outdoors**

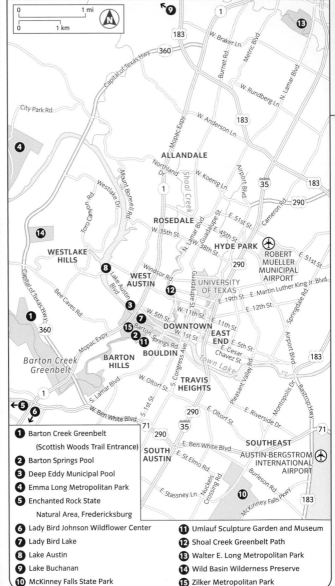

1. Barton Creek Greenbelt
   (Scottish Woods Trail Entrance)
2. Barton Springs Pool
3. Deep Eddy Municipal Pool
4. Emma Long Metropolitan Park
5. Enchanted Rock State
   Natural Area, Fredericksburg
6. Lady Bird Johnson Wildflower Center
7. Lady Bird Lake
8. Lake Austin
9. Lake Buchanan
10. McKinney Falls State Park
11. Umlauf Sculpture Garden and Museum
12. Shoal Creek Greenbelt Path
13. Walter E. Long Metropolitan Park
14. Wild Basin Wilderness Preserve
15. Zilker Metropolitan Park

Most Austinites pride themselves on being outdoorsy and adventuresome. The typical citizen is more likely to have a kayak in the garage than a BMW, and hip moms have three-wheel jogging strollers instead of ordinary baby buggies. Weekends mean time for camping and fishing, and somewhere on the shores of a glistening lake, there's a barbecue grill just waiting for you. You haven't really seen Austin until you've seen her stunning rivers, lakes, and hill country, so go west, young man—and nature lovers all. START: **Take Bus 30-Northbound to Barton Creek Greenbelt Entrance at Zilker Park.**

❶ ★★ Barton Creek Greenbelt. Almost 8 miles (13km) of trails wend through dense wooded areas featuring refreshing waterfalls, swimming holes, and rocks to climb along the way. With entrances in residential areas and along Lady Bird Lake at Zilker Park, the greenbelt trails also feature public restrooms and free parking at several points along the path. The Scottish Woods Trail entrance at the west end of the greenbelt leads into the beautiful 1,021-acre (413-hectare) Barton Creek Wilderness Park and takes you past Sculpture Falls. Very pretty. Pet friendly, too. *2201 Barton Springs Rd. www.ci.austin.tx.us. Bus: 30.*

❷ ★★★ kids Barton Springs Pool. The cool waters of this natural spring-fed swimming pool, which American Indians called "The Sacred Springs," cover three acres in what is now Zilker Metropolitan Park, creating one of Austin's coolest (68°F/20°C) and most beloved spots. The pool is open year round—except on Thursdays, when they close for cleaning. Actor Robert Redford (1936–) claims he learned to swim here. *See p 35,* **❷**.

❸ ★ kids Deep Eddy Municipal Pool. This historic, man-made swimming pool at the end of Lake Austin Boulevard is the oldest swimming pool in Texas and has a bathhouse built during the Depression era by the Works Progress Administration. Deep Eddy was first created by cold springs flowing along the banks of the Colorado River in a spot where a large boulder formed

Miles of trails pass through the densely wooded Barton Creek Greenbelt.

The Deep Eddy municipal pool is the oldest swimming pool in Texas.

an eddy. In 1915, A.J. Eilers, Sr. bought the land surrounding the swimming hole and built the concrete pool. Today, it remains a favorite swimming hole for locals and visitors alike and is listed as a landmark on the National Register of Historic Places. *401 Deep Eddy Ave.* ☎ *512/472-8546. www.deepeddy. org. Free admission. Daily 6am–7pm (check website for seasonal changes to pool hours). Bus: 4, 21 & 22.*

❹ Emma Long Metropolitan Park. Located just over 6 miles (9.7km) off scenic FM 2222 on City Park Road, this popular family park rests on the shores of Lake Austin and comprises a total of 1,150 acres (465 hectares). The park features boat ramps, sand volleyball courts, a sandy beach, and a designated swimming area. It also has restrooms, hot showers, dressing areas, and even 20 camping sites available, with water and electricity hook-ups. *1706 City Park Rd.* ☎ *512/ 346-1831. www.ci.austin.tx.us. Fri– Sun & holidays $8/vehicle, Mon– Thurs $5/vehicle. Daily 7am–10pm.*

❺ ★★★ kids Enchanted Rock State Natural Area, Fredericksburg. Although this giant granite dome is located in the Texas Hill

County about 2 hours from Austin, it is still a popular day-trip destination for outdoor enthusiasts. Designated a National Natural Landmark in 1970 and placed on the National Register of Historic Places in 1984, the Rock is one of the largest batholiths (underground rock formations uncovered by erosion) in the U.S., and this pink granite rock dome sprawls across 640 acres (259 hectares) and rises 425 feet (130m) above ground. The place was sacred to Tonkawa Indians who claimed to see ghost fires from the tops—inspiring legends and children's stories ever since. *16710 Ranch Rd. 965, Fredericksburg.* ☎ *830/685-3636. www.tpwd.state. tx.us. $6 adults and those ages 13 and above. Children 12 and under, free; seniors who are Texas residents 65 and older, $3. Daily 8am– 10pm. Closed to the public on specific public hunt dates in Jan (see website or telephone).*

❻ ★★ Lady Bird Johnson Wildflower Center. With 178 acres (72 hectares) of wildflowers, the Wildflower Center is a living research center and garden paradise founded by former First Lady "Lady Bird" Johnson and actress Helen Hayes, who were both dedicated to the preservation of native Texas plants and flowers. Visit the enchanting butterfly garden and the impressive natural stone-and-glass visitor's center, or browse the gift shop, whose proceeds (and admission prices) help fund this pretty non-profit center. The center often hosts free lectures, educational programs, and guided walks. *See p 18,* ⓫.

❼ ★★★ Lady Bird Lake. This section of the Colorado River that flows at the foot of downtown Austin was, for many years, known as Town Lake, until a 2007 ruling by the City Council changed the name

The Lady Bird Johnson Wildflower Center is filled with native plants and flowers.

so as to honor the former First Lady who changed the lake from an eyesore into "Austin's scenic and recreational centerpiece," according to one council member. For the most part, locals still call it Town Lake, and it remains central to Austin outdoor recreation More than 7 miles (11km) of hike-and-bike trails crisscross the lake over footbridges and run alongside it, on scenic paths through wooded areas, parks, soccer fields, and open spaces. It's the Saturday morning place to be, yearround, for families with strollers, joggers, cyclists, and those who just want to take Fido on a nice long walk. A map of the hike-and-bike trails can be downloaded at the Austin City website *www.ci.austin. tx.us.*

8 Lake Austin. One of the seven highland lakes created by the Colorado River northwest of Austin, Lake Austin is a reservoir created by the Lower Colorado River Authority and is a scenic spot in the Hill Country that begins on the edge of Austin. A great spot for recreational fishing, the lake has been stocked with largemouth bass, catfish, and sunfish. It is also an attraction for those who like to picnic, hike, or bicycle along its banks, and it is an area marked by resorts, spas, and restaurants with views of the water. With a surface area of nearly 1,600 acres (648 hectares), the lake is home to the scenic Austin landmark Pennybacker Bridge on the Capital of Texas Highway (aka Hwy. 360)—commonly known as The 360 Bridge—whose weathered steel arches span the lake. *Take Hwy. 360 N. & exit at the Pennybacker Bridge. www.highlandlakes.net.*

Paddle boats and canoes on Lady Bird Lake.

9 Lake Buchanan. The second-largest of the seven Highland Lakes, Lake Buchanan, about 60 miles north of downtown Austin, has a shoreline of 124 miles (200km), and is 30 miles (48km) long and 5 miles (8km) in width at its widest section. Sailing is a big sport here, and all kinds of watercraft, large and small (including houseboats), are available for rent at many spots along its banks, including **Silver Creek Resort** (☎ 512/756-4854) and **Lake Buchanan Adventures** (☎ 512/756-9911). A popular excursion is the **Vanishing Texas River Cruise** (☎ 512/756-6986). **Canyon of the Eagles** (☎ 512/334-2070) is a 940 acre eco-friendly resort established by the Lower Colorado River Authority—and a popular place to hike and enjoy stunning views. Buchanan Dam, a multiple-arch dam, spans more than 2 miles (3.2km). Picnics, resorts, RV spaces, cabins, parks, picnic tables, and restaurants may be found by the lake, and a granite gravel shore creates a beach-entry for those who like to swim or dive. A privately owned lighthouse stands watch over this lake, where bald eagles are often sighted. *www.highland lakes.com. Take US-183 N. to TX-29W.*

10 ★ McKinney Falls State Park. This southeast Austin park is set on 744 acres (301 hectares) and is named for Thomas F. McKinney (1801–1873), who came to Texas in the early 1820s as one of Stephen F. Austin's (1793–1836) first 300 colonists. In the park are the preserved ruins of McKinney's trainer's cabin and his own homestead. The park is home to clean camping grounds and is a good spot for hiking, mountain and road bike excursions, picnics, fishing, and bird watching. Swimming is available in the park at Onion Creek. The **Smith Visitors' Center** provides information on McKinney's homestead and the park's recreational offerings. Facilities include 84 campsites with water and electricity, walk-in water sites, picnic sites, 3.5 miles (5.6km) of paved trails, 4 miles (6.4km) of multi-use trails for hiking and mountain biking, and a dining hall which may be rented for day use. During summer, the park is sometimes used as the site of a literary day camp sponsored by the independent Austin book store, BookPeople (see p 62). *5808 McKinney Falls Pkwy.* ☎ *512/243-1643. www.tpwd. state.tx.us. Entrance fee $5 adults; children 12 and under, free. $12/ tent/night & entrance fees (4 people*

A little pocket of quiet beauty in the Umlauf Sculpture Garden and Museum.

per tent, maximum); $16/night campsites w/electric (30-amp) & water hookups (no more than 2 tents per site); $20/night premium campsites w/electric (50-amp) & water hookups (no more than 2 tents per site); $40/night (plus 6% occupancy tax) screened shelters w/4 sets of bunk-bed frames.

⓫ ★★ **Umlauf Sculpture Garden and Museum.** One of the most serene little parks in the city, where art and nature quietly comingle and a small museum beckons. *See p 41.*

⓬ **Shoal Creek Greenbelt Path.** Passing through nice neighborhoods along Shoal Creek, the trails here let you feel like a local as you run beside those who live nearby. *See p 22.*

⓭ **Walter E. Long Metropolitan Park.** Grab a fishing pole and a picnic basket, and spend the day at this pretty little park that encompasses the Walter E. Long Lake (formerly Dekker Lake). Rent a kayak or canoe, or a small motorboat for fishing. You can swim here, but there are no lifeguards on duty. There are 2.6 miles (4.2km) of trails to hike, and the park features two volleyball courts, lots of picnic tables and barbecue pits, and a nice long fishing pier. The $8 admission doesn't seem like much for a day of fun in the sun with the family for a barbecue or a cool refreshing swim. *6614 Blue Bluff Rd. ☎ 512/926-5230. www.austinparks.org. Mon–Thurs $5/vehicle, Fri–Sun & holidays $8/vehicle; walk-ins $1 adults. Season passes available. Daily 7am–10pm. No credit cards.*

Fishing at the Walter E. Long Metropolitan Park.

⓮ ★★ **Wild Basin Wilderness Preserve.** Seven visionary women in the 1970s fought hard to found this area now known as the Wild Basin Wilderness Preserve just north of Westlake Hills in Austin. The 227-acre (92-hectare) preserve was completed in the early 1980s and now serves as an interdisciplinary laboratory for St. Edward's University. More than 3 miles (4.8km) of hiking trails through the hills stay open from sunrise to sunset each day, and trail maps are available at the Environmental Education Center and at kiosks on both ends of the trail head. The preserve often hosts family events, concerts, adult workshops, and children's and school programs, as well. Pets, food, picnic items, and bicycles are not allowed on the trails. *805 N. Capitol of Texas Hwy. (approx. 1 mile/1.6km north of Bee Caves Rd. or approximately 3 miles/4.8km south of the Loop 360 bridge over Lake Austin). ☎ 512/327-7622. www.wildbasin.org. $3 adults, $2 seniors & children 5–12.*

⓯ ★★★ kids **Zilker Metropolitan Park.** A park for all ages—home to the fabulous Barton Springs Pool, the Zilker Hillside Theatre, playgrounds, parks, trails, and more. *See p 12,* ❽.

Austin's Best **Dining**

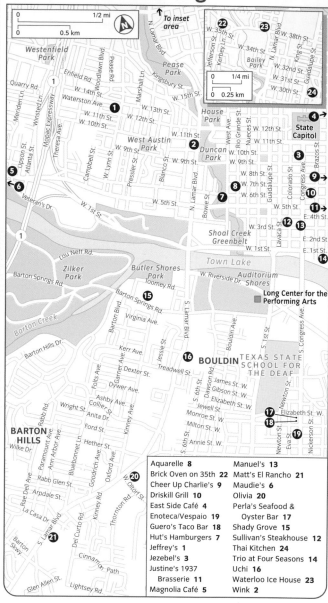

Aquarelle **8**
Brick Oven on 35th **22**
Cheer Up Charlie's **9**
Driskill Grill **10**
East Side Café **4**
Enoteca/Vespaio **19**
Guero's Taco Bar **18**
Hut's Hamburgers **7**
Jeffrey's **1**
Jezebel's **3**
Justine's 1937
  Brasserie **11**
Magnolia Café **5**

Manuel's **13**
Matt's El Rancho **21**
Maudie's **6**
Olivia **20**
Perla's Seafood &
  Oyster Bar **17**
Shady Grove **15**
Sullivan's Steakhouse **12**
Thai Kitchen **24**
Trio at Four Seasons **14**
Uchi **16**
Waterloo Ice House **23**
Wink **2**

Austin Dining Best Bets

Best **Barbecue**
★★★ The Salt Lick $$, *18300 FM 1826, Driftwood (p 80)*

Best **Breakfast Tacos**
★ Guero's Taco Bar $, *1412 S. Congress Ave. (p 77)*

Best **Brunch**
★ Magnolia Café $, *2309 Lake Austin Blvd & 1920 S. Congress Ave. (p 78)*

Best **Burger**
★ Huts Hamburgers $, *807 W. 6th St. (p 77)*

Best for **Families**
★ Brick Oven on 35th $–$$, *1608 W. 35th St. (p 76)*

Best **French (Classic or Modern)**
★★ Aquarelle $$$–$$$$, *606 Rio Grande St. (p 76)*

Best **Impress-Your-Date Spot**
★★★ Jeffrey's $$$–$$$$, *1204 W. Lynn St. (p 78)*

★★★ The Driskill Grill $$$–$$$$, *604 Brazos St. (p 76)*

Best **Neighborhood Eatery**
★★ Hyde Park Bar & Grill $$, *4206 Duval St. (p 78)*

Best **Pizza**
★★ Enoteca/Vespaio $$, *610 S. Congress Ave. (p 77)*

Best **Outdoor Dining**
★ Shady Grove $$, *1624 Barton Springs Rd. (p 80)*

Best **Seafood**
★ Perla's Seafood & Oyster Bar $$$, *1400 South Congress Ave. (p 79)*

Best **Splurge**
★★★ Hudson's on the Bend $$$–$$$$, *3509 Ranch Road 620 N. (p 77)*

Best **Sushi**
★★ Uchi $$–$$$, *801 S. Lamar Blvd. (p 81)*

Best **Tex-Mex**
★ Maudie's $$, *2608 W. 7th St. (at Lake Austin Blvd.) (p 79)*

Best **Stylish Steak House**
★★ Sullivan's Steakhouse $$$$, *300 Colorado St. (p 80)*

★★ Trio at Four Seasons $$$$, *98 San Jacinto Blvd. (p 81)*

Best **Vegetarian & Vegan**
★ Cheer Up Charlie's $, *1104 E 6th St. (p 76)*

The classy Driskill Grill.

Austin Dining A to Z

Authentic French cuisine is served at Aquarelle.

★★ **Aquarelle** MARKET DISTRICT
FRENCH This intimate little *maison*
has been serving pleasant prix-fixe
and pricey-but-delectable á la carte
offerings for over 10 years just off
6th Street. *606 Rio Grande St.*
☎ *512/479-8117. www.aquarelle
restaurant.com. Entrees $28–$38.
AE, DISC, MC, V. Dinner Tues–Sat.
Closed Sun & Mon. Bus: 4, 21 & 103.*

kids **Brick Oven on 35th**
BRYKER WOODS *ITALIAN* The original Brick Oven on 35th Street is
homey and warm—like their food.
Not to be confused with the Brick
Oven Pizza chain, this place has a
low-key look, fabulous fettuccini,
and crayons for the kids. *1608 W.
35th St. (between Jefferson St. & Kerbey Lane).* ☎ *512/453-4330. www.
brickovenon35th.com. Entrees $11–
$13. AE, DISC, MC, V. Dinner daily.
Bus: 21, 982, 983 & 987.*

Cheer Up Charlie's EAST SIDE
VEGETARIAN This earthy East Side
food trailer features raw vegan
organic chocolates, cool drinks (try
the Bare Bones Coconut), slushy
smoothies (try the Bruce Lee), beer,

wine, and hardy vegan nosh fare.
Sometimes, there's a movie or live
music on the patio. *1104 E 6th St.*
☎ *512/431-2133. Entrees $2–$10.
AE, DISC, MC, V. Breakfast, lunch &
dinner Mon–Sat. Closed Sun. Bus: 4.*

★★ **Driskill Grill** DOWNTOWN
AMERICAN Glittering crystal, white
tablecloths, low lighting, fine wines:
This historic hotel's upscale eatery
with dark wood accents, soft candlelight, and mirrored walls makes
an elegant dinner spot, and the din
of 6th Street reverie lies just beyond
its quietly closed doors. *604 Brazos
St.* ☎ *512/391-7162. Entrees $22–
$39. AE, DISC, MC, V. Dinner Tues–
Sat. Closed Sun & Mon. Driskill Bar
Sun–Thurs noon–midnight, Fri & Sat
noon–2am. Bus: 2, 3, 4, 10, 17, 18,
19, 37 & 137.*

★★ **East Side Café** EAST SIDE
AMERICAN With eclectic farm-to-
table fare—like wild mushroom
crepes and roasted veggie enchiladas—this cafe in an old East Side
house offers a bounty of fresh gar-
den-good eats, fresh fish entrees,
and bright spunky wines. *2113*

Manor Rd. ☎ 512/476-5858. Entrees $8.75–$28. AE, DISC, MC, V. Lunch Sat & Sun, dinner daily. Bus: 21 & 641.

★★ **Enoteca/Vespaio** SOCO *ITALIAN* Enter Enoteca, part Italian deli and bakery, part casual intimate cafe, with a fresh lively breakfast/ brunch/dinner menu, good wines, and the best pizza I've had since Italy. Adjacent is sister-restaurant Vespaio for upscale dining and a wall of fine wines. *1610 S. Congress Ave.* ☎ *512/441-7672. www.austin vespaio.com. Enoteca entrees $9–$19; Vespaio entrees $17–$31. AE, DISC, MC, V. Enoteca brunch Sun, lunch & dinner Mon–Sat. Vespaio dinner daily (bar opens 5pm). Bus: 1L, 1M, 9 & 483.*

★ **Guero's Taco Bar** SOCO *TEX-MEX* This hot Tex-Mex spot is always hopping. Outdoor seating and cold margaritas in the heart of SoCo. I go for breakfast there on Saturday mornings—but then, so does everyone else, so it can get crowded. *1412 S. Congress Ave. (at Elizabeth St.)* ☎ *512/707-8232. www.guerostacobar.com. Entrees $5–$14. AE, DISC, MC, V. Breakfast Sat & Sun, lunch & dinner daily. Bus: 1L, 1M & 486.*

★★ **Hudson's on the Bend** LAKEWAY *AMERICAN* Considered one of Austin's finest restaurants, this quiet old house, far from town

Enoteca is both a deli and bakery.

East Side Café emphasizes fresh ingredients.

and near Lake Travis, offers soft music, fresh flowers, white table-cloths, good wine, and a menu celebrating savory wild game dishes. Splurge and plan to spend big. *3509 RR 620 N.* ☎ *512/266-1369. www. hudsonsonthebend.com. Entrees $18–$49. AE, DISC, MC, V. Dinner daily. No bus service.*

Huts Hamburgers MARKET DISTRICT *AMERICAN* Kind of a dive, but in a good way, Huts is an old Austin tradition for hand-battered onion rings, thick shakes, and plump juicy hamburgers. Try the buffalo burger—a carnivore's delight—and

78

the veggie burger, too. *807 W. 6th St.* ☎ *512/472-0693. www. hutsfrankandangies.com. Entrees $6–$15. AE, DISC, MC, V. Lunch & dinner daily. Bus: 4, 21 & 103.*

★★ **Hyde Park Bar & Grill** HYDE PARK *AMERICAN* "When you come to the fork in the road, take it," said Yogi Berra, and here an enormous outdoor-art fork marks the spot to take friends to lunch or dinner. Known since 1982 for to-die-for-delicious buttermilk-batter fries and fresh fare, the original Hyde Park location is my favorite. *4206 Duval St.* ☎ *512/458-3168. www.hydepark barandgrill.com. Entrees $9–$16. AE, DISC, MC, V. Brunch Sun, lunch & dinner daily. Bus: 7-Northbound.*

★★★ **Jeffrey's** WEST LYNN/ CLARKSVILLE *CONTINENTAL* If my date took me to Jeffrey's, I knew he was a keeper. Tasteful upscale dining, great bar bites (think crispy oysters on Yucca chips), fine wines, chance celebrity sightings, low lighting, skinny suits and ties, little black dresses—ah, I remember it well. *1204 W. Lynn St.* ☎ *512/477-5584. www.jeffreysofaustin.com. Entrees $20–$45. AE, DISC, MC, V. Dinner daily (bar opens 5pm). Bus: 9.*

★ **Jezebel's** DOWNTOWN *FRENCH/ AMERICAN* Civilized downtown dining on the Avenue. With an attentive staff, customized prix-fixe dinners and wine-pairing options, eclectic urban ambiance, swank crystal, and white tablecloth touches—Jezebel is a wickedly wonderful temptress. *914C Congress Ave.* ☎ *512/499-3999. www.restaurant jezebel.com. Entrees $20–$46, prix-fixe $75–$125; wine-pairing dinners starting from $35. AE, DISC, MC, V. Dinner Mon–Sat. Bus: 1L & 1M.*

★★ **Justine's 1937 Brasserie** EAST AUSTIN *FRENCH* Despite its iffy East Side location, Justine's is a woozy dark bohemian bistro with gaga-good French fare and cloud-like crème brûlée. I love the ambience here. With waits longer than *War & Peace* on weekends, make early reservations. *4710 E. 5th St.* ☎ *512/385-2900. www.justines 1937.com. Entrees $10–$17. AE, DISC, MC, V. Dinner Wed-Mon. Closed Tues. Bus: 4.*

Magnolia Café CENTRAL & SOCO *DINER* For pancakes and the kind of food Mom would make when you came home from college with your laundry, The Magnolia Café is open 24/7, serving up sweet short stacks of satisfaction. *2304 Lake Austin Blvd.* ☎ *512/478-8645; 1920 S. Congress Ave.* ☎ *512/445-0000. www. themagnoliacafe.com. Entrees under*

Jezebel's tempts with attentive staff and urban ambience.

Manuel's Mexican dishes are a perfect way to fuel up for a late night.

$10. AE, DISC, MC, V. Daily 24-hr. Bus: 4 & 22.

★ **Manuel's** DOWNTOWN *MEXICAN* Mexican food has never seemed so sophisticated. This long-time-favorite urban supper spot is known for creamy Enchiladas Suizas and Enchiladas de Mole. Manuel's sparkles with bright conversation and pretty people on Congress Avenue at night. A popular spot before club hopping *310 Congress Ave.* ☎ *512/472-7555. www.manuels. com. Entrees $8–$22. AE, DISC, MC, V. Brunch Sun (w/live music), dinner daily; happy hour daily 4–6pm. Bus: 1L, 1M, 5, 7, 9, 20, 30, 101, 127, 483 & 462.*

Matt's El Rancho SOUTH AUSTIN *MEXICAN* This Tex-Mex margarita Mecca is a long-revered Austin institution—though I don't quite understand why. Still, scads of locals swear by it, and Matt's has been around since 1952, so they must be doing something right. *2613 S. Lamar Blvd.* ☎ *512/462-9333. www. mattselrancho.com. Entrees $8–$19. AE, DISC, MC, V. Dinner Wed–Mon. Closed Tues. Bus: 3, 29, 331 & 338.*

★ **Maudie's** LAKE AUSTIN *TEX-MEX* Chips and salsa, hot *queso*, consistently good Tex-Mex fare, and cold margaritas—my mouth is watering already. *2608 W. 7th St. at Lake Austin Blvd. & 5 other locations.* ☎ *512/474-7271. www.maudies. com. Entrees $5.25–$9.75. AE, DISC, MC, V. Breakfast, lunch & dinner daily. Bus: 21 & 663.*

Olivia SOUTH AUSTIN *AMERICAN* Trendy, urban, with fashionable wines, fresh fish, and so-so specials: I'm not as wowed by this place as my friends are. Maybe it's the urban retro *Mad Men* look they love or off-beat menu selections like lamb sliders. The bar mixology and sommelier's selections are always spot-on, and the surroundings are smart, so we keep going back. Named one of the Top Ten Best New Restaurants in America by *Bon Appetit* in 2009, and Chef James Holmes' name seems to be on everyone's lips lately. *2043 S. Lamar Blvd.* ☎ *512/803-2700. www.olivia-austin.com. Entrees $15–$39. AE, DISC, MC, V. Brunch Sun, lunch Fri & Sat, dinner daily (bar opens 5pm). Bus: 3, 331 & 338.*

★ **Perla's Seafood & Oyster Bar** SOCO *SEAFOOD* Bright, light, and sparkling like the sea, this trendy seafood restaurant and oyster bar has fresh food, airy ambience, and happening alfresco dining out front on South Congress Avenue. *1400 S. Congress Ave.* ☎ *512/ 291-7300. www.perlasaustin.com.*

Olivia was named one of the Ten Best New Restaurants in America by Bon Appetit.

Entrees $17–$38. AE, DISC, MC, V. Brunch Sat & Sun, lunch Mon–Fri, dinner daily (bar opens 3pm). Bus: 1L, 1M & 486.

★★★ The Salt Lick DRIFTWOOD

BARBECUE Even if you've never been to Texas, you may have read about this bastion of barbecue bliss in the *New York Times*. With tangy lick-your-fingers barbecue sauce slathered on brisket, ribs, and chicken, and heaping helpings of hardy side dishes, The Salt Lick is worth the scenic 20-mile (32km) drive south of town. With long, hot outdoor waits on weekends, it's wise to bring a cooler of cold brew, if you're so inclined—it's in a dry community, which means they're not permitted to sell alcohol, so BYOB. *18300 FM 1826, Driftwood.* ☎ *512/858-4959. saltlickbbq.com. Most sandwiches & plates $8–$15. No credit cards. Lunch & dinner daily. No bus service.*

Shady Grove BARTON SPRINGS

AMERICAN Historic Route 66 meets Barton Springs Road at this nostalgia-driven eatery with popular backyard patio dining. The restaurant's outdoor Starlight Theatre features old movies, Texas comfort foods, and sandwich and picnic-style fare, and live music on weekends in the spring and fall. It's located in front of a former RV park where, a few years back, rich and famous actor Matthew McConaughey (1969–) amused himself by living in a trailer. *1624 Barton Springs Rd.* ☎ *512/474-9991. www.theshadygrove.com. Entrees $7–$10. AE, DISC, MC, V. Dinner daily. Bus: 3, 338 & 484.*

★★ Sullivan's Steakhouse

WAREHOUSE DISTRICT *STEAK* Think fat raw oysters on the half-shell, lean linguine tossed amid clusters of succulent black mussels, broad fresh lobster tails, and thick steaks: Sullivan's is an upscale chain with a "shaken not stirred" chilled martini vibe and a tony young money-eyed crowd. Actor Dennis Quaid (1954–) met his current cute blonde wife here at the bar. See what I mean? *300 Colorado St.* ☎ *512/495-6504. www.sullivansteakhouse.com. Entrees $31–$50. AE, DISC, MC, V. Lunch Mon–Fri, dinner daily. Bus: 3, 10, 17 & 29.*

Thai Kitchen NORTH UNIVERSITY

THAI Award-winning authentic Thai cuisine and great carry-out for over 15 years, with three nice but slightly natty little family-owned locations. Try the Indian Noodle Soup (No. 12 on the noodle

The nostalgic Shady Grove screens classic films at its outdoor Starlight Theatre.

Sullivan's Steakhouse offers a relaxed, upscale dining experience.

menu)—hotter and more healing than Mom's chicken soup. *3009 Guadalupe St.* ☎ *512/474-2575. www.thaikitchenofaustin.com. Entrees $7–$12. MC, V. Lunch & dinner daily. Bus: 1L, 1M, 3, 21 & 481.*

★★ Trio at Four Seasons

DOWNTOWN *STEAK* With stylish contemporary decor, a swank seafood-and-steaks-style menu, extensive wine list, and top-notch bar, Trio sits overlooking Lady Bird Lake in the Four Seasons. Offering a sophisticated ambiance, fabulous food, and wine "happy hour" specials from 5 to 8pm Monday to Saturday. Trio guests can opt for alfresco dining, too. *98 San Jacinto Blvd.* ☎ *512/685-8300. www.fourseasons.com/austin. Entrees $28–$44. AE, DISC, MC, V. Breakfast, lunch & dinner daily. Picnic baskets to carry out. Bus: 17-Eastbound, 22 & 127.*

★★★ Uchi SOUTH AUSTIN *ASIAN*

Expensive Asian-fusion fare that's a favorite with locals, Uchi offers sparse, cool, casual ambience, fresh ceviche, sashimi, "cutting-edge" sushi, and delectable dishes like pork cheeks and *wagyu* beef. Cold sakes include hard-to-find high-end brands. Chef/owner Tyson Cole was named Best New Chef in 2005 by *Food & Wine* magazine, and his new restaurants, **Uchiko** (4200 N. Lamar Blvd.) and **Canteen** (W Hotel–ACL) are

slated to open in late 2010. Make reservations or expect long waits. *801 S. Lamar Blvd.* ☎ *512/916-4808. www.uchiaustin.com. Entrees $12–$30. AE, DISC, MC, V. Dinner daily. Bus: 3, 338 & 484.*

★ Waterloo Ice House ROSE-

DALE *AMERICAN* I often went here for hamburgers, fab onion rings, and cold bottled root beer with my boyfriend back in my college days. Years later, we've changed, but Waterloo hasn't—it's still just as good. Cold beer, live music, a deck for outdoor dining, roomy booths, a jukebox, and good veggie burgers, too. *1106 W. 38th St. (at Medical Pkwy.)* ☎ *512/451-5245. www. waterlooicehouse.com. Most entrees under $10. AE, DISC, MC, V. Breakfast, lunch & dinner daily (breakfast Mon–Fri till 11am, Sat & Sun till 2pm). Bus: 3, 22, 982, 983 & 987.*

★ Wink CASTLE HILL *AMERICAN*

Good eats and trendy style go together like a wink and a smile in this intimate eatery tucked away next to a dry cleaner at the foot of Castle Hill. With an unpredictable menu bringing out the best flavors in fresh dishes and just-flown-in fish, Wink is always an "in" place to eat in Austin. Make reservations. *1014 N. Lamar Blvd.* ☎ *512/482-8868. Entrees $16–$32. AE, DISC, MC, V. Dinner Mon–Sat. Closed Sun. Bus: 338.*

Austin **Lodging**

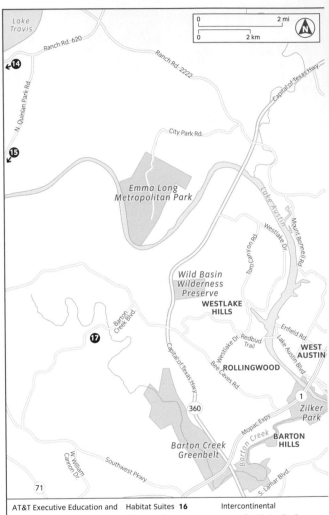

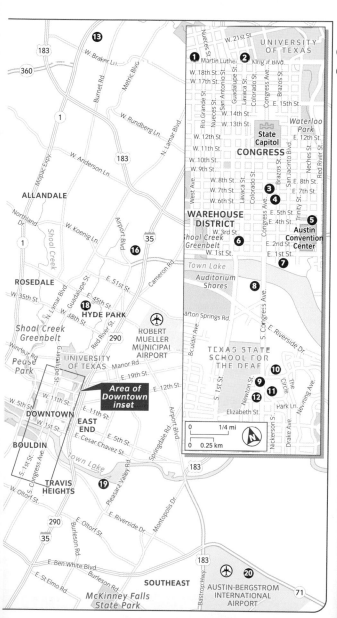

Lodging Best Bets

Best for **Austin City Limits Fans**
★★ The W Hotel–ACL $$$–$$$$,
200 Lavaca St. (p 89)

Best for **Chance Celebrity
Sightings**
★★★ The Four Seasons $$$$$, *98
San Jacinto Blvd. (p 86)*

Best for **Longhorn Lovers**
★ AT&T Executive Education and
Conference Center $$, *1900
University Ave. (p 85)*

Best **Neighborhood B&B**
★ Adams House $$, *14300 Ave. G
(p 85)*

Best **Hotel for Shopaholics**
★★ The Westin Austin at the
Domain $$–$$$, *11301 Domain Dr.
(p 89)*

Best for **Serenity Seekers**
★★★ Lake Austin Spa Resort
$$$$$, *1705 S. Quinlan Park Rd.
(p 88)*

Best for **Vagabonds & Free
Spirits**
★★ Hostelling International–
Austin $, *2200 S. Lakeshore Blvd.
(p 86)*

Best **Mecca of Minimalist
Style**
★★ Kimber Modern $$$, *110 The
Circle (near S. Congress Ave.) (p 88)*

Best **Place to Be Treated Like
a Rock Star (& Best Beds)**
★★★ Hotel St. Cecilia $$$–$$$$$,
*112 Academy Dr. (near S. Congress
Ave) (p 87)*

Best **Place to Go Green**
★ Habitat Suites $–$$, *500 E.
Highland Mall Blvd. (p 86)*

Best **Place to Land after a
Long Flight**
★ Hilton Austin Airport $$, *9515
New Airport Dr. (p 86)*

Best **Place to Tee Off**
★★★ Barton Creek Resort and
Spa $$$$, *8212 Barton Club Dr.
(p 85)*

★★ Lakeway Resort and Spa $$$,
101 Lakeway Dr. (p 88)

Best **Place to Wear Cowboy
Boots with a Suit**
★★ The Driskill $$$$, *604 Brazos
St. (at 6th St.) (p 85)*

Most **Romantic**
★★★ Mansion at Judge's Hill
$$–$$$, *1900 Rio Grande St. (p 89)*

Trendiest Hotel
★★ Hotel San Jose $$, *1316 S.
Congress Ave. (p 87)*

The architectural aesthetics of Kimber Modern make the hotel feel like a work of art.

Austin Hotels A to Z

★ **AT&T Executive Education and Conference Center** UT CAMPUS This on-campus hotel was built in 2008 to cater to business-conference attendees, Longhorn parents, returning alumni, and all who wish to enjoy all the University has to offer. Pleasant rooms have views of the Main Building Tower, the State Capitol, or a central courtyard. *1900 University Ave. (at MLK, Jr. Blvd).* ☎ *877/744-8822 or 512/404-3600. www.meetattexas. com. 297 units. Doubles $139–$239. AE, DISC, MC, V. Bus: 1L, 1M, 5, 982, & 983.*

Adams House HYDE PARK This pleasant B&B sits in one of my favorite Austin neighborhoods, Hyde Park, not far from the Elisabet Ney Museum (see p 17). Built in 1911, and enlarged and elevated to a two-story revival home in 1931, this B&B features fine furnishings and kind hosts. A separate bungalow at the back offers privacy. *4300 Ave. G.* ☎ *512/453-7696. www.theadams house.com. 5 units. Doubles $99– $110, suite & bungalow $149; w/ breakfast. AE, MC, V. Bus: 5 & 656.*

Austin Motel SOCO If it didn't look so kitschy and cool from the street and weren't on South Congress Street, I don't think I'd stay here. Still, this off-beat 1938 motel with its kidney-shaped pool does have a certain nostalgic allure and retro room rates that can't be matched. The decor is offbeat, and the area can be noisy, so this affordable motel is only as cool as you want it to be. Love the location, though. *1220 S. Congress St. (at Nellie St).* ☎ *512/441-1157. www.austinmotel. com. 41 units. Singles $80, doubles & suites $100–$168. AE, DISC, MC, V. Bus: 1M, 1L, 9 & 486.*

Poolside at the Austin Motel.

★★ **kids Barton Creek Resort and Spa** BEE CAVES Golfers come for the four 18-hole championship courses and the Chuck Cook Golf Academy, and ladies love the spa. Programs for kids make it family-friendly, too. The resorts' rooms are attractive and well-appointed, and the grounds and facilities are superior. *8212 Barton Club Dr. (at Barton Creek Blvd.).* ☎ *866/572- 7369 or 512/329-4000. www.barton creek.com. 312 units. Doubles $260– $380; suites from $500. Spa & golf packages available. AE, DC, DISC, MC, V. No city bus service.*

★★ **The Driskill** DOWNTOWN Built in 1886 by a Texas cattle baron and renovated in 2000, this tall, dark, handsome 6th Street hotel is classic Texan to the core. Its dim romantic piano bar and first-rate gleaming wood, brass, and candlelight Driskill Grill are favorites of downtowners after dark. *604 Brazos St. (at 6th St.).* ☎ *800/252-9367 or 512/474-5911. www.driskillhotel.com. 189 units.*

The Best of Austin

Doubles $150–$340. AE, DC, DISC, MC, V. Bus: 2, 3, 4 & 10.

★★★ **The Four Seasons** DOWNTOWN   When big-name celebrities come to town, they stay at this high-end hacienda overlooking Lady Bird Lake and the downtown skyline. With its alluring Texas-sized lobby, swank bar and restaurant, outdoor pool, hot health club, and exquisite spa, this Four Seasons has been dubbed "Austin's Living Room" by its casual, well-heeled crowd. Attorneys hobnob here over cocktails after work and wonder if that's really Angelina Jolie (1975–) seated at that far table. Restaurant Trio (see p 81) is a steak, seafood, and fine-wine lover's dream come true. *93 San Jacinto Blvd. (at 1st St./ César Chavez St.). ☎ 512/478-4500. www.fourseasons.com/austin. 291 units. Doubles starting at $420. AE, DC, DISC, MC, V. Bus: 3, 10, 17 & 482.*

★ **Habitat Suites** NORTH CENTRAL   One of the greenest best-kept secrets in Austin, this standard-looking three-story residential hotel is an eco-friendly outpost for families and environment-conscious travelers. Spacious rooms have in-room

"Austin's Living Room"—The Four Seasons.

kitchens, and organically grown vegetables are often available. Sheets, towels, and cleaning products are of natural materials, so this hotel is ideal for those with chemical sensitivities. The pool is chemical-free, too—a salt generator cleans and sanitizes the water. *500 E. Highland Mall Blvd. ☎ 800/535-4663 or 512/467-6000. www.habitatsuites. com. 96 units. 1-bedroom suite $137, 2-bedroom suite $207; w/breakfast. Mon–Sat complimentary afternoon wine & snacks. AE, DC, DISC, MC, V. Bus: 10 & 7.*

The Hilton Austin DOWNTOWN   Adjacent to the convention center, this Hilton is often brimming with conventioneers. Located near 6th Street, with a great health club and spa, the hotel serves both business and leisure travelers well. Step across the street to see the O. Henry House and Susanna Dickinson museums (see p 21, ❸). An Alamo survivor, Dickinson's house moved there when the hotel was built—it used to sit where the hotel coffee shop now stands. *500 E. 4th St. (at Neches St.). ☎ 512/482-8000. www.hilton.com. 800 units. Doubles $199–$219. AE, DC, DISC, MC, V. Bus: 100.*

★★ **Hostelling International– Austin** LADY BIRD LAKE   This award-winning facility located beside the hike-and-bike trails of Lady Bird Lake offers great views, a laundry room, kitchen, two male dorms, one female dorm, one co-ed dorm, and a four-bed coed en-suite dorm and a two-person private room that share a bathroom and kitchen. Best of all, it offers free Internet and Wi-Fi. Solar-panels and low-flow shower heads are but a few of the hostel's many "green" eco-friendly features. A 15% lodging tax is applied to all reservations. *2200 S. Lakeshore Blvd. ☎ 800/725-2331 or 512/444-2294. www.hiaustin. org. 47 beds divided into 6 rooms.*

$22 adults, $19 AYH members, $11 children under 13; private rooms $25 & $43 ($22 & $40 member rates). AE, MC, V. Free parking. Bus: 7 & 20.

★★ **Hotel San Jose** SOCO This diminutive urban boutique hotel features the kind of *Mad Men* time-warp vibe many would love to get stuck in: minimalist, mid-century, retro everything with big flat-screen televisions, plush bedding, and all the über-trendy touches you'd expect. Originally a 1930s motor court, this hip little hotel offers a chic sanctuary in the heart of SoCo, across from the Continental Club. Request a "grand standard" room in back to avoid traffic noise and partying passerby. *1316 S. Congress Ave. ☎ 800/574-8897 or 512/852-2350. www.sanjosehotel.com. 40 units. Doubles $95–$105 w/shared bathroom, double w/private bathroom $160–$260, suites $280–$375. AE, DISC, MC, V. Bus: 1M & 1L.*

★★ **Hotel St. Cecilia** SOCO This shrine to the patron saint of music and poetry features six swank poolside bungalows on the grounds of an historic house in SoCo, with five suites, three studios, and an old Hollywood vibe that permeates the tony private grounds, striking subtle rock-n-roll chords. Celebrities visiting Austin have always stayed at the Four Seasons (and many still do), but these days, some hide out here in the bungalows—how Chateau Marmont of them. Even though a much-cooler-than-thou crowd may lounge in the lobby and do laps in the pool, almost-affordable weekday rates make a stay here accessible to uncool travelers like me. *112 Academy Dr. (near S. Congress Ave.). ☎ 512/852-2400. www.hotel saintcecilia.com. 14 units. Doubles $275–$540 w/breakfast. AE, DC, DISC, MC, V. Bus: 1M & 1L.*

The Hyatt Regency Austin DOWNTOWN On the banks of Lady Bird Lake, this high-rise Hyatt features great views of the lake and the city skyline. Best of all, Capital Cruises offers bat tours and lake excursions on a dock below the hotel's back door. Rent kayaks, canoes, paddle boats, or even a mountain bike to explore hike and-bike trails along the lake. *208 Barton*

The Hyatt Regency lobby.

InterContinental Stephen F. Austin caters to the downtown business traveler.

Springs Rd. (at Congress Ave.). ☎ 512/477-1234. www.austin.hyatt. com. *448 units. Doubles $249–$314. AE, DC, DISC, MC, V. Bus: 30 & 5.*

InterContinental Stephen F. Austin DOWNTOWN

Built to compete with the Driskill in 1924, and fully restored in 2000 when the Driskill did its latest renovation, this hotel features amenities with discriminating downtown business travelers in mind. The hotel is home to a restaurant, bar, indoor pool, health club, and business center, too. I like it that the hotel is now 100% smoke-free. *701 Congress Ave. (at 7th St.)* ☎ *888/424-6835 or 512/457-8800. www.austin.inter continental.com. 189 units. Doubles $139–$389. AE, DC, DISC, MC, V. Bus: 1M & 1L.*

★★ Kimber Modern SOCO

With its sophisticated, stark Euro-minimalist style, this little SoCo treasure is perhaps Austin's best-kept secret. Is it a boutique hotel, a private retreat, or just an adult's tree house hidden by oak trees? You decide. With Pare Eames desk chairs and Philippe Starck bathroom fixtures, this architecturally alluring den of designer furnishings and amenities oozes severe, austere

style and reminds me of a chic hotel I know in Stockholm. Can't beat the location just behind The Continental Club in SoCo on a residential street. *110 The Circle (near S. Congress Ave.).* ☎ *512/912-1046. www.kimber modern.com. 6 units. Doubles $250–$320. AE, MC, V. Bus: 1L, 1M, 5, 6, 7, 9, 20, 30 & 101.*

★★★ Lake Austin Spa Resort NORTHWEST AUSTIN

This resort offers the quintessential laidback, lovely Austin experience—but it'll cost you. The rooms (rows of sweet little connected cottages) didn't wow me—though the rates did. Still, the draw here isn't a room—it's the whole decadent, superior spa-resort experience. The lush lakeside grounds, pools, facilities, programs, restaurant, reading room, water-sport options and oh-so splendid spa, and all the classes and amenities that go with it are well worth the cost. *1705 S. Quinlan Park Rd. (FM620).* ☎ *800/847-5637 or 512/372-7300. www.lakeaustin.com. 40 units. $500 adults w/all meals, classes & activities; spa treatments/ personal trainers extra. AE, DC, DISC, MC, V. No city bus service.*

★★ kids Lakeway Resort and Spa LAKEWAY

With arresting views

of Lake Travis and the Hill Country, this conference resort is a serene sanctuary from the bustle of Austin business and traffic. Set 18 miles (29km) northwest of downtown Austin, the resort features manicured lawns, attentive guest services, pleasant decor, and award-winning restaurants. Sailing, tennis, golf, and great kids' programs are a draw, and I adore being pampered in the flawless spa. The restaurant is upscale, and the sports bar and grill is a favorite with guys. *101 Lakeway Dr.* ☎ *512/261-6600. www.dolce-lakeway-hotel.com. 173 units. Doubles $198–$265. AE, DC, DISC, MC, V. No city bus service, though transfers to/from airport are available.*

★★★ The Mansion at Judge's Hill WEST CAMPUS
Proud UT parents and Longhorn alums, businessmen, and couples are all regular returning guests of this impeccable Victorian mansion in the "West Campus" area. The inn features fine dining, attentive service, and wraparound porches overlooking the city. The newer, adjacent North Wing features stately French Quarter–style rooms. The bar and restaurant are sublime—elegant but not stuffy. *1900 Rio Grande St. (at MLK, Jr. Blvd./19th St.).* ☎ *800/311-1619 or 512/495-1800. www.mansionat judgeshill.com. 48 units. Doubles $189–$299 North Wing, $129–$219 mansion. AE, DC, DISC, MC, V. Bus: 19 & 3.*

★★ THE W HOTEL–ACL WAREHOUSE DISTRICT
As of December 2010, the trendy W Hotel chain will now have an Austin address. This 36-floor skyscraper in the 2nd Street District features 252 guest rooms and 156 condominiums. Part of Block 21, a $250-million mixed-use development, the W's neighbors will include the new Austin City Limits (see p 27, ❶) television studio and theater, a 2,200 seat live music

venue, retail space, restaurants, and an open-air public plaza. Magic Johnson (1959–) is part of the Block 21 development team, and Willie Nelson and his nephew are partners in the music venue. *200 Lavaca St.* ☎ *888/625 4988. www.whotels. com/austin. 250 units. See website for rates & credit card information. Bus: 1L, 1M, 3, 5, 9, 19, 29, 101, 103 & 110.*

★ The Westin Austin at the Domain NORTH AUSTIN
If you like to shop, this is the hotel for you. Practically sitting on the parking lot of the Domain, an upscale shopping village in north Austin, this property's swank restaurant, bar, and lobby areas stand out from what is otherwise your basic nice, neat hotel. Although the pool (and most rooms) has appalling views of parking lots, the rooms' beds and bedding are divine. *11301 Domain Dr.* ☎ *512/832-4197. www.westinaustin athedomain.com. 340 units. Doubles $109–$309. AE, DC, DISC, MC, V. Bus: 147 & 240.*

Guests pamper themselves at the Lake Austin Spa Resort.

Austin Arts & Nightlife

Alamo Drafthouse Cinema **8**
Antone's **14**
Austin Lyric Opera **31**
Austin Museum of Art **5**
The Backyard **21**
Ballet Austin **25**
Beauty Bar **11**
The Beverly S. Sheffield
   Zilker Hillside Theatre **29**
Bob Bullock Museum **3**
The Broken Spoke **30**
Cedar Door **26**
Cedar Street Courtyard **16**
Continental Club **33**
Dallas Nightclub **1**
Driskill Bar **7**
The Elephant Room **23**
Emo's **9**
Esther's Follies **10**
Jack S. Blanton
   Museum of Art **4**
La Zona Rosa **13**
The Long Center for the
   Performing Arts **32**
Lucky Lounge **15**
Malaga Tapas & Bar **24**
Mean-Eyed Cat **12**
Mexic-Arte Museum **18**
Oilcan Harry's **20**
The One World Theatre **22**
The Paramount Theatre **6**
Rain on 4th **19**
Speakeasy **17**
Texas Memorial Museum &
   Natural Science Center **2**
Trio at the Four Seasons **27**
The Zachary Scott Theatre **28**

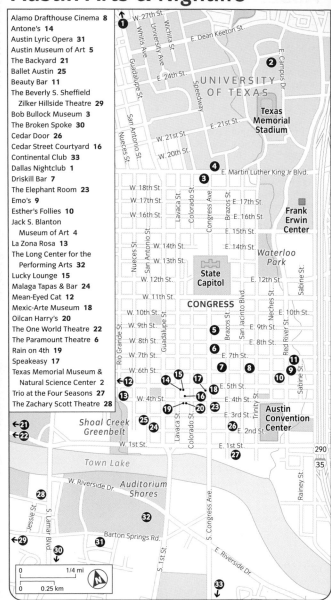

Austin Arts & Nightlife
Best Bets

Best **Dance Club**
★ Beauty Bar, *617 E. 7th St. (p 95)*

Best **Gay & Lesbian Bar**
★ Rain on 4th, *217 W. 4th St. (p 96)*

Best **Jazz**
★★★ The Elephant Room, *315 Congress Ave. (p 96)*

Best **Art Museum**
★ Blanton Museum of Art, *200 E. MLK, Jr. Blvd. (p 94)*

Best **Museum for Kids Crazy about Dinosaurs**
Texas Memorial Museum & Natural Science Center, *2400 Trinity St. (p 17)*

Best **Outdoor Venue**
★★ The Backyard, *13472 Bee Cave Pkwy. (p 92)*

Best **Performing Arts Venue**
★★★ The Long Center for the Performing Arts, *701 West Riverside Dr. (p 28)*

Best Place to **Channel Stevie Ray Vaughan**
★★★ Antone's, *213 West 5th St. (p 32)*

Best Place for a **Dinner-&-a-Movie Date**
★★★ Alamo Drafthouse Cinema, *320 E. 6th St. (p 92)*

Best Place to **Laugh till your Face Hurts**
★ Esther's Follies, *525 East 6th St. (p 96)*

Best Place to **Meet for Drinks**
★★ Cedar Door, *201 Brazos St. (p 94)*

Best Place to **Two-Step**/Best **Jukebox**
★★★ The Broken Spoke, *3201 S. Lamar Blvd. (p 24)*

Coolest **Austin Classic**
★★★ Continental Club, *1315 S. Congress Ave. (p 32)*

Coolest **Small Concert Venue**
★ One World Theatre, *7701 Bee Cave Rd. (p 93)*

The architecturally stunning Long Center for the Performing Arts.

Arts & Nightlife A to Z

A performance by the innovative Ballet Austin.

Dance
★ Ballet Austin DOWN-
TOWN   Artistic director Stephen Mills' acclaimed ballet company appears at various Austin performing arts venues when not touring or participating in international dance festivals. *501 W. 3rd St. ☎ 512/476-9151. www.balletaustin.org. Tickets $24–$74. Bus: 171 & 3.*

Theater/Concert Venues
★★ Alamo Drafthouse Cinemas DOWNTOWN   For one-stop dinner-and-a-movie dates, this artsy independent theater offers a bar; good brews; decent food (really); and indie, art house, and first-run films for movie-goers 18 and up. During Baby Day matinees on Tuesdays, parents can bring along noisy bundles of joy. Special screenings include fun food and film events (like Chinese

The Alamo Draft House is a great dinner-and-date destination for fans of indie films.

food and a Kung Fu movie), costume nights, audience-interactive shows and festivals, and guest lectures—and the pizza's not bad, either. A new location is coming soon to the Circle C area in South Austin. *13729 Research Blvd. ☎ 512/459-7090; 1120 S. Lamar Blvd. ☎ 512/707-8262; 320 E. 6th St. ☎ 512/476-1320; 2700 W. Anderson Lane ☎ 512/219-5408. Tickets $6.75–$9; Mon all seats $6.75, Thurs after 6pm ladies $6. 6th St. & Trinity RITZ theater location bus: 2, 3, 19, 37 & 137.*

★★ The Backyard BEE CAVE   My favorite airy outdoor venue for big-name bands—in a place that doesn't scream concert scene and that is committed to green initiatives. Bob Dylan (1941–), David Bowie (1947–), Willie Nelson, Paul Simon (1941–), and others have played the Backyard. They say it's only a three-song drive from downtown to their new Bee Cave–area location, but hit traffic, and it could take a whole CD. *13472 Bee Cave Pkwy. (at Hwy. 620/FM 2244).*

93

Arts & Nightlife A to Z

☎ 512/263-4146. Tickets for local acts $6–$12, national acts $20–$50. No bus service.

★★★ **Long Center for the Performing Arts** RIVERSIDE/BARTON SPRINGS The nonprofit group Arts Center Stage led Austin's Lester E. Palmer Auditorium through a multi-million-dollar renovation, transforming it into an architecturally arresting community performing arts venue, opened in March 2008. Facilities are some of the finest in Texas. *701 W. Riverside Dr.* ☎ *512/457-5100. www.thelongcenter.org. Tickets $20–$100. Buses: 5, 29 & 30.*

★★ **One World Theatre** WEST-LAKE HILLS A pleasantly unexpected venue, this non-profit theater offers an impressive eclectic calendar of performers, from Sergio Mendes (1941–) to Cowboy Junkies, Duncan Sheik to Judy Collins (1939–). The alluring 300-seat theater stands adjacent to a Tuscan-villa-type space where full bar and three-course dinners are offered before each show. However, concerts are sometimes all too brief, as two shows may be seated in one evening—an unpleasant surprise if you didn't expect it and paid a lot for tickets. *7701 Bee Cave Rd.* ☎ *512/330-9500. Tickets $12–$71 (often $56–$71); dinner $35 w/tax & tip. Bus 30.*

★★★ **The Paramount Theatre.** The Grand Dame of Austin venues, The Paramount is one of the oldest and most beloved theaters in town. *See p 43,* ❽.

The Zachary Scott Theatre SOUTH AUSTIN One of Austin's oldest theaters, incorporated in 1933, the Zachary Scott Theatre operates two venues at the edge of Zilker Park, presenting plays, musicals, lectures, and special events. *John E. Whisenhunt Stage, 1510 Toomey Rd.; Kleburg theatre-in-the-round, 1421 W. Riverside Dr.*

☎ 512/476-0541 (box office) or 512/476-0594. www.zachtheatre. org. Tickets $22–$54. Buses: 3 & 338.

★★★ 🅺🅸🅳🆂 **The Beverly S. Sheffield Zilker Hillside Theatre** ZILKER PARK The Zilker Summer Musical is the longest-running outdoor musical production with pay-what-you-wish admission in the United States. Since 1959, highly professional summer musicals have been performed beneath the stars in Zilker Park before the Hillside Theatre stage. Spread out your blanket to save a spot at sundown with the family, and bring a cooler or visit the concession stand and restrooms nearby. Fabulous for families, it's affordable, too (donations appreciated but not required); there's not a better show in town. Blankets may be spread out at 6pm to reserve a spot; the show starts at dark. *2100 Barton Springs Rd. (in Zilker Park, across from Barton Springs Pool).* ☎ *512/479-9491. www.zilker.org. Free admission (donations accepted). Parking $3. Bus: 3 & 338.*

Museums
Austin Museum of Art–Laguna Gloria MAYFIELD PARK/DOWNTOWN Originally established in 1961 on the lush 12-acre (4.9-hectare) grounds of a lakeside private family estate, the Austin Museum of Art–Laguna Gloria is one of Austin's most attractive art museums and art schools. Peacocks stroll outside the stunning 1916 Italianate-style villa which houses the museum, once the home of a prominent Texan, Clara Driscoll (1881–1945). Today, AMOA also has a bright downtown space on Congress Avenue for exhibitions and seminars. *Laguna Gloria, 3809 W. 35th St.* ☎ *512/458-8191; downtown, 823 Congress Ave.* ☎ *512/495-9224 or* ☎ *512/495-9224, ext. 313 (Laguna Gloria tours).*

www.amoa.org. Laguna Gloria free admission (suggested donation $3); downtown adults $5; seniors & students w/ID $4 and children 12 and over; free for children under 12 & AMOA members. Laguna Gloria free parking; bus: 9. Downtown bus: 1L, 1M, & 5.

★★ Blanton Museum of Art UT

CAMPUS   One of the largest university-owned art museums in the United States, the Blanton is home to more than 18,000 works from Europe, Latin America, and the U.S., and it operates as part of UT's College of Fine Arts. *200 E. MLK, Jr. Blvd.* ☎ *512/471-7324. www.blanton museum.org. $5 adults, $4 seniors 65 & older, $3 youth 13–25, free for children 12 & younger; free admission on Thurs. Parking $3 w/validation. Buses: 100, 103, 110 & 142.*

Bars & Cocktail Lounges
★★ Cedar Door DOWN-

TOWN   This dearly beloved bar has moved so many times that I'm beginning to feel like its stalker. It almost lost me after changing addresses for the fourth time, but this nomadic Austin institution (since 1975) has never lost its cool. Decks with heaters and misters make outdoor areas popular year-round, and folks said their award-winning Mexican Martini Mix drinks

were so good somebody should bottle the stuff. So they did. Buy one at the bar. *201 Brazos St.* ☎ *512/473-3712. www.cedar dooraustin.com. Bus: 3, 10, 17, 482 & 483.*

★★Cedar Street Courtyard

WAREHOUSE DISTRICT   Cool cocktails, hot nightly bands, and a great spot during South by Southwest (SXSW), this narrow courtyard bar offers long leisurely happy hours and an outdoor setting. This means that in virtually smoke-free Austin, you'll have a place to puff on that Cohiba or light up your Lucky Strikes. Live music nightly. *208 West 4th St.* ☎ *512/495-9669. www. cedarstreetaustin.com. Bus: 3, 10, 17, 29 & 110.*

★★ Driskill Bar DOWNTOWN

I could get lost in the arms of the oversized tufted-leather sofas or stare at a fireplace as flames gleam against brass lamps and shiny bottles of bracing spirits in this old hotel piano bar. Texas politicians, lawyers, and well-heeled locals like to hold court in this lobby-like lounge. Who wouldn't? (LBJ's ghost is said to hang out here, too.) *See p 76.*

★ Malaga Tapas & Bar WARE-

HOUSE DISTRICT   Bathed in soft glowing light, warm colors, and a woozy wine buzz, and with savory

The Italianate-styled Austin Museum of Art.

Two of many Johnny Cash portraits on display in the Mean-Eyed Cat.

tapas to nibble and nosh, this tony tapas spot is the creation of Spanish-born award-winning chef/owner Alejandro Duran. His paella can't be beat, and the first and third Wednesdays of the month are Flamenco nights. *440 W. 2nd St. ☎ 512/236-8020. www.malaga austin.com. Bus: 3, 10, 17, 29 & 110.*

★★★ **Mean-Eyed Cat** OLD WEST AUSTIN What's not to love about a Johnny Cash–themed beer joint with a pool table inside and a laid-back music venue on the back patio? The Man in Black's mug is all over this place, and so are lyrics to "Mean-Eyed Cat" and more. Restroom doors are labeled "Johnny" and "June." I just love that. *See p 21,* ❶.

★★★ **Trio at the Four Seasons** DOWNTOWN Sophisticated yet casual, modern yet warm, Trio's wine bar happy hours are a treat. *See p 81.*

Dance Clubs
Beauty Bar DOWNTOWN A crowded, loud, sweaty, hipster dance club that spins indie, '80s, and hip-hop, with cheap beer and whiskey specials, drinks, and questionable goings-on on the front

porch late at night. *617 E. 7th St. ☎ 512/391-1943. www.beautybar. com. Cover $5. Bus: 2, 3, 4, 37 & 137.*

★★★ **The Broken Spoke** SOUTH AUSTIN Want to see a real, bona fide Texas cowboy dancehall? Well, here it is—authentic and then some. *See p 24,* ❿.

Dallas Nightclub CRESTVIEW/ALLENDALE Urban cowboy boot-scoot boogie types will love this kikker-meets-city-slicker dancehall. Try the Two-Step, Cotton-Eyed Joe, Schottische, and line dancing. Thursday is Salsa Night. Free dance lessons (Salsa on Thurs/Country on Fri). With cowboy boots, Wranglers, belt buckles, beer—you'll know you're in Texas at Dallas. *7113 Burnet Rd. ☎ 512/452-1300. www. danceatdallas.com. Cover Wed $2 men, ladies free; Thurs– Sat $3 men, $2 ladies. Closed Sun–Tues. Bus 3.*

Lucky Lounge WAREHOUSE DISTRICT Neighborhood lounge with loud music, a cool vibe, and cold drinks. *209A W. 5th St. ☎ 512/479-7700. Bus: 3, 10, 17 & 29.*

★ **Speakeasy** WAREHOUSE DISTRICT First, there are the stairs: 59 of them to get to this three-tier club after entering through an alley (how

Prohibition-era is that?). Even if you take the elevator, when you get to patio-and-palm-tree-pretty Terrace 59 on top, it'll take your breath away. Striking city views and swing dance on weekends. Did I mention it's haunted? *412 Congress Ave.* ☎ *512/476-8017. Cover $5–$10. www.speakeasyaustin.com. Bus: 1L, 1M, 5 & 483.*

Comedy Clubs
★★ **Esther's Follies** 6TH STREET Your face is going to hurt from laughing at this wacky vaudeville venue on 6th Street (think *Saturday Night Live* meets *Hairspray*) known for hilarious, irreverent, and oh-so-current comedy. Named for svelte swimming '40s film star Esther Williams (1921–), this you-forget-how-funny-it-can-be club has been making Austin's sides hurt for over 30 years. *525 East 6th St.* ☎ *512/320-0553. www.esthers follies.com. Tickets $20 general admission, $25 pre-paid reserved seating; Thurs & Fri $18 students & military w/ID. Bus: 2, 3, 37 & 137.*

Music Clubs
★★★ **Antone's** WAREHOUSE DISTRICT Austin's best-known blues club. *See p 32,* ⑮.

★★★ **Continental Club** SOCO Kind of a dive? Sure. But it's a hopping SoCo music venue and a long-time favorite among locals. *See p 32,* ⑭.

★★★ **The Elephant Room** DOWNTOWN For almost 20 years, this has been my favorite club in Austin, with the best jazz this side of the Spotted Cat in New Orleans. *See p 33,* ⑯.

★★ **Emo's** 6TH STREET A loud alternative lounge off 6th Street with stages indoors and out, this popular club features nightly bands that take loud indie, rock, punk, hardcore, alt-country, and metal to

their sweaty zenith. With costly covers and cult-like loyalty among keep-Austin-cool crowds, Emo's is your basic drunk-and-disorderly dive off 6th Street. *603 Red River St. (at 6th St.).* ☎ *512/505-8541 www.emos austin.com. Cover/tickets $5–$25. Bus: 2, 3, 37 & 137.*

★ **La Zona Rosa** WAREHOUSE DISTRICT With an exciting, eclectic line-up each month on the open-air stage out back, La Zona Rosa hits all the right notes. From world music to zydeco, alternative rock to Americana, this all-ages-allowed place is perfect for a hot night with cold Coronas and wedges of lime while Marsha Ball (1949–) makes Jerry Lee Lewis–like moves on her piano. *612 W. 4th St.* ☎ *512/263-4164. www.lazonarosa.com. Tickets $8–$12 local acts, $20–$50 national acts. Bus: 4, 21, 103, 484 & 663.*

The Gay & Lesbian Scene
★ **Oilcan Harry's** WAREHOUSE DISTRICT Called the "Gay Epicenter of Austin" and locally known as "The Can," this place has been around for years and is still your best bet for a basic dance-and-flirt spot with sassy bartenders and a loud, outrageous boys-will-be-boys-and-girls scene. A little more civilized scene than some other clubs. *211 W. 4th St.* ☎ *512/320-8823. www.oilcanharrys.com. No cover. Bus: 3, 10, 17, 29 & 110.*

★★ **Rain on 4th** WAREHOUSE DISTRICT Often voted the number one gay and lesbian club in Austin, this place features a packed elevated dance floor, DJs, videos, and all the usual suspects—karaoke queens included. The later it gets, the dirtier the dancing—consider yourself warned. *217B W. 4th St.* ☎ *512/494-1150. www.rainon4th.com. No cover. Bus: 3, 10, 17, 29 & 110.* ●

The Best of San Antonio

The Best in One Day

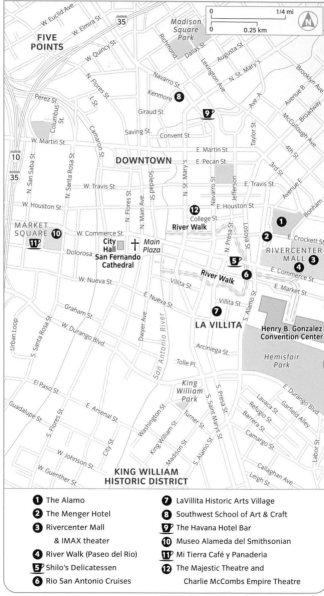

FIVE POINTS

Madison Square Park

DOWNTOWN

MARKET SQUARE

City Hall
San Fernando Cathedral
Main Plaza

River Walk

River Walk

RIVERCENTER MALL

LA VILLITA

Henry B. Gonzalez Convention Center

Hemisfair Park

King William Park

KING WILLIAM HISTORIC DISTRICT

❶	The Alamo
❷	The Menger Hotel
❸	Rivercenter Mall & IMAX theater
❹	River Walk (Paseo del Rio)
❺	Shilo's Delicatessen
❻	Rio San Antonio Cruises
❼	LaVillita Historic Arts Village
❽	Southwest School of Art & Craft
❾	The Havana Hotel Bar
❿	Museo Alameda del Smithsonian
⓫	Mi Tierra Café y Panaderia
⓬	The Majestic Theatre and Charlie McCombs Empire Theatre

Previous page: The 750-foot-high Tower of the Americas.

For a sprawling modern metropolis, San Antonio has a quaint Old World sensitivity that's vaguely Spanish, decidedly Mexican, and truly Texan. It's no wonder that here, in the shadow of the Alamo where so many died in the fight for Texas independence, a strong proud spirit endures, honoring all that is old and beautiful about the Lone Star State. Known for its rambling River Walk, spicy Tex-Mex fare, and colorful diverse cultures, this sizzling urban oasis is, by population, the seventh-largest city in the nation. START: Take Red- or Blue-line streetcar to Alamo Plaza.

A miniature diorama of the Alamo.

❶ ★★ **The Alamo.** Smaller than you'd expect, this Spanish mission (San Antonio de Valero), built in 1744, squats in the center of downtown. With its famous facade, it is a sacred place honoring those who died here in 1836 during its bloody siege in Texas's fight for independence from Mexico. Today, the historic complex features tree-shaded grounds, the mission chapel, a research center, a museum, and a gift shop. There is not a lot to see inside the chapel itself—disappointing some visitors—but in the Low Barracks building, a brief film gives a historical context to the mission, and docent storytellers give a riveting free talk about the battle, leaving you feeling as though you've stood on hallowed ground. ⏱ *30–45 min. 300 Alamo Plaza.* ☎ *210/225-1391.*

www.thealamo.org. Free admission (donations accepted). Mon–Sat 9am–5:30pm, Sun 10am–5:30pm. Closed Dec. 24 & 25. Free history talks & self-guided walks; call ahead to schedule private, after-hours tours. Streetcar: Red & Blue lines to Alamo Plaza.

❷ ★ **The Menger Hotel.** Standing in the shadow of the historic mission, and built just 23 years after the Alamo fell, the historic Menger Hotel is a San Antonio treasure which opened in 1859. Enter the Crockett Street side door of the hotel's Teddy Roosevelt Bar, where Rough Riders were recruited. From there, enter the hotel and follow a corridor where historic photos, artifacts, and hotel memorabilia are all on display. Pass through the lobby and notice the adjacent courtyard of towering palm trees and exploding blossoms of bright bougainvillea before peeking into the elegant Colonial Room. In the older, original lobby, be sure to look up at the stained-glass ceiling in the atrium. The Mae West and King Ranch suites are both remarkable in the historic (and supposedly haunted) side of the hotel (I don't recommend rooms in the "newer" part). Presidents and kings have stayed here, and I spent my honeymoon night in a suite with a balcony overlooking Alamo Plaza. ⏱ *15 min. 204 Alamo Plaza.* ☎ *210/223-4361. www. mengerhotel.com. Streetcar: Red & Blue lines to Alamo Plaza.*

The Rivercenter Mall can be used to reach the River Walk.

3 ★ **kids Rivercenter Mall & IMAX theater.** Step out the southside doors of the Menger and cross a pedestrian walkway to enter the mall, a convenient portal to the River Walk. There, in the Rivercenter, an IMAX theater offers a 38-minute docu-drama, *Alamo: The Price of Freedom,* bringing to life the historic battle. Newer movie releases (some in 3-D) are also shown. Artifacts from the 1800s and an Alamo diorama are displayed near the theater gift shop. 🕐 *1½ hr. Rivercenter Mall, 849 E. Commerce St.* ☎ *800/354-4629 or 210/247-4629. www.imax-sa.com. $12 adults, $11 seniors & children 12–17, $7.95 children 3–11. Streetcar: All lines to Alamo & E. Commerce sts.*

Travel Tip

Hop on board a river-taxi shuttle to locations along the River Walk. "Rio taxis" run daily from 9am to 9pm. Tickets are available from boat drivers or at various hotels along the River Walk.

4 ★★★ **River Walk.** No visit to San Antonio would be complete without exploring the city's most enchanting attraction, the River Walk, or *Paseo del Rio.* This rambling corridor of quiet walkways first began in 1939 as a project of the WPA (Works Progress Administration) and today features romantic arched bridges, a canopy of shade tree branches, and lush landscaping. Flanking both sides of the slender green San Antonio River, restaurants, clubs, art galleries, and shops line narrow walkways. Float on a river barge, dine beneath colorful umbrellas, and sway to the sounds of Jim Cullum's (1941–) Jazz Band at the **Landing** (see p 169) after dark. At this writing, a "museum reach" expansion of the River Walk is underway, and popular restaurants such as **Osteria Il Sogno** (see p 156) have opened there in the shadow of the **Old Pearl Brewery** (see p 111). Enter at Rivercenter or at any bridge stairwell. 🕐 *1½ hr. Administration offices, 110 Broadway St.* ☎ *210/227-4262. www.thesanantonioriverwalk.com. Bus: 302 & Yellow streetcar line.*

5 ★★★ **Schilo's Delicatessen.** As Mexican and Spanish as San Antonio may seem, there's also a strong German influence here from immigrants who came in the mid-1800s. Stop at this affordable and well-loved landmark German deli for breakfast or a bite of bratwurst, and don't miss the huge slabs of scrumptious cheesecake. Pronounced "shy-low's," this is the perfect pick-me-up place for a cup of coffee and a slice of strudel. *424 E. Commerce St.* ☎ *210/223-6692. $–$$.*

⑥ ★★★ kids Rio San Antonio Cruises. To get your bearings on the River Walk, it's best to board a boat. Buy your ticket under the Commerce Street bridge just below Schilo's, and take a 35- to 40-minute cruise covering 2½ miles (4km) of the San Antonio River on a slow-moving river barge. Boat drivers provide entertaining and informative narratives about the history of the River Walk. Pass the Arneson River Theatre and La Villita, a historic arts village, along the way, as well as numerous hotels and restaurants you'll want to visit. Buy tickets and board boats at any of four locations on the River Walk. Tickets and maps are available on their website. This company also provides river-taxi shuttle service and "boat dining" from numerous restaurants and hotels. Along the River Walk, stop under the Market Street bridge and Alamo Street to buy tickets at the Historia stop. Or walk to the

The deli and baked goods display at Schilo's Delicatessen.

Clearwater stop at Rivercenter Mall (Commerce and Bowie streets). ⏱ *1 hr. Administration office, 205 N. Presa Building B.* ☎ *800/417-4139 or 210/244-5700. www.riosan antonio.com. $8.25 adults; $6 Bexar County residents, seniors (60+) & U.S. military; $2 children 1–5. Daily 9am–9pm. Bus: 301 & Red streetcar line.*

⑦ ★ La Villita Historic Arts Village. Located on the banks of the San Antonio River, up the steps

A boat cruise down the San Antonio River alongside the River Walk.

La Villita's colorful folk art and souvenirs.

Daily 10am–6pm. Streetcar: Red & Blue lines to LaVillita.

❽ ★ Southwest School of Art & Craft. Formerly the Southwest Craft Center, its exhibition galleries, studios, and classrooms focus on contemporary art, while it also hosts lectures, concerts, and performing arts events. The center is housed in the historic convent, quiet gardens, and walled grounds that served as the first girls' school in San Antonio, opened by Ursuline nuns in the mid-19th century. The Ursuline Sales Gallery features unique crafts items and art. Check out the wacky Art*O*Mat, a converted vending machine containing art and jewelry created by 20 different artists, with items just $5 each. The Visitor's Center Museum in the First Academy Building is a good source of information on the school and its historic grounds. In the adjacent Navarro Campus, see the large exhibition galleries, as well as art studios to tour when classes aren't in session. ⏱ *1 hr.* *See p 98.*

❾ ★★★ The Havana Hotel Bar. Smell the history—but no cigars—in this small, dark, and handsome best-kept-secret Cuba-themed bar. Set in the basement of the enchanting little Hotel Havana, the bar's tobacco-colored walls and worn-leather chairs add an other-world, other-century, Hemingway-was-just-here-a-minute-ago vibe that leaves me weak in the knees. Now a non-smoking area, so leave the Cohbias in Cuba.*1015 Navarro St.* ☎ *210/ 222-2008. $.*

from the little outdoor **Arneson River Theatre** rests San Antonio's first neighborhood, La Villita ("little village"). Spanish soldiers stationed at The Alamo once lived in huts on this spot, which later would become a community of brick, stone, and adobe houses in the 1800s. In 1836, the Mexican Army General Santa Anna (1794–1876) positioned his cannon line here during his siege of the Alamo. Later, German and French immigrants settled here. Today, historic structures (the village is listed on the National Register of Historic Places) house galleries, restaurants, and shops with folk art, jewelry, clothing, home decor, Mexican imports, and more. Be sure to peek inside the **Little Church** (418 Villita St., Bldg. #1300; ☎ 210/226-3593), built in 1979—a popular site for weddings. Walking tour maps are available throughout the site. ⏱ *1 hr. 401 Villita St. (from the River Walk enter at the Arneson River Theatre). La Villita is located near the corner of S. Alamo and Nueva sts.* ☎ *210/207-8610. www.lavillita.com.*

❿ ★ Museo Alameda del Smithsonian. The building's bright flamingo-pink and margarita-lime colors will catch the eye of visitors to Market Square. Step inside to see the largest museum dedicated to Latin American art and culture in the nation. This Smithsonian affiliate features 20,000 square feet (1,858 sq. m) of exhibition space divided into 11 galleries, and unique exhibits celebrating the history, traditions, artifacts, and art of San Antonio's vibrant and colorful cultures. Visiting exhibits often focus on the Mexican American heritage of the majority of San Antonio citizens. The museum space is also bold and arresting, with elaborate, contemporary stainless steel panel walls reminiscent of colonial Latin American iron work and sculpture. 🕑 *1 hr. 101 S. Santa Rosa St. (at Commerce St., in Market Sq.).* ☎ *210/229-4300. www.thealameda. org. Free admission (suggested donation $4 adults, $3 seniors, $2 students & military w/ID, $12 families). Tues & Thurs–Sat 10am–6pm, Wed 10am–8pm, Sun noon–6pm. Streetcar: Red & Yellow lines to Market Sq.*

11 ★★★ **kids** **Mi Tierra Café y Panadería.** In Market Square is an exploding piñata of sweet colors, strings of twinkling lights, and consistently good Tex-Mex fare. Mariachis stroll past tables while waiters balance big trays of steaming enchiladas and handmade tortillas. An SA tradition since 1941, Mi Tierra's is still open 24 hours and stays busy all the time. *218 Produce Row.* ☎ *210/225-1262. $–$$.*

12 ★★★ **The Majestic Theatre & Charlie McCombs Empire Theatre.** San Antonio's most beloved theater, the Majestic Theatre, stands downtown just blocks from the Alamo and adjacent to another fabulous old former movie house, **The Empire Theatre.** *Majestic Theatre, 224 E. Houston St.; Empire Theatre, 226 N. St Marys St.* ☎ *210/226-3333 (box office) or 210/226-5700 (administration). www.majestic empire.com. Streetcar: Red line to corner of Houston & Navarro sts.*

The flamingo-pink walls of the Museo Alameda del Smithsonian.

The Best **in Two Days**

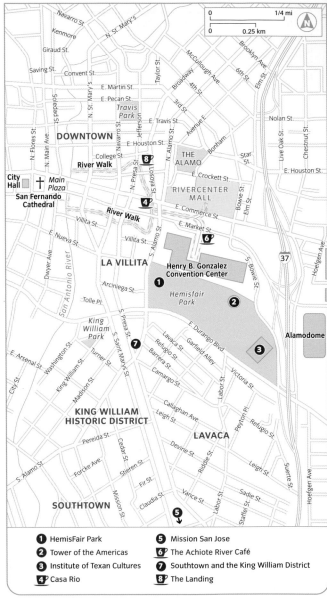

0   1/4 mi

0   0.25 km

Navarro St.

Kenmore

Giraud St.

Saving St.

Convent St.

N. St. Mary's

N. St. Mary's Ave.

Taylor St.

Broadway

McCullough Ave.

6th St.

Brooklyn Ave.

Elm St.

E. Martin St.

E. Pecan St.

4th St.

3rd St.

Avenue E

Nolan St.

Live Oak St.

Chestnut St.

DOWNTOWN

Travis Park

Jefferson

E. Travis St.

E. Houston St.

Bonham

Star St.

E. Houston St.

N. Flores St.

N. Main Ave.

N. Navarro St.

N. Alamo St.

College St.

River Walk

N. Presa St.

Losoya St.

8

THE ALAMO

E. Crockett St.

City Hall

Main Plaza

San Fernando Cathedral

Villita St.

River Walk

4

RIVERCENTER MALL

E. Commerce St.

Bowie St.

Elm St.

E. Nueva St.

Villita St.

S. Alamo St.

E. Market St.

6

37

Hoefgen Ave.

LA VILLITA

San Antonio River

Dwyer Ave.

Arciniega St.

Tolle Pl.

Henry B. Gonzalez Convention Center

1

Hemisfair Park

2

King William Park

7

E. Arsenal St.

S. Presa St.

S. Saint Marys St.

E. Durango Blvd.

Lavaca St.

Garfield Alley

Refugio St.

Barrera St.

Camargo St.

Labor St.

Victoria St.

S. Bowie St.

Alamodome

3

Washington St.

King William St.

Madison St.

Turner St.

City St.

KING WILLIAM HISTORIC DISTRICT

Pereida St.

Cedar St.

Callaghan Ave.

Leigh St.

Devine St.

LAVACA

Riddle St.

Labor St.

Leigh St.

Peyton Pl.

Refugio St.

Suerte St.

Hoefgen Ave.

S. Alamo St.

Forcke Ave.

Stieren St.

Fir St.

Mission St.

Claudia St.

Vance St.

Sadie St.

Staffel St.

SOUTHTOWN

5
↓

- **1** HemisFair Park
- **2** Tower of the Americas
- **3** Institute of Texan Cultures
- **4** Casa Rio
- **5** Mission San Jose
- **6** The Achiote River Café
- **7** Southtown and the King William District
- **8** The Landing

Put on your walking shoes for Day Two in the Alamo City. You'll hop on a streetcar, see the lay of the land from the top of a high tower, criss-cross pretty parks, stroll through a museum, and go on a mission, exploring ancient sites. But don't worry: I've built-in time to rest tired feet with stops along the River Walk, where cold drinks, hot salsa, and crispy corn tortilla chips provide a quick pick-me-up as you hit the trail in search of a good time in Old San Antonio. START: **Take Red-line streetcar to HemisFair Park (W. Market & S. Alamo sts.).**

❶ ★ kids HemisFair Park. Built for the 1968 World's Fair and to commemorate San Antonio's 250th anniversary, HemisFair Park features playgrounds, parks, waterfalls and fountains, educational museums, the children's **Magik Theatre** (see p 122), and the **Tower of the Americas** (see p 105). **The Maximilian Schultze House Cottage Gardens** (514 HemisFair Park— no phone), created and maintained by the Master Gardeners of Bexar County, is also worth a look. 🕐 *1 hr. 200 S. Alamo St. No phone. www.sanantonio.gov. Streetcar: Red, Blue & Yellow lines to HemisFair Park (S. Alamo & Market sts.).*

❷ ★ ★ kids Tower of the Americas. The celebrated centerpiece of HemisFair Park is the city's definitive skyline feature, a tower rising 750 feet (229m) high, built in 1968 for the World's Fair. With multimillion-dollar renovations in 2004 and 2006, the Tower of the Americas boasts an observation deck near the top, nearly 59 stories high. Take the glass elevator there to enjoy spectacular views, especially by night. The tower has a ground-level cafe and gift shop, an observation deck, a revolving restaurant, a cocktail lounge, and a thrilling **"Skies Over Texas" 4-D film "ride."** The slowly revolving **Chart House** is part of the Landry's restaurant chain. 🕐 *1 hr. 600 HemisFair Plaza Way.* ☎ *210/223-3101. www.toweroftheamericas.com. $11 adults, $9.95 seniors & military, $8.95 children. Sun–Thurs 10am–10pm, Fri & Sat 10am–11pm. Streetcar: Yellow line to S. Alamo & Nueva sts.*

❸ ★ ★ kids Institute of Texan Cultures. This entertaining museum and educational center, home to one of several campuses of UT San Antonio, features exhibits highlighting the influence of more than 20 different ethnic and cultural groups on Texan culture. Buildings in the large complex include a

The Tower of the Americas is the defining feature of San Antonio's skyline.

The historic Mission San Jose.

one-room school, an adobe home, a windmill, and the multimedia Dome Show Theatre. Family-friendly shows, events, and exhibits are offered throughout the year. Upstairs, an historic photo archive is open to the public on weekdays. ⏱ *1½ hr. 801 S. Bowie St.* ☎ *210/ 458-2300. www.texancultures.com. $8 adults; $7 seniors; $6 military w/ ID, college students & children 3–11; free for children under 3. Mon–Sat 9am–5pm, Sun noon–5pm. Closed Thanksgiving, Dec 25, Jan 1, Easter & during special festivals such as the Texas Folklife Festival (held in June). Streetcar: Yellow line to Bowie St. & Institute of Texan Cultures.*

4 ★ **Casa Rio.** Some say the food is overrated, but there's not a more pleasant spot along the River Walk to sit under colorful umbrellas and try some authentic Tex-Mex fare. In lieu of a full meal, a basket of crispy tortilla chips, a bowl of hot "chile con queso" (cheese dip), and a frozen margarita make a nice snack before hitting the Mission Trail. *430 E. Commerce St.* ☎ *210/225-6718. $–$$.*

5 ★★★ **Mission San Jose.** San Antonio is home to five historic Spanish missions (including the Mission San Antonio de Valero, or "Alamo") built by Catholic priests and native peoples along the San Antonio River in the early 1700s. City-owned hike-and-bike trails create a nice route loosely connecting four of the walled medieval-style fortresses, which rest surprisingly near one another along a 6-mile (9.7km) stretch (see p 114). A popular mission along the trail is the "Queen of the Missions," Mission San Jose y San Miguel de Aguayo (aka "Mission San Jose"), featuring an ornate "Rose Window" in its chapel. The largest of the four missions run by the National Park Service (the Alamo is not a national park property), San Jose was established in 1720 and was home to a busy and productive community of priests, nuns, and mission Indians. Beautifully restored in the 1930s by the WPA (Works Projects Administration), Mission San Jose appears today much as it did over 250 years ago. On Sundays, this Texas and U.S. National Historic Site offers a bilingual "Mariachi Mass" (featuring mariachi bands) at noon, as well as morning services in English and Spanish. The **Park Visitor Center** stands adjacent to Mission San Jose and features an informative short film, as well as a small museum and bookstore. Park rangers and docents conduct free mission tours. ⏱ 1½ hr. 6701 San Jose Dr. ☎ 210/922-0543 (Mission San Jose), 210/534-8833 (Mission HQ) or 210/932-1001 (Visitor's Center). www.nps.gov/saan. Free admission. Daily 9am–5pm. Closed Thanksgiving, Dec 25 & Jan 1. Bus: 42 to Roosevelt Ave. & Dagley (White) St.

6 ★ **The Achiote River Café.** Indulge in *antojitos* (literally, "little cravings" in Spanish, or "appetizers" in English) at the outdoor tables along the river, then stroll through the mid-century-style lobby for a

A mural decorating a studio on Southtown.

quick look at the adjacent new Grand Hyatt hotel (see p 160) and high-rise condo residence. *600 E. Market St. ☎ 210/224-1234. $–$$$.*

7 ★★ **kids** **Southtown and the King William District.** A few blocks from the city center is a bohemian enclave built up along South Alamo Street called Southtown. This hip arts and entertainment district of distinctive galleries, restaurants, bars, warehouses, converted lofts, and specialty shops sits next door to its stately—but not stodgy—neighbor, the King William Historic District. Known for its regal Victorian mansions and pretty little turn-of-the-20th-century bungalows, King William borders a quiet bend in the green San Antonio River and makes for a nice self-guided walking tour (see p 132). In Southtown, salsa and merengue clubs, photography studios, Tex-Mex restaurants, sushi bars, microbrew pubs, and tea rooms draw locals for late-night fun on First Fridays every month, when places stay open late and a block-party vibe sets in. Be sure to walk (or take the streetcar on) South Alamo Street as far as the **Blue Star Arts Complex** (see p 160) and **Blue Star Brewery** (see p 160) to see some interesting art and enjoy a cold one before Day Two in San Antonio draws to an end. ⏱ 2 hr. S. Alamo St. (from Durango Blvd. to Probant St.). Streetcar: Blue line to S. Alamo & Barrera sts.

8 ★★★ **The Landing.** Great River Walk spot, good drinks, tiny tables . . . and all that Jim Cullum jazz on the River Walk. Sip a mint julep and taste their stuffed jalapenos—a fiery hot San Antonio specialty. *123 Losoya St. ☎ 210/223-7266. $.*

The Best in Three Days

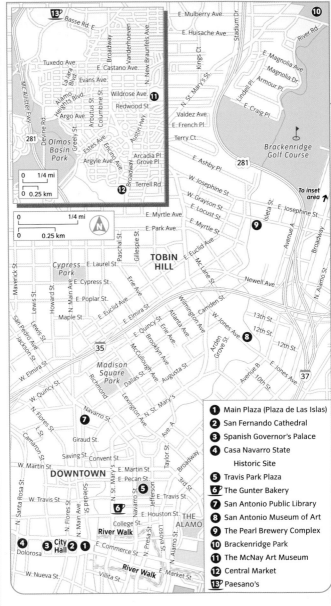

1. Main Plaza (Plaza de Las Islas)
2. San Fernando Cathedral
3. Spanish Governor's Palace
4. Casa Navarro State Historic Site
5. Travis Park Plaza
6. The Gunter Bakery
7. San Antonio Public Library
8. San Antonio Museum of Art
9. The Pearl Brewery Complex
10. Brackenridge Park
11. The McNay Art Museum
12. Central Market
13. Paesano's

If Austin is a liberal college town with an eye on all things hip and contemporary, San Antonio is, conversely, more "old school"—with an inclination toward history, culture, and diversity. With that in mind, you begin Day Three with a visit to some historic sites downtown before you branch out to more contemporary art museums, parks, and places locals love best. Today, the fun is spread all over the city, so you may have to drive a bit—something most Texans do every day. **START: Take Yellow-line streetcar to Main Plaza & W. Market St.**

❶ Main Plaza (Plaza de Las Islas). Following a recent $18-million-dollar revitalization, San Antonio's Main Plaza is today more vibrant than ever, standing at the colorful center of San Antonio life. Established in 1731 by settlers from the Canary Islands whose homes encircled this spot, this plaza has seen times of war and peace—from battles and peace treaties with Apaches, to a battle with Santa Anna's troops, to present-day celebrations, symphony and dance events, and outdoor concerts. Nearby stands the Romanesque-style Bexar County Courthouse, built in 1892. ⏱ *10 min. 115 Main Plaza (at W. Market St.).* ☎ *210/225-9800. www.sanantonio.gov/main plaza. Streetcar: Yellow & Blue lines to Main Plaza & W. Market St.*

❷ ★ San Fernando Cathedral. This majestic cathedral is the site of the earliest marked graves in the city and the oldest continuously functioning religious community in Texas. The sanctuary is also the state's oldest standing church building. Three walls of the original church, which was founded by the Canary Island settlers in 1738, are still visible in the rear of this 1868 Gothic Revival cathedral, which not long ago underwent a major renovation. Remind the kids that several prominent Texans throughout history have been buried within the sanctuary walls. Spooky, I know—but little boys love that kind of thing. ⏱ *15 min. 115 Main Plaza.* ☎ *210/227-1297. www.sfcathedral. org. Streetcar: Yellow & Blue lines to Main Plaza & W. Market St.*

The colorful Main Plaza.

❸ ★ Spanish Governor's Palace. Its a misnomer: No Spanish governors ever resided here. Rather, this recently renovated, early-1700s Spanish Colonial–style home or "palace" (a National Historic Landmark) was the residence and headquarters of the captain of the Presidio de Béxar. From the house, the commander had a view of his troops conducting drills in **Military Plaza** across the street. This supposedly haunted one-story white house comprises 10 rooms surrounding a central courtyard and large fountain. Note the home's large front doors—legend has it that the history of Spanish America is told in ornate symbols carved there. ⏱ *30 min. 202 E. Nueva St.* ☎ *210/224-0601. $2 adults, $1.50 seniors & military, $1 children 7–13; free for children under 7. Tues–Sat 9am–5pm, Sun 10am–5pm. Closed Mon. Streetcar: Yellow & Blue lines to W. Commerce & Camaron sts.*

❹ ★ Casa Navarro State Historic Site. This small museum of the Texas Historical Commission was once the home of an important figure in Texas history, José Antonio Navarro (1795–1871). This rancher and merchant was a signatory of the 1836 Texas Declaration of Independence and, later, a senator in the Texas State Legislature. Navarro and his wife both died here. Today, this 1850s whitewashed stucco-and-limestone structure is a small museum with period furnishings and personal mementos, and is open to the public. This is no longer considered a Texas State Park, so park passes are not accepted. ⏱ *30 min. 228 S. Laredo St.* ☎ *210/226-4801. www.visitcasanavarro.com. $4 adults, $3 students w/ID & children 6–18, free for children 5 & under. Tues–Sun 9am–4pm. Streetcar: Yellow & Blue lines to Flores & Commerce sts.*

❺ ★ Travis Park Plaza. The area where this park now sits in downtown San Antonio was once the upper farmlands of Mission San Antonio de Valero (the Alamo). By 1873, the area here was called Travis Plaza, named for William Travis (1809–1836), the commander of Texas troops at the Alamo. Today, this city park is surrounded by hotels such as the St. Anthony and other downtown buildings, and is home to the popular outdoor music festival called "Jazz'SAlive." ⏱ *10 min. Travis Park (Travis, Navarro, Pecan & Jefferson sts.). Streetcar: Yellow line to Navarro St. (between Travis & Pecan sts.).*

The Casa Navarro State Historic Site.

6 ★ **The Gunter Bakery.** Fresh-baked cookies, brownies, pastries, and salads make this a nice stop across the street from the Majestic Theatre (see p 170). Be sure to stroll through the adjacent Sheraton Gunter Hotel lobby. The famous Delta Blues guitarist Robert Johnson, who legend says sold his soul to the Devil in exchange for talent, held three recording sessions at the hotel in Nov. 1936. *205 East Houston St.* ☎ *210/227-3241. $.*

7 **San Antonio Public Library.** Why make this library a tour stop? Because art lovers will want to see the magnificent Fiesta Tower colored-glass art sculpture suspended from the ceiling of the library atrium. Created by celebrated artist Dale Chihuly (1941–), this arresting piece, "Fiesta Tower 2003," is more than 20 feet (6.1m) tall and 9 feet (2.8m) wide, and is the pride of the Alamo City. Removed in 2009 for repair work on the ceiling and skylight, the stunning sculpture is scheduled for reinstallation in 2011—but call ahead to be sure. Other interesting art pieces are featured, as well. ⏱ *20 min. 600 Soledad St.* ☎ *210/207-2500. www. mysapl.org. Free admission. Mon–Thurs 9am–9pm, Fri & Sat 9am–5pm, Sun 11am–5pm. Streetcar: Blue line to San Antonio Public Library.*

8 **San Antonio Museum of Art.** An old Lone Star Brewery built in 1904, in 1981, several castle-like buildings of the old brewery were transformed into architecturally arresting exhibition spaces housing Latin American folk art, pre-Columbian art, Spanish Colonial art, and much more. The museum's Lenora and Walter F. Brown Asian Art Wing is the largest Asian art collection in Texas and one of the largest in the Southwest. Be sure to note the Dale

A mosaic bull decorating the San Antonio Public Library.

Chihuly Persian Ceiling art piece in the museum. Thanks to the new River Walk "Museum Reach" expansion, you can now travel to the museum via river taxi. ⏱ *1½ hr. 200 W. Jones Ave.* ☎ *210/978-8100. www.samuseum.org. $8 adults, $7 seniors, $5 military & students w/ID, $3 children 4–11; free for children under 4. Free general admission, unless hosting a special exhibit, Tues 4–9pm. Tues 10am–9pm, Wed–Sat 10am–5pm, Sun noon–6pm. Closed Mon. Bus: 7, 8, 9 & 14.*

9 **The Pearl Brewery Complex.** The old, 22-acre (8.9-hectare) Pearl Brewery, which closed in 2001, is now undergoing a booming revitalization. The Museum Reach expansion of the River Walk instigated the transformation of the site into an entertainment complex with studios, galleries, shops, warehouse lofts, chic restaurants, and exciting art installations along the river. The towering original brewery structure, built in 1883 on the east bank of the San Antonio River, is one of the city's most prominent and recognizable features. ⏱ *30 min. 312 Pearl*

The revitalized Pearl Brewery Complex is now an entertainment hub.

Pkwy. ☎ 210/212-7260. www.pearl brewery.com. Bus: 20.

⑩ ★★★ kids Brackenridge Park. This is San Antonio's favorite Saturday spot—a park with rustic stone bridges and shaded walkways that wend through lush landscaping under a canopy of trees. Visit the **Japanese Tea Garden,** or "Sunken Garden," created in 1817. A bowl of limestone cliffs (once a cement quarry) is home to the park's

Enjoying some shade in a gazebo at the Brackenridge Park.

Sunken Garden Theater. A 60-foot-tall (18m) waterfall and ponds loaded with water lilies adorn the spot. Across from the entrance to the **San Antonio Zoo & Aquarium** (☎ 210/734-7184), get on board the **SA Zoo Eagle** (☎ 210/735-7455), an old-fashioned kiddie train. The 1800s-style choo-choo chugs along a pretty 2-mile (3.2km), 20-minute track through the park. The zoo itself is hardly notable, though my kids and I find it pleasant enough. ⏱ 1 hr. 3700 N. St Marys St. (main entrance 2800 block of N. Broadway St., near the Witte Museum). ☎ 210/207-3000. www. sanantonio.gov/sapar. Train tickets $3 adults, $2.50 children 3–11; free for children under 3. Park open daily 5am–11pm; train runs 9:30am–5pm. Bus: 7, 8 & 9.

⑪ ★★★ The McNay Art Museum. My favorite way to spend the day in San Antonio is to wander the grounds and galleries of this exquisite modern art museum housed in an historic home. The 1929 Spanish Colonial Revival–style mansion just north of Brackenridge Park rests on 23 acres (9.3 hectares) of landscaped grounds dotted with large sculpture pieces. The house was once the private residence of an oil heiress, art collector, and artist who bequeathed her home, art collection, and much of her fortune to establish the museum. The museum collection focuses primarily on 19th- and 20th-century art, including works by **Cézanne** (1839–1906), **Picasso** (1881–1973), **Gauguin** (1848–1903), **Matisse** (1869–1954), **Monet** (1840–1926), **O'Keeffe** (1887–1986), and others. The museum's well-designed modern sculpture wing is a nice plus. Visit the gift shop, and then enjoy a picnic lunch on the grounds as you watch brides have their portraits done in the gardens. ⏱ *1½ hr. 6000 N. New Braunfels Ave.* ☎ *210/824-5368. www.mcnayart.org. $8 adults (additional fee added during special exhibitions); $5 students w/ID, seniors (65 & over) & active military; free for members & children 12 & under. Tues, Wed & Fri 10am–4pm; Thurs 10am–9pm; Sat 10am–5pm; Sun noon–5pm. Free docent tours at 3pm on first Sun of month (must be scheduled in advance through website). Bus: 8 & 14.*

⓬ ★★ **Central Market.** Like its nearby competitor **Whole Foods** (255 E. Basse Road, ☎ 210/826-4676), Central Market, the rich relation of the popular Texas H-E-B grocery chain, is an upscale, fresh, and gourmet food market that is a delightful destination in the popular Alamo Heights area along Broadway Street. Grab a bite in the cafe or just nibble on samples in the store. But watch your wallet—it's easy to spend a wad here only to find your brown paper bag is still half-empty (or half-full, depending on your point of view.) ⏱ *30 min. 4821 Broadway St.* ☎ *210/368-8600. www.central market.com. Bus: 9, 10, 14 & 209.*

⓭ ★★★ **Paesano's.** With a cult-like following since owner Joe Cosniac came to town for the World's Fair in 1969 with his secret shrimp paesano recipe, Paesano's has been a well-loved, often-lauded San Antonio institution. (See p 156.) *555 E. Basse Rd.* ☎ *210/828-5191. $$–$$$$.*

The McNay Art Museum displays works by artists such as Cezanne, Picasso, and Matisse.

114

The Historic Mission Trail

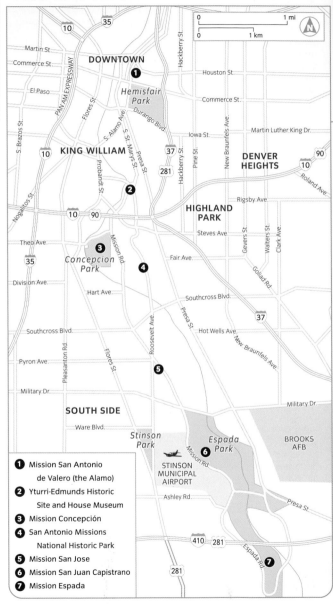

1. Mission San Antonio
   de Valero (the Alamo)
2. Yturri-Edmunds Historic
   Site and House Museum
3. Mission Concepción
4. San Antonio Missions
   National Historic Park
5. Mission San Jose
6. Mission San Juan Capistrano
7. Mission Espada

Perhaps San Antonio's best-kept secret is its spectacular historic missions, standing like a small gathering of monastic brothers holding hands along the banks of the San Antonio River. Like sparkling beads in a beloved rosary, these missions are strung just a few miles from one another in a serene rural setting, tucked away from the traffic and business of town Their beauty and size may surprise visitors, and the quiet time for reflection and rest, so often overlooked during vacation tours, is easy to enjoy while following the Mission Trail. **START: Take bus 301, 305, or either a blue or red streetcar, disembark at Alamo Plaza between Crocket & Houston streets.**

Visitors exploring the Mission San Antonio de Valero (the Alamo).

1 ★★ **kids** **Mission San Antonio de Valero (the Alamo).** Though it's not part of the National Parks Service and not set along what locals call the Mission Trail, the Alamo is included in this tour because it played such a pivotal role in Texas history. Although Mission San Antonio de Valero was first established in April 1718 by the governor of Spanish Texas, Martín de Alarcón, the mission compound that would come to be known as the Alamo didn't stand at its current location until 1744, and no piece of the chapel that would become San Antonio's most famous landmark

actually stood on that spot until 1758, after the mission's 1744-built tower and sacristy collapsed. By the 19th century, the mission complex at this site would come to be called the Alamo—the Spanish name for cottonwood tree. The Alamo is today best known as the site of a historic battle in the fight for Texas's Independence from Mexico, when in the spring of 1836, Mexican General Antonio Lopez de Santa Anna and his army laid siege to the mission fortress, killing almost all of the "Texian" defenders there. It wasn't until 1905 that the Daughters of the Republic of Texas, a group primarily established to save and restore the

Alamo, took official custody of the mission. The leader in the quest to save the Alamo (from being razed for a hotel) was a wealthy woman named Clara Driscoll (1881–1945), whose Lake Austin–area home now houses the **Austin Museum of Art–Laguna Gloria** (see p 93). Today, the Alamo, with its famous chapel, Low Barracks, and walled verdant grounds, is a museum attracting more than 4 million visitors each year. *See p 114.*

❷ ★★★ kids Yturri-Edmunds Historic Site and House Museum. Originally part of the Mission Concepción grounds, this house museum and historic site now stands along the Mission Trail. Here, the Yturri-Edmunds home, the Old Mill, the Oge Carriage House from the King William District (see p 137), and the 1855 Postert House (a small caliche-stone and block-rubble structure) were moved to this ⅔-acre (.3-hectare) tract. The land was bequeathed to the San Antonio Conservation Society by Ernestine E. Edmunds, granddaughter of Spaniard Manuel Yturri Castillo, who received the land grant in 1824 from the Mexican government. Built circa 1840 to 1860, the Yturri-Edmunds home is one of the few adobe block houses remaining in San Antonio. This historic site and six-room house museum is open to the public by appointment only, but it is well worth a stop. Visitors are able to learn what life may have been like in the early 1800s for those living in the shadow of the missions. *128 Mission Rd. (Yellowstone St. at Mission Trail).* ☎ *210/534-8237. www. saconservation.org/tours/yturri.htm. $6 adults, free for children under 12; discounts available for seniors & students (call for information). Open by appointment only.*

❸ ★★ kids Mission Concepción. The first of the four missions

Texas's oldest un-restored mission, the Mission Concepción.

you'll come to as you head south on the Mission Trail is Mission Nuestra Señora de la Purisima Concepción de Acuña, or Mission Concepción, as it is commonly known. Built in 1731, this mission looks much as it did more than 250 years ago, for it is Texas's oldest un-restored mission. While time, wind, and weather have washed away most traces of the colorful geometric designs that graced the front of the church, still, remnants of colorful frescos remain visible inside several of its rooms, and one can glimpse a hint of its detailed designs and colors on its rugged facade. In 2005, Mission Concepción celebrated the 250th anniversary of its dedication, and its active congregation may proudly claim that this is the only mission church in San Antonio whose walls have never fallen through age and neglect. *807 Mission Rd. (at Felisa St.). Free admission. Daily 9am–5pm.*

❹ ★★ San Antonio Missions National Historical Park. Established in 1983, the San Antonio Missions National Historical Park was created for the maintenance and

Strategies for Visiting the Missions

In 1718, Spanish representatives and Franciscans established the first Catholic mission along the San Antonio River, and within 13 years, a total of five Franciscan missions had been established along its banks. Now, almost 3 centuries later, visitors may hike or bike to retrace the footsteps of the native peoples and friars who lived within the walls of these fascinating fortress-like compounds.

There is a well-maintained, paved pathway connecting four of the missions as part of San Antonio Missions National Historical Park. The hike and bike trail follows the river as it passes by each mission—some missions lying a good distance from the path itself. More than just pretty churches, the missions were active communities established to convert the native peoples to Christianity.

Standing surprisingly close to one another (most fewer than 3 miles/4.8km apart), the Missions are easiest to visit by car. For those who'd rather walk or cycle, it's a 16-mile (26km) round-trip trek. However, if you begin at Mission Concepción and walk to Mission Espada, it's only about 8 miles (13km). Another option is to travel between only two of the missions for a shorter excursion. Although I usually drive to each mission, on a spring day, there is no better way to get a fresh glimpse of San Antonio's history than by bike, breezing along this best-kept-secret trail. Bicycle rentals are available in town at Alamo Bike Rental (1016 N. Flores St., ☎ 210/226-BIKE) and Andu Blue Star Bike Shop (1414 S. Alamo St., ☎ 210/858-0331), and parking, water fountains, and restrooms are offered along the trail at most of the missions.

operations of the four missions along the trail (this does not include the Alamo). The headquarters for these operations may be found at Roosevelt Avenue and Mission Road. From there, drive—or hike and bike—from mission to mission. However, because complete signage is not in place, it's a good idea at each site to ask for directions to the next site. For information about each of the individual missions, contact the Park headquarters office or see their informative website, which includes a page just for kids. *202 Roosevelt Ave. ☎ 210/534-8833. www.nps.gov/saan. Free admission. Daily 9am–5pm. Bus: 42 & 242 to Roosevelt & McDonald aves.*

❺ ★★★ kids Mission San Jose. Perhaps San Antonio's favorite mission along the trail is Mission San José y San Miguel de Aguayo (Mission San Jose), established in 1720, and it truly is the largest and most beautiful of the Texas missions. This is an excellent place for children and adults alike to get a well-rounded picture of what life in a mission community must have been like, as the entire property was reconstructed—right down to the granary, mill, and Indian quarters—to educate and delight guests who will want to spend time entering each building and walking in the shade of its archways. Almost fully restored to its original design in the 1930s by

The beautiful stone arches of Mission San Jose, the largest of the Texas missions.

the WPA (Works Projects Administration), this mission is today perhaps best known for its beautiful "Rose window" and popular Mariachi Mass services held here every Sunday at noon (Mariachi bands lead the music, so services are lively—come early if you want a seat). If you only have time to see one mission on this trip, this is the one you won't want to miss. It's also the site of the missions' excellent (and blessedly air-conditioned) park visitor center, with an informative short film, an attractive small museum and gift shop, and clean restrooms. Kids can pick up free Junior Ranger activity books in the visitor center. This is a good place to start if you want to drive from the first mission and then walk to the next mission or two. *6701 San Jose Dr. (at Mission Rd.).* ☎ *210/932-1001. Free admission. Daily summer 9am–7pm, fall–spring 9am–5pm.*

⑥ ★★★ Mission San Juan Capistrano. Founded originally in 1716 at another location in east Texas, Mission San Juan (as it is known to locals) was moved to its present location in 1731. Simpler in stature than its sister missions to the north, a stone church, friary, and granary were built and completed on this site in 1756; however, plans for a larger church were abandoned as the missions' population declined. The original simple chapel and the rural setting give visitors a sense of how isolated the missions may have seemed to those who lived there centuries ago, and this mission, which was once a self-sustaining community, now seems a secluded and serene spot. The Yanaguana Trail, a short (.3-mile/.5km) accessible walking trail, wends through shady woods leading from the Mission complex to the San Antonio River. Several overlooks provide pretty vistas along the way. *9101 Graf Rd. (at Ashley Rd.).* ☎ *210/932-1001. Free admission. Daily 9am–5pm.*

⑦ ★★★ Mission Espada. The final and southernmost mission along the trail is the lovely Mission San Francisco de la Espada, with its

A shady walkway through the Mission complex at the Mission San Juan Capistrano.

Mission Espada's arched Spanish bell towers.

three-part arched Spanish bell towers. Founded as San Francisco de los Tejas in 1690 near present-day Weches, Texas, this was the first mission in Texas. In 1731, the mission moved to this site along the San Antonio River and was renamed, and today Mission Espada looks as though it's the oldest and most isolated of the missions along the trail. Much smaller than some of the other mission chapels, Mission Espada's church is home to an active parish integral to the local community—as are the other three mission churches on the trail. When I visited, a small parish festival was taking place, and demonstrations on life in the mission community were underway, along with horse-drawn carriage rides. One of the most arresting features of this mission is the Espada Aqueduct, located about a mile (1.6km) north of the mission. This was part of the community's original *acequia* (irrigation ditch) system, and is the only remaining Spanish aqueduct in the United States. *10040 Espada Rd.* ☎ *210/627-2021. Free admission. Daily 9am–5pm.*

Wilde about the Missions

You may not associate him with San Antonio and its missions, but Oscar Wilde, the famous Irish writer, playwright, poet, and humorist, visited the Alamo City in the summer of 1882, and was smitten. "There are in Texas two spots which gave me infinite pleasure…Galveston and San Antonio … It was in San Antonio, however, that I found more to please me…". Following a visit to Mission San Jose that June, 27-year-old Wilde described the door and window of the mission church as "the finest he had seen in America." Wilde is said to have been particularly impressed with the "Rose Window" on the south side of the sacristy, created by sculptor Pedro Huizar. Wilde is quoted as saying of the missions, "Those old Spanish churches, with their picturesque remains and dome and their handsome carved stonework, standing amid the verdure and sunshine of a Texas prairie, gave me a thrill of strange pleasure."

San Antonio with Kids

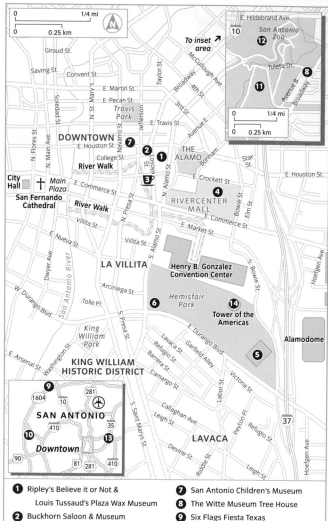

1. Ripley's Believe it or Not & Louis Tussaud's Plaza Wax Museum
2. Buckhorn Saloon & Museum and Texas Ranger Museum
3. Rainforest Café
4. Rivercenter IMAX theater
5. The Institute of Texan Cultures
6. Magik Children's Theatre
7. San Antonio Children's Museum
8. The Witte Museum Tree House
9. Six Flags Fiesta Texas
10. SeaWorld
11. Brackenridge Park
12. San Antonio Zoo & Aquarium
13. Splashtown
14. Tower of the Americas

Why do kids love San Antonio? Because, in many ways, parts of this picturesque city—downtown on the River Walk, on the grounds of the Alamo, and along the Mission Trail—look like a real, live theme park. Maybe they love it because it's also home to SeaWorld and Fiesta Texas—two Texas-sized attractions sure to make them squeal. There's also a couple of IMAX theaters, kid-friendly museums, boat rides, train rides, water parks, a zoo, and so much more. Where to begin? Why, at the mouth of a dinosaur, of course! START: **Take a Red- or Blue-line streetcar to Alamo Plaza.**

Ripley's Believe It or Not collection of the odd.

❶ ★ **Ripley's Believe It or Not & Louis Tussaud's Plaza Wax Museum.** If a tour of the Alamo made your kids yawn, the open mouth of an enormous roaring T-Rex should wake them up. Enter the lobby of these Siamese-twin-like "museums" (complete with video arcade, gift shop, and snack bar), and a massive mechanical dinosaur greets you at the door. The wax museum has all the usual suspects (a bleeding Jesus, Julia Roberts, *Planet of the Apes* characters, Marilyn Monroe, etc.), and the Ripley's exhibits have the requisite shrunken heads and headless chickens. The whole thing gives me the creeps and scared my son when he was younger—but now he's 11, so he

begs to go back. 🕐 *1 hr. 301 Alamo Plaza.* ☎ *210/224-9299. sanantonio. ripleys.com. One attraction $19 adults, $10 children 4–12; both attractions $22 adults, $13 children 4–12. Mon–Thurs 10am–8pm, Fri & Sat 10am–midnight, Sun 10am–11pm. Streetcar: Red & Blue lines to Alamo Plaza.*

❷ ★ **Buckhorn Saloon & Museum, and Texas Ranger Museum.** With its rather cheesy portrayal of the Wild West and all things Texas, this place is a bit eccentric—a downtown storefront space chock-full of taxidermy animals, cowboy gear, and oddities presented with an educational slant, of sorts—still, if you're a kid, it's probably kind of neat. Feeding the big Texas cowboy culture myth in a way tourists expect and kids love, this touristy spot is arguably over-rated . . . and pricey. The facility includes a re-creation of an old Buckhorn saloon, a curio shop, and an antique Texas bar. Best of all, it's not far from the River Walk and the Alamo, so the kids can run around like wild horses when they get out-side. Look for printable discount coupons on the museum website. ⏱ *1 hr. 318 E. Houston St.* ☎ *210/247-4000. www.buckhornmuseum.com. $18 adults, $17 seniors (55 & over) & military, $14 children 3–11. Early Sept to late May daily 10am–5pm), late May to early Sept daily 10am–6pm. Streetcar: Red & Blue lines to Houston & Presa sts.*

③ Rainforest Café. Sure, it's a big chain restaurant, but kids go ape for this multi-storied jungle-themed eatery where mechanical monkeys, elephants, tigers, and more come to life and a thunder-storm revs up on the ceiling every few minutes. I like this location because it's housed in an old downtown building near kid-friendly attractions and the River Walk—and because I can get an elephant-sized salad while the kids nosh on dino-saur-shaped chicken nuggets. *110 East Crockett St.* ☎ *210/277-6300. $–$$.*

④ ★★ Rivercenter IMAX the-ater. Located in the Rivercenter Mall along the glorious River Walk, this IMAX theater runs a daily show about the historic fall of the Alamo, giving kids a better idea about the history of the places they'll visit in San Antonio. But the cinema also shows first-run movies and educa-tional documentaries—many in 3-D. *See p 120.*

⑤ ★★ Institute of Texan Cul-tures. A favorite spot for school field trips, this HemisFair-area museum is geared toward making educational experiences fun and interesting. ⏱ *1 hr. See p 120.*

⑥ ★★ Magik Children's The-atre. This professional little family-friendly theater provides delightful productions for youngsters and

Kids playing on the Witte Museum's Move It!, an interactive exhibit.

Riding a rollercoaster at Six Flags Fiesta Texas.

their parents alike. Located in HemisFair Park (see p 105), it offers daytime productions geared to children as young as 3, and evening performances for families with kids age 6 and up. ⏱ *1 hr. Beethoven Hall, 420 S. Alamo St.* ☎ *210/227-2751. www.magiktheatre.org. $10 adults, $9 seniors & military, $8 children 3–17, $2 children under 3. Box office Mon–Fri 9am–5pm, Sat 10am–3pm; performances Tue–Fri 9:45 & 11:30am, Fri 7pm, Sat 2pm. Streetcar: Red & Blue lines to HemisFair Park.*

7 ★★ **San Antonio Children's Museum.** I love it that, within walking distance of numerous downtown hotels and River Walk attractions, kids have a place to run, play, and learn cool stuff. This multilevel museum features all the fun permanent exhibits you'd expect— a play grocery store, cages full of colored balls, things to climb on— along with changing educational exhibits and hands-on arts and craft offerings. I've seen better children's museums in other cities, but this one isn't bad at all. ⏱ *1½ hr. 305 E. Houston St.* ☎ *210/212-4453. www.sakids.org. $7 adults & children 2 & over, $6 military w/ID; free for children under 2. Tues–Thurs 10am–4pm, Fri 10am–5pm, Sat 10am–6pm, Sun noon–5pm. 1-hr. lot parking validated at museum. Streetcar: Red line to Houston & Navarro sts.*

8 ★★ **The Witte Museum Tree House.** When I took my daughter to the Louvre, she ran straight to the Mona Lisa in the back of the museum. When I brought her to the Witte, she (and every other kid in the place) ran straight to the big Science Treehouse in the back— a fun, four-level 15,000-square-foot (1,394-sq.-m) interactive science center exhibit. Like the Louvre, the Witte offers much more than its most well-loved piece; this well-organized, family-friendly museum focuses on Texas history, natural science, and anthropology, and has lots of attention-grabbing exhibits. ⏱ *1 hr. 3801 Broadway St.* ☎ *210/357-1900. www.wittemuseum.org. $8 adults, $7 seniors & military, $6 children 4–11, free for children under 4; free to public Tues 3–8pm. Mon & Wed–Sat 10am–5pm, Tues 10am–8pm, Sun noon–5pm. Bus: 7, 9 & 14 to Broadway St. & Tuleta Dr.*

9 ★★★ **Six Flags Fiesta Texas.** This 200-acre (81-hectare) theme park was built in the bowl of an abandoned limestone quarry surrounded by 100-foot (30m) cliffs on the outskirts of town in northwest San Antonio. Thrill-seekers will love the rides: the Tornado (a wet and wild tunnel of tubing fun); the Superman Krypton Coaster, with six stomach-turning inversions; the Rattler, one of the world's fastest and highest wooden roller coasters; the 60-plus-mph (97km/h) Poltergeist roller coaster; and Scream!, a 20-story space shot/turbo drop. Kids go for the virtual-reality simulators and laser games, and the Lone Star Lagoon wave pool is a good way to cool off on a hot day. Of course, there are food booths, shops, craft demonstrations, and live music and dance productions—along with laser firework shows on summer evenings. Before the Six Flags chain took over, Fiesta Texas was an independent park with "town" areas representing different cultural groups, and these attractions may still be found here—along with lots of Time Warner's Looney Tunes cartoon characters in the souvenir shops. Parking is expensive ($15 a day), and so is everything else, from park passes to popcorn and cold drinks. But isn't that the theme of most theme parks these days? Discounted 2-day and season passes are available. Check the Web for coupons and discounts. *17000 I-10W (at Loop 1604 & I-10).* ☎ *800/ 473-4378 or 210/697-5050. www.six flags.com/fiestatexas. $50 adults, $35 children less than 48 in. tall; free for children 2 & under. Hours vary throughout the season, and the park is closed Nov–Feb. It is also closed during weekdays in Sept–Oct. Call ahead or check website for current information Bus: 94.*

❿ ★★★ **SeaWorld.** In a place as hot and humid as South Texas, spending the day in and around water is always a good idea. This SeaWorld park sprawls over 250 acres (101 hectares), making this the largest of the Anheuser-Busch–owned parks and the largest marine theme park in the world. Set in the hills northwest of San Antonio, not too many miles from Six Flags, and full of fun rides, wet and wild fun, and shows and attractions, it might be hard to decide which theme park to enjoy with the kids while you're in the area. If I had to choose, though, for my travel dollar value, I'd cast my vote for this one since it's shadier, cooler, and more educational and engaging than your basic roller-coaster theme park, even if it costs a few bucks more. Internet purchase discounts are available. *10500 SeaWorld Dr. (from Loop 410 or Hwy. 90W, exit Hwy. 151W).* ☎ *800/ 700-7786. www.seaworld.com. $59 adults, $50 children 3–9; free for children under 3. Parking $15–$20. Early Mar to late Dec days and hours vary. Call ahead or check website for current information. Bus: 64.*

A killer whale show at SeaWorld.

Feeding time at the San Antonio Zoo & Aquarium.

⑪ ★★ Brackenridge Park. This pretty park features footbridges, a Japanese "Sunken Garden," a little amphitheater, and a miniature train. A pleasant place for a picnic or a nice morning walk. ⏱ *1 hr. See p 120.*

⑫ ★★ San Antonio Zoo & Aquarium. Yes, it's all happening at the zoo. This pleasant, tree-shaded zoo and aquarium is open year-round (my friends went on Christmas morning!). With fun things like a "Caterpillar Flight School" (butterfly exhibit) and the San Antonio Zoo Eagle miniature train ride, youngsters will enjoy this Brackenridge Park treasure. Still, if they've been to SeaWorld or, say, the zoo in San Diego, this park won't wow them. My kids liked it better when they were younger and seeing the monkey cage was still a big deal. Once every spring and fall, the zoo offers a nifty "Open Roars and Snores" overnight adventure in the park. ⏱ *1–2 hr. 3903 N. St Marys St.* ☎ *210/734-7184. www.sazoo-aq. org. $10 adults, $6.50 disabled adults, $8 seniors (62 & over) & children 3–11, $5 disabled children 3–14; free for children under 3. Daily (including holidays) 9am–5pm. Bus: 7.*

⑬ ★★ Splashtown. Just your basic big outdoor family water park—but still, in a city this sizzling hot in summer, the whole family is going to want to spend a day here. This centrally-located 8-acre (3.2-hectare) water park features 50-plus rides and attractions, including the largest wave pool in the Lone Star State. Expect long lines in summer and steep climbs to the big slides and such. For a more impressive water park just outside San Antonio, check out **Schlitterbahn** (see p 186) in New Braunfels. ⏱ *3 hr. 3600 North Pan Am Expwy. (Exit 160, Splashtown Dr., off I-35).* ☎ *210/227-1100. www.splashtownsa.com. $27 adults & children over 4 ft. tall, $20 children under 4 ft. tall. Apr–May, 11am–7pm open weekends only; June–Aug, open weekdays 11am–8pm & weekends 11am–9pm; Sept 1 until mid-Sept open on weekends only, 11am–7pm. Closed mid-Sept–Mar.*

⑭ ★★ Tower of the Americas. What kid wouldn't love a glass elevator to the top of a tall tower where he or she can run around in circles on the observation deck? With a snack bar and scary-cool simulator "4-D" theater "ride" at the base, and a restaurant on top, my kids are crazy about this famous San Antonio landmark attraction. *See p 120.*

San Antonio **Romance**

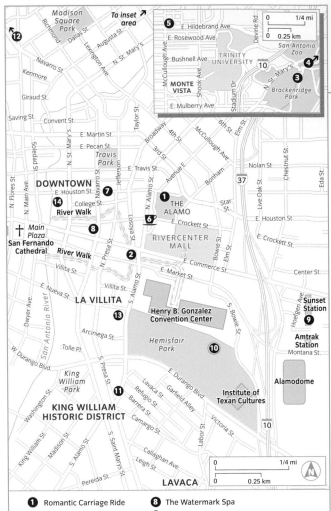

1. Romantic Carriage Ride
2. Rio San Antonio Cruises
3. Brackenridge Park
4. The McNay Art Museum
5. Olmos Bharmacy
6. The Menger Hotel
7. Majestic Theatre
8. The Watermark Spa
9. Sunset Station
10. Tower of the Americas
11. Southtown
12. Emilie and Albert Frederich Wilderness Park
13. Restaurant Insignia Bar at The Fairmount
14. Vbar

"Water has perfect memory," writes Maya Angelou, and in this city, where a quiet slender river rambles at every turn, couples are sure to remember the romance-soaked, wistful memories they'll make here. From carriage rides past the Alamo at night to dinner at a tiny cafe table on the River Walk, salsa dancing in Southtown to a couple's massage at a serene spa—Texas' sexiest city offers sweet sultry heat and the unforgettable thrill of romance. START: **Take a Red- or Blue-line streetcar to Alamo Plaza.**

❶ ★ Romantic carriage tours by day or after dark. Several carriage companies offer romantic rides starting in the lovely heart of it all at Alamo Plaza. See downtown area sites or take a special tour to see the attractive Victorian homes of the King William District. Snuggle up under a blanket in winter or catch an evening breeze off the river in summer while a driver takes the reins and shares stories of the city's history and lore. Make reservations for Valentine's Day. ⏱ *30 min. Alamo Plaza. Bluebonnet Carriage Tours 20–75 min.* ☎ *210/599-2474. www.bluebonnetcarriage. com. Yellow Rose Carriage Co. 20–60 min.* ☎ *210/225-6490. www.yellow rosecarriage.com. $35–$75. Streetcar: Red & Blue lines to Alamo Plaza.*

❷ ★★★ Rio San Antonio Cruises. What could be more romantic than a lazy cruise along the shady, tree-lined river that runs through the city? San Antonio's most famous attraction is also its most romantic one—and the best way to see the River Walk (and a whole lot more of the city) is by boat. An affordable adventure that's often crowded and touristy by day, a river cruise by night, depending on the time of year and the number of folks on board, can be oh-so romantic—especially during December, when the River Walk drips with twinkling colored lights. ⏱ *30 min. See p 126.*

❸ ★ Brackenridge Park. A picnic in Brackenridge's green **Japanese Tea Gardens** (aka the Sunken Gardens) is the perfect spot for a loaf of bread and a jug of wine. Perhaps you'll come upon a concert in the Sunken Garden Theater in the park or you'll wander into the zoo to see the animals, birds, and

An evening carriage ride.

Brackenridge Park's picturesque greenery.

butterflies. Quiet garden paths, shady lawns, and a loved one—how sweet it is! 🕐 *1 hr. See p 126.*

④ ★★★ The McNay Art Museum.

I love strolling the grounds at this delightful museum to see the original Monet paintings and the early original Picassos, too—and, of course, my man Matisse always melts my heart as though it were Icarus's wax wings. But the things I love best are the McNay's verdant grounds and the glorious Old World Spanish-style hacienda where an independent woman lived and loved art all her life. After her death, her home became this enchanting museum where so many San Antonio brides have their portraits made on the lawns. I like to picnic here and watch their delicate veils dance in the wind. 🕐 *1½ hr. See p 126.*

⑤ ★★★ Olmos Bharmacy.

A San Antonio landmark soda fountain for years, the old Olmos Pharmacy was transformed into Olmos Bharmacy—a nice little soda fountain by day and hot little club by night where Tango Milonga Wednesdays are not to be missed (see p 169). Want to tango in other parts of town? In **Stone Oak**, the popular brasserie **Pavil** (see p 169) offers private tango classes, free introductory lessons, beginner and intermediate classes, and open practice and dance times—an affordable, fun, sexy way to get close to someone special. **Antigua Bar and Grill** (☎ 210/587-7470) and **Calle Ocho** (☎ 210/788-6945) are two other hot spots where sweat and seduction tango tightly in the sultry San Antonio night. 🕐 *2 hr. See p 168.*

⑥ ★★ The Menger Hotel.

Share a cup of coffee in the courtyard. You'd spend more at Starbucks for a cup of Joe, and the atmosphere is ever-so-much more charming in this historic hotel next to the Alamo, so why not take a unique coffee break together here? I adore breakfast or Sunday brunch in the Menger's Colonial Room restaurant, but on a pretty day, there's no lovelier place for a perk-me-up pot on a silver tray than in the palm-tree-shaded courtyard off the lobby. With bursts of colorful bougainvillea blooms in summer and a flowing Spanish fountain year-round, romance can blossom any old time at the Menger. 🕐 *30 min. See p 98.*

7 ★★★ **Majestic Theatre.** With stars in the ceiling, stars on the stage, and a Spanish-style village set in its walls, this beguiling old performing arts venue, and aptly named theater, sets the stage for a romantic night out. Hear Tony Bennett (1926–) croon, take in a touring Broadway play, or hear the San Antonio Symphony perform—the calendar is full of special events and touring shows throughout the season. There's nothing quite like a night on the town at the Majestic. ⏱ *2 hr.* See p 98.

8 ★★★ **The Watermark Spa.** A couple's massage may be a new concept to some men, but talk your guy into it anyway, ladies. One of San Antonio's most sublime spas may be found at the lovely award-winning, independent Watermark Hotel & Spa (see p 129, **8**), found along the River Walk. With separate areas for men and women where you can sit in a sauna or soak in a whirlpool, his-and-her "sanctuary lounges" where you can rest in the dark, and quiet couples' spaces

Two can tango at Olmos Bharmacy.

where you can await your tandem spa treatments together, the Watermark offers a posh, private place for the kind of pampering that's sure to soothe the savage beast and bring out the best in you both. ⏱ *1 hr.*

9 ★★ **Sunset Station.** A large, historic special events center with

One of the captivating statues at the McNay Art Museum.

The Watermark Spa pampers couples with tandem treatments.

four popular music and theater venues, restaurants, and more. 🕐 *1 hr. See p 126.*

⑩ ★★ Tower of the Americas.
Love lifts us up where we belong when we ride glass elevators to the top of this famous building. The revolving bar and hip restaurant in this 750-foot (229m) HemisFair-area observation tower make for a great date-night spot with breathtaking views of the city below. 🕐 *30 min. See p 126.*

⑪ ★★ Salsa in Southtown.
Latin American music and dancing is all the rage in the **Southtown Arts and Entertainment District** along South Alamo Street near the King William District. Several clubs swing to a Cuban, Argentinean, Mexican, and Brazilian beat. Whether you come to dance to *cumbia* at a Mexican ballroom or you try the merengue, there's a place for you in San Antonio most every night and weekend. First Fridays of the month are the main event in Southtown, of course—shops, galleries, restaurants, and clubs stay open late, and special openings and art events flood the area. Check all that out,

then try tapas and dance lessons at spots like **Azuca Nuevo Latino Restaurant and Bar** (see p 152) and tacos and salsa at **Rosario's Café y Cantina** (see p 157). 🕐 *1 hr.*

⑫ ★★★ Emilie and Albert Friedrich Wilderness Park.
A walk in the woods can be more romantic than a white-linen-and-crystal restaurant on a lovely spring or fall day. Situated along the Balcones Escarpment, 20 miles (32km) northwest of downtown, this heavenly 633-acre (256-hectare) Hill Country habitat operated by the San Antonio City Parks and Recreation Department boasts hiking trails for hard-core outdoor enthusiasts and lazy-paced wanderers alike. The park is maintained in a way that allows visitors to observe and enjoy both wildlife and plant life in an undisturbed, natural environment. 🕐 *1 hr. 21395 Milsa Rd.* ☎ *210/564-6400. www.sanaturalareas.org. Free admission. Daily 7:30am–sunset. No city bus service.*

⑬ ★★★ Restaurant Insignia Bar at the Fairmount.
How civilized to rendezvous over drinks at a handsome, high-end hotel restaurant

and bar—you know, the kind where the dining room glitters with bulbous wine glasses, where the dimly lit bar is sleek with broad windows overlooking a city street, and striped awnings offer shade from the hot summer sun. This two-story, 45-foot-tall (14m), 3.2-million-pound (1.5-million-kg) brick 1906 hotel was moved 5 blocks to its current location near **La Villita** (see p 166) and the entrance to **HemisFair Park** (see p 105, ❶) back in 1985, and *The Guinness Book of World Records* claims it's the heaviest building in the world to have ever been moved. While that's impressive—half the town turned out to see it happen—what surprises me most is how great it still looks after all these years. ⏱ *30 min. 401 S. Alamo St.* ☎ *210/223-0401. www.thefairmount hotelsanantonio.com. Sun–Thurs 11am–10pm, Fri & Sat 11am–11pm. Streetcar: Red & Blue lines to S. Alamo & E. Nueva sts. (near Hemis-Fair Plaza).*

❹ ★★ **Vbar.** Cocktails and conversation could hardly come together in a more hip setting than at the swank, streamlined digs of Hotel Valencia. This hot boutique hotel on

Drinking and mingling at the Vbar.

Houston Street is a little too trendy for my tastes—think chain metal curtains and cold chrome accoutrements. Still, its dark, sleek hotel bar couldn't be hotter with its little leather barstools, a seen-and-be-seen vibe, and views of the River Walk. It's so very little black dress, stilettos, and dirty martini dangerous. Gotta love it. ⏱ *30 min. See p 131, ❹).*

The historic Sunset Station.

Southtown & the King William Historic District

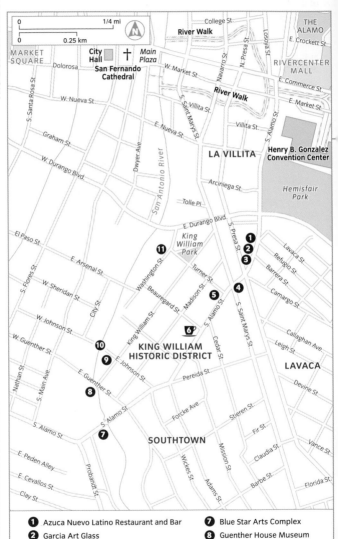

1	Azuca Nuevo Latino Restaurant and Bar	**7**	Blue Star Arts Complex
2	Garcia Art Glass	**8**	Guenther House Museum
3	Rendon Photography & Fine Art	**9**	Edward Steves Homestead
4	Texas Highway Patrol Museum	**10**	O. Henry Bridge/Johnson
5	Jive Refried Vintage and Art		Street Footbridge
6	Madhatters Tea House & Café	**11**	The Oge House

Think of Southtown as San Antonio's Left Bank. This hip bohemian arts and entertainment district has a sexy Latin American sensibility with a slice of stoic German on the side. I like to think of Southtown as a young hipster with a sweet elderly next-door neighbor—the King William Historic District, with its grand Victorian-era mansions and well-groomed gardens. South Flores and South Presa streets border Southtown, west and east; Durango and Lone Star boulevards are demarcation lines to north and south, and the area actually encompasses three neighborhoods—Blue Star, King William, and Lavaca. There's no way to see it all in one short walking tour, so I'll keep it simple and stick to the main drag along South Alamo Street. **START: Walk south along S. Alamo St. from the Southtown sign.**

Travel Tip

On the first Friday night of each month, shops and galleries stay open late, and many host special receptions and exhibit openings, during Southtown's First Fridays ArtWalk. Area clubs and restaurants also celebrate with live music. Parking can be problematic, so get there before sundown to find a spot.

Garcia Art Glass offers free glass blowing demonstrations and the chance to see artists at work.

❶ ★★ Azuca Nuevo Latino Restaurant and Bar. This restaurant is mentioned in several tours in this book, but it's one of the most popular spots in the neighborhood and a good place to start your Southtown stroll. Good music, drinks, food, and dancing—all Latin American style. See p. 152.

❷ ★★ Garcia Art Glass. The studio and gallery of talented glass blower and designer Gini Garcia is a hot design and fabrication center specializing in one-of-a-kind blown glass lighting and sculpture pieces, including table-scapes and wall art. Colorful and arresting, the pieces are as pretty as they are pricey. From 10am to 3pm, see free glass-blowing demonstrations and artists at work—the artists break for a lunch hour at noon. Unlike most spots in Southtown, this gallery isn't open after hours for the First Fridays ArtWalk. Garcia has a downtown River Walk location, too. *715 S. Alamo St. ☎ 210/354-4681. www.garciaartglass.com. Mon–Sat 10am–6pm.*

❸ ★★ Rendon Photography & Fine Art. Showcasing works of art and commercial photography, this fine-art gallery features striking contemporary photographs with an

A wood panel painting at the Blue Star Arts Complex.

emphasis on local and multicultural subjects (see both of Al Rendon's stunning *Conjunto* and *Charreada* series), architectural features, local landmarks, and more. Music lovers will enjoy Rendon's *Rock 'n Roll* series, featuring candid photographs of musical artists like Rod Stewart (1945–), Tina Turner (1939–), and Led Zeppelin. Paintings and sculpture are often also on exhibit. The gallery often hosts special exhibitions and receptions during First Fridays ArtWalk evenings. 🕐 *10 min. 733 S. Alamo St.* ☎ *210/288-4900. www.alrendon.com. Wed–Sat 2–6pm; First Friday of each month 6–9pm.*

❹ ★ **Texas Highway Patrol Museum.** From the outside, this little storefront-style place looks too cool to be a museum, but that's what it is—a 2,000-square-foot (186-sq.-m) space honoring Texas State Troopers. On display are items like vintage Texas Highway Patrol uniforms, photographs of Bonnie and Clyde, and an odd assortment of officer memorabilia. Its Hall of

Honor pays tribute to 74 troopers who fell in the line of duty, featuring photographs and profiles of the troopers and explaining the incidents surrounding their heroic deaths. A short, interesting stop, it won't take long to tour this unusual little museum. 🕐 *20 min. 812 S. Alamo.* ☎ *210/231-6030. www.thpm. org/museum.htm. Free admission (suggested donation $2 adults). Tues– Fri 10am–4pm. Closed Sat–Mon.*

❺ ★ **Jive Refried Vintage and Art.** With original and vintage clothing, crazy jewelry, and accessories, this fusty little retro shop is an interesting stop, though some customers say the staff's rack-side manners need refining. Still, cute trendy clothes, bangles, and unique bags are enough to make me overlook any attitude. Store owner Agosto Cuellar is a local designer known for reworking vintage garments, so clothes are trendier than those of most other hipster vintage shops. *919 S. Alamo St.* ☎ *210/257-5132. jiverefried.blogspot.com. Mon–Sat noon–6:30pm, Sun 1–5pm.*

❻ ★★ **Madhatters Tea House & Café.** I like this cool, casual "in community" place, with its laid-back vegetarian and traditional tea-room fare ordered deli-style at the counter. Serving a stellar assortment of teas (try the Moroccan Mint) and offering free Wi-Fi, this spot smack-dab in the center of Southtown sometimes features live music and stays open late for First Fridays. Though they offer "high tea," Madhatters isn't about scones and Limoges teacups—rather, it's an eclectic sandwich stop. And their cellphone-free-zone policy is as refreshing as a glass of iced tea. *320 Beauregard St.* ☎ *210/212-4832. $–$$.*

7 ★★★ kids **Blue Star Arts Complex.** Historic warehouse buildings have been tastefully transformed into an arts-oriented, mixed-use space housing galleries and studios, retail and performance spaces, studio/loft apartments, and sleek design offices, making this your best-bet art stop. Here, the **Blue Star Contemporary Arts** space (☎ 210/227-6960) is a non-profit art center dedicated to the development of regional, national, and international contemporary art. the **Blue Star Brewing Company** (see p 166) provides a nice place to sit and sip a cold one after browsing through the many Blue Star galleries, folk-art outposts, and eclectic shops. With music on weekends and art every day, Blue Star is always a sure thing. ⏱ *30 min. 116 Blue Star.* ☎ *210/225-6742. www.bluestararts complex.com.*

Walk northeast on S. Alamo St. toward Guenther St. Turn left on Guenther, and continue until you see the Guenther House on your left.

8 ★★ **Guenther House Museum.** This mansion was once the home of the nearby Pioneer Flour Mill's founding family. Built in 1860 as a humble one-story residence, from rocks quarried near what is now the San Antonio Zoo, the house was remodeled and enlarged by the family's youngest son in 1902. Today, the enchanting house looks much as it did then and is a delightful little museum, restaurant, and retail shop adjacent to the still-operating Pioneer Flour Mill. Rooms are decorated with period pieces, and the restaurant and "Roof Garden" areas are ladies-lunch lovely and tea-room-like. The San Antonio River Mill store and library/museum areas are interesting. Afterward, be sure to walk past the still-active Pioneer Flour Mill to see the building's unexpected castle-like turrets. ⏱ *30 min. 205 E. Guenther.* ☎ *800/235-8186 or 210/227 1061. Free admission to museum & store Mon–Sat 8am–4pm, Sun 8am–3pm; restaurant daily 7am–3pm.*

The Edward Steves Homestead is one the few historic homes to offer tours.

King William Historic District

This is the first designated Historic Neighborhood District in Texas. The main area of this district comprises just two streets, King William (originally named for King Wilhelm I, King of Prussia in the 1870s) and Madison streets, each covering 5 blocks. Locally quarried limestone was used to build many of the stately Victorian-era homes here and along neighboring Washington Street in this German-immigrant enclave established in the 1840s, which in the early 1900s was called "Sauerkraut Bend." During WWI, anti-German sentiment prevailed, and King Wilhelm Street was renamed Pershing Avenue; however, after the War, it was given back its name, but this time with an English spelling. For a more detailed walking tour of the King William neighborhood, pick up a brochure from the San Antonio Conservation Society headquarters at 107 King William St. (☎ **210/224-6163**), or download its printable walking tour and history map from www.saconservation.org.

Go a few steps northeast to King William St. and turn right. Go almost 1 block; the Steves Homestead appears on your left before you come to E. Johnson St.

9 ★ Edward Steves Homestead. One of very few homes in the King William Historic District to allow visitors inside, this San Antonio Conservation Society Foundation Property and House Museum is an elegant three-story mansion on the east bank of the San Antonio River. Built in 1876 for Edward Steves (1829–1890), founder of the Steves Lumber Company, the house, a stately ashlar limestone home, offers a 30- to 45-minute docent-led tour giving guests a sense of what life may have been like for rich San Antonio families in this neighborhood at the turn of the 20th century. ⏱ *30 min. 509 King William St. ☎ 210/225-5924. www. saconservation.org. $6 adults, $4 seniors, $3 students & active military w/ID; free for children under 12. Daily 10am–4:15pm, last tour at 3:30pm. Closed major holidays.*

At the corner of King William and E. Johnson sts., turn left.

10 ★★★ kids O. Henry Bridge/ Johnson Street Footbridge. The bridge that once spanned the San Antonio River on Commerce

The view of the San Antonio River from the Johnson Street Footbridge.

The Oge House on Washington Street offers an inside glimpse of a beautifully preserved mansion.

Street (from 1880 to 1914) was called the O. Henry Bridge after William Sidney Porter (who employed the pen name O. Henry) mentioned it in some of his stories. However, in 1914, the iron span was moved to the Johnson Street site, where it now stretches across the river in the King William Historic District. The bridge was later removed during extensive river redevelopment in the 1960s, but the quiet wooded area there along the river banks is now home to an enchanting little footbridge, with tall gothic spire structures standing at each entrance, which replicates the original bridge. In O. Henry's short story "A Fog in Santone," the author writes, "There was a little river, crooked as a pot-hook, that crawled through the middle of the town, crossed by a hundred little bridges . . . " O. Henry's longtime Austin residence is now a small house museum in the Capitol City (see p 46). San Antonio river barges can't travel south of the Nueva Street dam, so the section of the River Walk that meanders through the King

William District and wends under this bridge is pedestrian-friendly and graciously quiet. *Johnson St. (between King William & City sts.).*

From the bridge, head southwest on E. Johnson St. Take the second left (Madison St.) and head about 3 blocks northeast on Madison. Note the attractive Victorian homes along the way until, on your left, you come to

⓫ ★★ The Oge House.

Although there are many B&Bs in the area, few are as pretty and professionally managed as this 1857 mansion on Washington Street. Best of all, the home has been meticulously preserved and restored, and offers a graceful glimpse of the beauty hidden behind the closed doors of the mansions in the neighborhood. This stately three-story house rests on a quiet section of the River Walk (not the touristy part downtown). Walk inside the lobby to get a brochure and make plans to stay here next time you're in town. ⏱ *10 min.* See p 132.

Best of **San Antonio Shopping**

Hanley Wood **13**
Hogwild Records,
  Tapes & CDs **20**
Invitations, Etc. **10**
Julian Gold **16**
Kathleen Sommers **19**
Learning Express Toys **2**
Lee Lee Loves Shoes **12**
Lin Marché Fine Linens **15**
Marti's **22**
Penner's **21**
Satel's **14**
Sugarplum Dreams **7**
Theo & Herb
  Designer Shoes **6**
Whole Earth
  Provision Co. **5**
The Twig **23**

Antiquarian Book Mart **18**
Bass Pro Shop **1**
Bric Brac 'n Brass **4**
Bussey's **8**

C. Aaron Peñaloza Jewelers **9**
Central Market **17**
Five Broads Off Broadway **11**
Grove Hill Ltd. **3**

Shopping Best Bets

Marti's specializes in imported Mexican goods.

Best **Designer Duds**
★ Julian Gold, *4109 McCullough Ave. (p 141)*

Best Place for **Classic Mexican Imports**
★ Marti's, *310 W. Commerce St. (p 144)*

Best Place for **Home Furnishings & Accessories**
★★★ Five Broads off Broadway, *518 Austin Hwy. (p 142)*

Best Place to **Build Your Dream Bed**
★★★ Lin Marche, *4307 McCullough Ave. (p 144)*

Best Place to **Bury Your Head in a Book**
★★ The Twig, *200 E. Grayson St. (p 140)*

Best Place to **Do a Male Wardrobe Intervention**
★★ Satel's, *5100 Broadway St. (p 140)*

Best Place to **Find a Bridal-Shower Gift**
★ Hanley-Wood, *5611 Broadway St. (p 143)*

Best Place to **Find Good Educational Toys**
★ Whole Earth Provisions, *255 E. Basse Rd. (p 145)*

Best Place to **Find That Little Black Dress**
★★ Kathleen Sommers, *2417 N. Main Ave. (p 141)*

Best Place to **Find the Perfect Gift**
★ Invitations Etc., *6434 N. New Braunfels Ave. (p 143)*

Best Place to **Give into Your Passion for Pretty Shoes**
★ Theo & Herb, *555 E. Basse Rd. (p 144)*

San Antonio Shopping A to Z

Books

Antiquarian Book Mart ALAMO HEIGHTS   Although it sits next door to the popular chain store Half-Price Books, this lovable used-books store features harder-to-find and more interesting titles, including a section on military history. *3127 Broadway St.* ☎ *210/828-4885. MC, V. Bus: 9, 10, 14, 209 & 214.*

★★ **kids The Twig** PEARL BREW-ERY/MUSEUM REACH   After years tucked away behind Cappy's restaurant in Alamo Heights, the little Twig Book Shop made a big move to the Full Goods building of the new Pearl Brewery Complex *(see p 111, ⑨).* Always a popular place for book signings and guest lectures, this popular San Antonio independent bookseller offers a wide array of subjects, including regional Texana lit, children's books, travel, photography, and coffee-table titles. A fun place for kids' story hour on Friday mornings at 10:30. *200 E. Grayson St.* ☎ *210/826-6411. http://thetwig.indiebound.com. AE, DISC, MC, V. Bus: 20.*

Fashion (Men's)

★★★ **Satel's** ALAMO HEIGHTS   The premier San Antonio shop for fine menswear since 1950, Satel's has set the standard for the city's best-dressed men. With suits, sports coats, sportswear, formal wear, dress shirts, and shoes, Satel's has got you covered. *5100 Broadway St.* ☎ *210/822-3376. www.satels.com. AE, MC, V. Bus: 9, 10, 14 & 209.*

★ **Penner's** DOWNTOWN   You've got to get a Guayabera shirt if you're going to fit in in San Antonio, and this is the place to find these popular, lightweight Mexican shirts. Since 1916, this family-owned business has carried the city's largest collection of Guayabera shirts, linen pants, and casual menswear. It's a good place to find offbeat "retro" shirts and hats, too, along with Hawaiian shirts and men's shoes. They also have a "Big Men's" department. *311 W. Commerce St. (near El Mercado/Market Sq.).* ☎ *210/ 226-2487. www.pennersinc.com. AE, DC, DISC, MC, V. Bus: 301.*

San Antonio's independent bookseller, the Twig Book Shop.

Julian Gold carries brand name shoes, clothes, and fashion accessories.

Fashion (Women's)

★★ Kathleen Sommers MONTE VISTA   In 1979, designer Kathleen Sommers, who already had a following with clients like Donna Karan, opened a store in a vintage building in San Antonio and built a loyal local following. In 1985, her designs became a hit throughout the U.S. This little Monte Vista neighborhood shop also carries Sommers' breezy, beautiful fashions—often in linen—along with accessories, jewelry, gifts, high-end bath and body products, candles, and books. The store carries plus sizes, too. *2417 N. Main Ave. (at Woodlawn Ave.).* ☎ *210/ 732-8437. www.kathleensommers. com. AE, DISC, MC, V. Bus: 90.*

Grove Hill Ltd. LINCOLN HEIGHTS   The perfect place to find that little black dress, some bangles and beads, a cute outfit for a patio party, or a cute top to wear with that denim skirt. Featuring fashion designs by Seven, Elliot Lauren, Michael Stars, Citizens of Humanity, Johnny Was—just to name a few. *355 E. Basse Rd.* ☎ *210/829-0011. AE, DISC, MC, V. Bus: 505 to the Quarry (Basse & Jones Maltsberger rds.).*

★★ Julian Gold OLMOS PARK Carrying top-name clothing, shoes, jewelry, and accessories by the likes of Armani, Escada, Bill Blass, and Emilio Pucci, and contemporary fashions by Nanette Lepore, Trina Turk, Theory, Elie Tahari, and more, this is the favorite go-to place of local fashionistas. *4109 McCullough Ave.* ☎ *210/824-2493. www.julian gold.com. MC, V. Bus: 5 & 204 to Olmos Circle.*

Fashion (Children's)

★★ Sugarplum Dreams ALAMO HEIGHTS   This lovely family-owned store carries everything from bibs and burp cloths to fabulous furnishings for a nursery or for a tot's

Satel's fine men's fashion.

adorable bedroom. Heirloom-quality items, including jewelry, silver spoons, and other lovely baby-shower gift items, are all here, too. The staff greets children with balloons and cookies, and they let the children play with the toys while you shop. *999 E. Basse Rd.* ☎ *210/826-5402. www.sugarplumdreams.com. AE, DISC, MC, V. Bus: 505.*

Flea Markets

★★ **kids Bussey's** SCHERTZ   It's something of a San Antonio Saturday tradition to drive up North I-35 to spend the morning at this flea market, checking out fun knock-off designer purses and shoes, booths brimming with cellphone chargers, racks of vintage vinyl, Mexican videos, DVDs, inexpensive toys, and cages containing hamsters, birds, snakes, and more for sale. Walk around eating sausage-on-a-stick, funnel cakes, and cotton candy, listening to Mexican pop music in the warm weather. Bussey's has been an area institution for over 30 years—with the same giant armadillo out front and more than 10,000

visitors each weekend browsing the 500-plus indoor/outdoor booths. *18738 I-35 N.* ☎ *210/651-6830. www.busseysfm.com. AE, DISC, MC, V. No city bus service.*

Home Furnishings

★★★ **Five Broads Off Broadway** ALAMO HEIGHTS   I adore this store. With a fresh take on classic furnishings, antiques, home accessories, lighting, and gifts, the "broads"—and one out-numbered man—who own the place have impeccable taste and fabulous inventory. They also carry Lee Industries custom furnishings. Suitably located at the edge of two stylish old-money neighborhoods, Alamo Heights and Terrell Hills, "Five Broads" is a find. *518 Austin Hwy.* ☎ *210/824-3483. www.5broads.com. MC, V. Bus: 14 & 214 to Austin Hwy. & Montclair Ave.*

Gifts & Fine Stationery

Bric Brac 'n Brass LINCOLN HEIGHTS   If you can't find a gift in here, go home—it's hopeless. Carrying everything from faux floral

The giant armadillo marks the front to Bussey's flea market.

Classic home furnishing at Five Broads Off Broadway.

arrangements, wreaths, picture frames, ceramics, French dinnerware, dolls, seasonal/holiday decorations, glass art, and curios, this is a home-decor Mecca and an idea-challenged gift-giver's answer to prayer. Located near the popular Alamo Quarry Market (aka "The Quarry"). *355 E. Basse Rd.* ☎ *210/828-6742. AE, DISC, MC, V. Bus: 505 to the Quarry (Basse & Jones Maltsberger rds.).*

★★★ Hanley Wood ALAMO HEIGHTS   So many San Antonio brides register here that it's the only place I go for a shower gift anymore. With tableware, barware, fine China, photo frames, Jon Hart bags and luggage, gifts, and accessories, I can't seem to get out of this store without buying myself a present, too. *5611 Broadway St.* ☎ *210/822-3311. www.hanleywoodtexas.com. AE, DISC, MC, V. Bus: 9, 10 & 209 to Broadway & St Dennis sts.*

★★ Invitations, Etc. ALAMO HEIGHTS   I got the most fabulous custom luggage tags here—but that's the kind of store this is. Not just cards, invitations, and stationery (though they have the best of those, as well), this store has everything from photo albums and

frames to leather datebooks and unique gifts. Located in Sunset Ridge, this shop is handy to lots of other great little stores. *6434 N. New Braunfels Ave.* ☎ *210/826-2329. www.inviteetc.com. AE, MC, V. Bus: 505 to Randolph Park & Ride.*

Gourmet Food & Wine

★★★ Central Market ALAMO HEIGHTS   If Austin loves its Whole Foods, San Antonio swoons over its Central Market store. Displaying a mind-blowing abundance of fresh produce, fine wines, fresh seafood and meats, bulk items, fresh baked goods, high-market and hard-to-find brand gourmand food products and ingredients—not to mention fresh flowers, gifts, and hand-made sushi—this is what a fresh market should look like. Expensive, yes—but shopping here is an experience in and of itself. Sometimes, I go just to look and sample cheeses and nab freebie nibbles on weekends. **Whole Foods Market** (☎ 210/826-4676) fans will be glad to know that San Antonio has their favorite store, too, at the Quarry. *4821 Broadway St.* ☎ *210/368-8600. www.central market.com. AE, DISC, MC, V. Bus 9, 10, 14 & 209 to Broadway St. & Patterson Ave.*

An abundance of cheeses at San Antonio's Central Market.

Jewelry & Precious Stones

★★★ C. Aaron Peñaloza Jewelers SUNSET RIDGE   Since 1924, the Peñaloza family has been a respected San Antonio name in jewelry, and C. Aaron Peñaloza continues his family's long tradition in fine jewelry with the Sunset Ridge store he opened in 1990. With the highest-quality jewelry and watches, and trustworthy service in casting, repair, engraving, and remolding, this is the jeweler I go to with my family's heirloom jewelry. *6430 N. New Braunfels Ave.* ☎ *210/822-4044. www.penaloza.com. AE, DISC, MC, V. Bus: 505 to Randolph Park & Ride.*

Linens & Bedding

★★★ Lin Marché Fine Linens OLMOS PARK   Lots of women adore fine linens, beautiful bedding, plush towels and nightgowns, scented sachet pillows and pretty soaps—and I'm one of them. This store has all that, along with table linens and accessories to lift your home to new levels of loveliness. Of course, flying high can be costly. People who like linens often like fine stationery, so be sure to stop next door in **Camilla Brink Stationers** (☎ 210/822-6565). *4307 McCullough Ave.* ☎ *210/826-6771. www.linmarche.com. AE, DISC, MC, V. Bus: 5 & 204 to Olmos Circle.*

Mexican Imports

★★ Marti's DOWNTOWN   For years, San Antonio society ladies would cross the border into Nuevo Laredo to sip margaritas at the Cadillac Bar and shop at Marti's. But hard times hit Nuevo Laredo, and some San Antonio customers stopped coming, so Marti's came to them, opening a new shop here, near El Mercado/Market Square. Now, ladies can find the fabulous Mexican imports, gold and silver jewelry, smart apparel, gifts, art, colorful home furnishings, and accessories without having to pull out a passport. *310 W. Commerce St.* ☎ *210/223-9100. www.martis.com. AE, DISC, MC, V. Bus: 17, 21, 22 & more. Streetcar: Yellow & Red lines to Commerce & Laredo sts.*

Music

★ Hogwild Records, Tapes & CDs TOBIN HILL   This little "indie" vinyl and CD music vendor is one of those places you'd like to lose yourself in on a Saturday afternoon. Located near San Antonio College, the store's hip selection of new and used music is popular with students and baby boomers alike. Bumper stickers cover the front door—this is no chain store, thank you very much. And, no, they don't carry cassettes or 8-track tapes. *1824 N Main Ave.* ☎ *210/733-5354. AE, DISC, MC, V. Bus: 90 to Main St. & Dewey Place.*

Shoes

★ Theo & Herb Designer Shoes LINCOLN HEIGHTS   *Sex & the City* re-introduced expensive designer shoes to American women, and Theo & Herb introduced them to San Antonio ladies. With designer footwear from Stuart Weitzman, Donald J Pliner, and Kate Spade, along with high-market handbags, Karen Hartley jewelry, and smart accessories, high fashion comes with a pretty price tag here. Still, twice a year, they throw a big sale with huge discounts and savings. *555 E. Basse Rd.* ☎ *210/824-6901. AE, DISC, MC, V. Bus: 647 to Treeline Park & Basse Rd.*

Lee Lee Loves Shoes ALAMO HEIGHTS *Texas Monthly* touted this store as the "best shoe and accessory store in the state." I like it because this store carries a selection of more affordable shoes, along with high-priced designer shoes. Locally owned by Leigh Landreth and Sherry Leeper, Lee Lee steps up to the plate. *5932 Broadway St.* ☎ *210/832-0066. www.leeleeshoes. com. AE, DISC, MC, V. Bus: 9 & 10 to Broadway St. & Montclair Ave.*

Sports & Outdoor Recreation

kids Bass Pro Shop NORTHWEST/THE RIM This family-friendly store is so big it could almost be its own stand-alone San Antonio suburb. Anchoring the Rim shopping center, it features sporting goods, fishing and hunting equipment, boats (for sale, charter, and rental), all-terrain vehicles, archery equipment, camping gear, golf gear, clothing, shoes, and more. Located not far from Six Flags Fiesta Texas (see p 123, ➒), the Westin La Cantera Resort (see

p 162), and the Shops at La Cantera. *17907 I-10 W.* ☎ *210/253-8800. www.basspro.com. AE, DISC, MC, V. Bus: 94 & 97 La Cantera at Rim Dr.*

★★★ Whole Earth Provision Co. LINCOLN HEIGHTS Hard-core campers and outdoor enthusiasts will adore this store, carrying everything you'll need (and more) for the perfect backcountry adventure. Featuring all the great gear campers, fishermen, hip travelers, and earth-conscious Texans (and their kids) could ask for, Whole Earth also carries clothing, backpacks, luggage, books, and toys. Their educational toys are a big hit with my kids. Part of a chain that was first born in Austin. *255 E Basse Rd.* ☎ *210/829-8888. www.wholeearthprovision. com. AE, DISC, MC, V. Bus: 505 to the Quarry (Basse & Jones Maltsberger rds.).*

Toys

★ kids Learning Express Toys LINCOLN HEIGHTS Bright, colorful educational toys and books your kids will love. *255 E. Basse Rd.* ☎ *210/930-4442. www.learning express.com. AE, DISC, MC, V. Bus: 505 to the Quarry (Basse & Jones Maltsberger rds.).*

C. Aaron Peñaloza Jewelers has been creating fine jewelry since 1924.

San Antonio's **Great Outdoors**

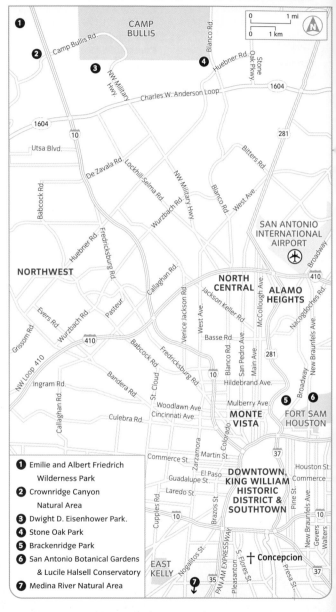

CAMP BULLIS

Camp Bullis Rd.

NW Military Hwy.

Blanco Rd.

Huebner Rd.

Stone Oak Pkwy.

Charles W. Anderson Loop

1604

1604

10

Utsa Blvd.

De Zavala Rd.

Lockhill-Selma Rd.

Bitters Rd.

Babcock Rd.

Wurzbach Rd.

NW Military Hwy.

Blanco Rd.

West Ave.

SAN ANTONIO INTERNATIONAL AIRPORT

NORTHWEST

Huebner Rd.

Fredericksburg Rd.

Pasteur

Callaghan Rd.

Venice Jackson Rd.

West Ave.

Jackson Keller Rd.

McCollough Ave.

Broadway

NORTH CENTRAL

ALAMO HEIGHTS

Nacogdoches Rd.

Evers Rd.

Wurzbach Rd.

410

Babcock Rd.

Fredericksburg Rd.

10

Basse Rd.

Blanco Rd.

San Pedro Ave.

Main Ave.

281

Grissom Rd.

NW Loop 410

Ingram Rd.

Bandera Rd.

St. Cloud

Woodlawn Ave.

Cincinnati Ave.

Hildebrand Ave.

Broadway

New Braunfels Ave.

Callaghan Rd.

Culebra Rd.

Mulberry Ave.

MONTE VISTA

FORT SAM HOUSTON

1. Emilie and Albert Friedrich Wilderness Park
2. Crownridge Canyon Natural Area
3. Dwight D. Eisenhower Park.
4. Stone Oak Park
5. Brackenridge Park
6. San Antonio Botanical Gardens & Lucile Halsell Conservatory
7. Medina River Natural Area

Commerce St.

Martin St.

Zarzamora

Colorado

El Paso

Guadalupe St.

Laredo St.

Cupples Rd.

Brazos St.

10

37

DOWNTOWN, KING WILLIAM HISTORIC DISTRICT & SOUTHTOWN

Houston St.

Commerce

Pine St.

New Braunfels Ave.

Gevers St.

Walters

10

Concepcion

EAST KELLY

Nogalitos St.

35

PAN AM EXPRESSWAY

Pleasanton

Flores St.

Presa St.

37

0   1 mi
0   1 km

If you can't stand the heat, stay out of San Antonio—or at least spend time in the city's many museums and water parks. But some like it hot, and if you're a sun worshiper and triple-digit temperatures are not a problem, you'll be just fine. Most locals don't mind sizzling summers because the fall, winter, and spring seasons are so sublimely mild. And even though Texans have a tendency to drive across the street rather than walk, we still like to hike, bike, and spend time outdoors. San Antonio is home to more beautiful nature preserves and parks than I have room to list here, so I've chosen just a few of the sweetest spots where locals go to commune with nature. **START: I-10 to the Dominion Drive exit, about ½ mile (.8km) past Loop 1604 on Milsa Rd.**

❶ ★★ Emilie and Albert Friedrich Wilderness Park. This stunning 633-acre (256-hectare) Hill Country natural area rests along the Balcones Escarpment 20 miles (32km) northwest of downtown. The park's mission allows the simple splendor of the place to take center stage by ensuring that natural elements remain beautifully undisturbed, so trails here are simple and unobtrusive. Enjoy an up-close and personal afternoon enjoying the many kinds of birds, animals, and plant life you'll spy in their natural environment. You'll find trails for novice and experienced hikers, alike. *See p 130.*

❷ ★ Crownridge Canyon Natural Area. Located just 19 miles (31km) from downtown, not far from the Six Flags Fiesta Texas theme park (see p 123), this preserve was developed as part of the Edwards Aquifer Protection initiative, and it features 1.3 miles (2.1km) of cement-stabilized ADA Level 1 accessible trails and Level 4 hiking trails through a number of habitats. The trail-head pavilion features several interpretive mosaic tile panels by artist Oscar Alvarado. These tell the story of the area's natural history, the park's rocks and plant life, the aquifer's recharge cycle, and the impact of human beings on the ecosystem.

Emilie and Albert Friedrich Wilderness Park offers trails with a range of difficulty levels.

The park also offers a rainwater-harvesting demonstration area and solar lighting. *7222 Luskey Rd.* ☎ *210/564-6400. www.sanantonio. gov/sapar. Free admission. Daily 7:30am–sunset. No city bus service.*

❸ ★ **Dwight D. Eisenhower Park.** With 5 miles (8km) of trails for hiking, jogging, and nature walks, 320-acre (130-hectare) Eisenhower Park is full of rolling Texas Hill Country landscapes featuring wooded dry creek beds and rock canyons. There are family-friendly amenities like a climbing rock wall and playground, shady picnic pavilions and barbecue pits, and nice restroom facilities. The huge Harris Pavilion and kitchen is a mass picnic area that large groups can rent. The park also has primitive camping sites if you want to reserve an overnight stay. Pets are welcome—as long as Fido stays on a leash and you pick up after him. No roller blades, scooters, or bicycles allowed, and hikers must stay on the trails. *19399 NW Military Hwy.* ☎ *210/564-6400. www.sanantonio.gov/sapar. Free admission. Daily 6am–sunset. No city bus service.*

❹ **kids Stone Oak Park.** One of the fastest-growing urban development areas in town is in the area called Stone Oak, which these days is known for heavy traffic jams during rush hours, quickly-built "McMansions," and Starbucks-style strip centers northwest of town. But what you may not know about Stone Oak is that it's also home to a delightful park, which opened in 2006, with hiking trails, pavilions, cave protection features, and picnic spots. Leave the ugly urban sprawl behind. Scenery like this is why folks moved to Stone Oak in the first place. *20395 Stone Oak Pkwy.* ☎ *210/564-6400. www.sanantonio. gov/sapar. Free admission. Daily 7:30am–sunset. Bus: 648.*

❺ ★★★ **kids Brackenridge Park.** From the Japanese Sunken Gardens; to the Sunken Garden Theater; to the brooks, footbridges, lush lawns, and San Antonio Zoo—it's all here near the heart of town. This is my favorite garden-party spot in a city full of so many lovely places to play. *See p 127.*

❻ ★★★ **kids San Antonio Botanical Gardens & Lucile Halsell Conservatory.** This exquisite 38-acre (15-hectare) setting of quiet gardens, ponds, and fountains celebrates native Texas plants and wildflowers amid pools, paved paths, a garden for the blind, a biblical garden, a children's garden, and the extraordinary

The Medina River Natural Area has miles of hiking trails and native plant displays.

The Lucile Halsell Conservatory is home to tropical flowers and desert plants.

$6.9-million conservatory complex of greenhouses that are home to tropical flowers and desert plants. The entrance to the gardens is through the stone 1896 Sullivan Carriage House, moved to the park from its original downtown site. There, visitors may browse the gift shop or enjoy a light lunch in the Carriage House Bistro known for delicious desserts. Especially to those visiting in spring, I highly recommend adding these gardens to your list of must-see San Antonio attractions. *555 Funston Place.* ☎ *210/207-3250. www.sabot.org. $7 adults; $5 seniors, students & military; $4 children 3–13; free for children under 3. Gardens & conservatory daily 9am–5pm; Bistro Tues–Fri 11am–2pm, Sat–Sun 9am–2pm. Closed Thanksgiving, Christmas, and New Year's Day. Bus: 7 to Botanical Gardens.*

❼ ★★★ Medina River Natural Area. Constructed on the site of what the city had first planned to develop as a reservoir, this 511-acre (207-hectare) Natural Area, flanking the north shore of the lovely green Medina River, is home to plants, mammals, snakes, birds, fish, and insects. With 6 miles (9.7km) of trails with varying degrees of difficulty along the river for hikers, and abundant native plant displays, this park is a fine place for fishing, hiking, and group camping. Pets on leashes, bikes, and geocaching are permitted. *15890 Hwy. 16 S.* ☎ *212/207-7275 (camping reservations) or 210/624-2575. www.sanantonio.gov/sapar. Free admission. Daily 7:30am–sunset. No city bus service.*

❽ ★★★ 𝗸𝗶𝗱𝘀 Hill Country State Natural Area. Wide open spaces don't get much better than this. The best place to play cowboy and experience a bit of Hill Country heaven rests about 50 miles (80km) from San Antonio near Bandera, Texas. This spectacular 5,370-acre (2,173-hectare) nature preserve sits surrounded by ranches, rivers, and rolling Texas hills. It's truly a stunning place with more than 40 miles (64km) of multi-use trails that cut across verdant valleys and cold spring-fed streams, and creep up steep limestone cliffs. Hikers, horsemen, and mountain bikers will love these trails—you know you've been to Texas when you've ridden a horse here. Dude ranches encircle the area like cowboys around a campfire. Primitive and backcountry camping areas are available. *10600 Bandera Creek Rd., Bandera.* ☎ *830/796-4413. www.tpwd.state.tx.us. No city bus service.*

San Antonio's Best Dining

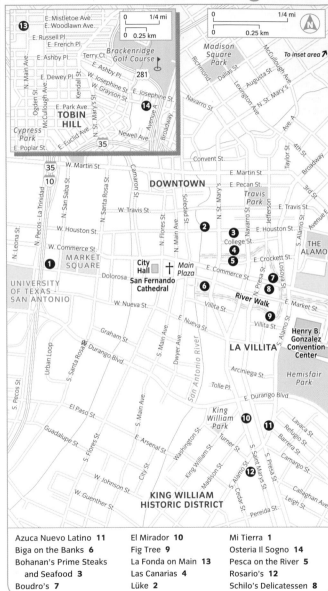

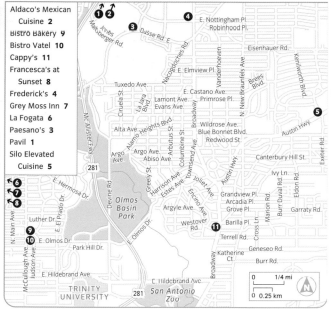

Aldaco's Mexican Cuisine **2**	
Bistro Bakery **9**	
Bistro Vatel **10**	
Cappy's **11**	
Francesca's at Sunset **8**	
Frederick's **4**	
Grey Moss Inn **7**	
La Fogata **6**	
Paesano's **3**	
Pavil **1**	
Silo Elevated Cuisine **5**	

San Antonio Dining Best Bets

Best **All-Night Eats**
★ Mi Tierra $$, *218 Produce Row*
(p 156)

Best **Brunch**
★★ Las Canarias $$$$, *112 College St.* (p 155)

Best **French**
★★★ Bistro Vatel $$–$$$, *218 E. Olmos Dr.* (p 153)

Best **Italian**
★★★ Paesano's $$–$$$, *555 E. Basse Rd.* (p 156)

Best-Loved **Alamo Heights Eatery**
★★ Cappy's $$–$$$, *5011 Broadway St.* (p 153)

Best **Oh-So San Antonio Spot**
★ La Fonda on Main $$, *2415 N. Main Ave.* (p 155)

Best **Outdoor Dining**
★★ Biga on the Banks $$–$$$$, *203 S. St Marys St.* (p 152)

Best **River Walk Romance Spot**
★★ Fig Tree $$$–$$$$$, *515 Villita St.* (p 154)

Best **Seafood**
★ Pesca on the River (Watermark Hotel) $$$–$$$$$, *212 W. Crockett St.* (p 156)

Best **Splurge**
★★ Bohanan's Prime Steaks & Seafood $$$$–$$$$$, *219 E. Houston St.* (p 153)

Best **Sunset Views**
★★★ Francesca's at Sunset $$$–$$$$, *16441 La Cantera Pkwy.* (p 154)

Best **Tex-Mex**
★ La Fogata $–$$$, *2427 Vance Jackson Rd.* (p 155)

San Antonio Dining A to Z

★ Aldaco's Mexican Cuisine
STONE OAK *MEXICAN* For great Tex-Mex food in a fun, contemporary place, Aldaco's is a sure thing. If you've never tried Tex-Mex, come here to fall in love with the simple, authentic flavors fusing these two cultures. Order chicken *flautas* (red or white corn tortillas filled with shredded chicken breast meat, rolled into a flute shape, and then deep fried) and a big frozen margarita—or try the fajitas if you're not sure about Mexican food. Dine on the patio at night for a dazzling view of city lights in Stone Oak. *20079 Stone Oak Pkwy.* ☎ *210/494-0561. www.aldacos.net. Entrees $9–$23. AE, MC, V. Brunch Sat & Sun, lunch & dinner daily. No city bus service. See map p 151.*

★★ Azuca Nuevo Latino
SOUTHTOWN *LATIN* Calling theirs "world cuisine," Azuca blends the best of traditional Latin American flavors with today's hottest trends in Caribbean and Latin fare. I like to sit out back on the patio—especially when live music rocks the bar area inside. Young, hip, busy, and bohemian, Azuca is one of Southtown's hottest spots, especially during First Fridays ArtWalk nights. *713 S. Alamo St.* ☎ *210/225-5550. www. azuca.net. Entrees $15–$27. AE, MC, V. Lunch Mon–Sat, dinner daily. Streetcar: Blue line to S. Alamo & Barrera sts. See map p 150.*

★★ Biga on the Banks
RIVER WALK *AMERICAN* Splurge at this iconic River Walk restaurant. Chef Bruce Auden is well known with local foodies who loved Biga, an earlier McCullough Avenue incarnation of this hot riverside bistro. The interior decor is just so-so, so be sure to reserve a table on the

The terrace at Biga on the Banks overlooks the River Walk.

terrace overlooking the River Walk. Try Chef Auden's apple-smoked salmon nachos. Biga's has a second hopping location in Stone Oak. *203 S. St Marys St.* ☎ *210/271-7603. www.biga.com. Entrees $19–$36. AE, DC, DISC, MC, V. Dinner daily. Bus: 301 & 305. Streetcar: Blue line to Market & St Marys sts. See map p 150.*

★★ Bistro Bakery
OLMOS PARK *BAKERY* Owner and famed local chef Damian Watel's mother, Lucile, runs this lovely French patisserie on Olmos Circle across from Watel's popular Bistro Vatel (see p 153). Serving croissants, tarts, baguettes, quiches, and strong coffee, as well as scrumptious daily takeout specials, this tiny get-it-to-go spot is my new favorite stop. *4300 McCullough Ave.* ☎ *210/824-3884. www.bistro vatel.com/bakery. Entrees under $10. AE, DC, DISC, MC, V. Breakfast*

& lunch Tues–Sun. Bus: 5 & 204 to Olmos Circle. See map p 151.

★★★ **Bistro Vatel** OLMOS PARK *FRENCH* Ask any discriminating foodie or in-the-know local, and they'll tell you this is the best restaurant in town. Chef Damian Watel has opened several San Antonio restaurants, but this pricey little gem on Olmos Circle remains my favorite. The prix-fixe dinner menu is always a splendid choice. Regulars rave about the duck breast with rhubarb, but I love the tasty veal tenderloin with truffle cream. *218 E. Olmos Dr.* ☎ *210/828-3141. www.bistrovatel. com. Entrees $16–$30; prix fixe $42. AE, DC, DISC, MC, V. Lunch Tues–Sat, dinner Tues–Sun. Bus: 5 & 204 to Olmos Circle. See map p 151.*

★★ **Bohanan's Prime Steaks and Seafood** DOWNTOWN *STEAKHOUSE* This family-owned downtown restaurant is known for its pricey prime steaks and seafood. Owner and Executive Chef Mark Bohanan takes Texas steakhouse fare to new heights, and his award-winning wine menu and flaming table-side dessert offerings make this spot sweeter still. *219 E. Houston St.* ☎ *210/472-2600. www. bohanans.com. Entrees $35–$100. AE, DISC, MC, V. Lunch Mon–Fri, dinner daily. Bus: 30. Streetcar: Red line*

to Houston & Navarro sts. See map p 150.

★ **Boudro's** RIVER WALK *SOUTH-WESTERN* Southern, southwestern, and a tad bit Cajun, too, Boudro's popular River Walk bistro is one of the things I like best about eating on the river. Their braised beef short ribs and blackened gulf seafood dishes keep me coming back. *421 E. Commerce St.* ☎ *210/ 224-8484. www.boudros.com. Entrees $16–$36. AE, DC, DISC, MC, V. Lunch & dinner daily. Bus: 301, 302 & 305. Streetcar: Blue & Yellow lines to Commerce & Losoya sts. See map p 150.*

★★ **Cappy's** ALAMO HEIGHTS *AMERICAN* If a restaurant were a family member, Cappy's would be a favorite uncle. This iconic Alamo Heights eatery is casual with consistently good food. From juicy Kobe beef hamburgers and salads at lunch to great steaks and seafood for dinner, Cappy's never fails to deliver. *5011 Broadway St.* ☎ *210/ 828 9669. www.cappysrestaurant. com. Entrees $16–$29. AE, DC, MC, V. Lunch & dinner daily. Bus: 9, 10 & 209 to Broadway St. (between Terrell & Elizabeth rds.). See map p 151.*

★ **El Mirador** SOUTHTOWN *MEXICAN* To die-for delicious homemade

Bistro Vatel is where one of the city's best prix-fixe dinner menus can be found.

soups make this Mexican food Mecca in Southtown the place where locals love to stand in line on Saturdays. But all week long, for breakfast, lunch, and supper, the authentic flavors of Mexico comingle with savory San Antonio–style dishes in this family-owned favorite restaurant. *722 S. St Marys St.* ☎ *210/225-9444. www. elmiradorrestaurant.com. Entrees $8.95–$25. AE, DISC, MC, V. Breakfast & lunch daily, dinner Mon–Sat. Bus: 34 & 242. Streetcar: Blue line to S. St Marys & King William sts. See map p 150.*

★★ Fig Tree LA VILLITA/RIVER WALK *AMERICAN*

Take me here for dinner, please. Tiny white lights in the trees and tables on little terraces overlooking the River Walk, sizzling steaks and fine wine, white tablecloths, and candlelight—it's so romantic I'm swooning already. A San Antonio institution in La Villita since what seems like forever, this place is a pricey little gem. *515 Villita St.* ☎ *210/224-1976. www. figtreerestaurant.com. Entrees $28–$43. AE, DC, DISC, MC, V. Dinner daily. Bus: 301 & 305. Streetcar: Blue line to S. Alamo St. (opposite Hilton Hotel at LaVillita). See map p 150.*

★★★ Francesca's at Sunset NORTHWEST *SOUTHWESTERN*

Last time here, I savored every bite of their fabulous farm-to-table fare—until I realized the restaurant had emptied and the polite waiters probably wanted to go home. Afterward, I couldn't decide what I'd enjoyed most—Francesca's award-winning wine list or Chef Ernie Estrada's superb cuisine (the lobster bisque is luscious). As contemporary, casual, and attractive as this Westin La Cantera Resort (see p 163) restaurant's Hill Country views at sunset, Francesca's gets my glowing review. *16441 La Cantera Pkwy.* ☎ *210/558-6500. www.westinla cantera.com/dining.html. Entrees $28–$39; wine-pairing dinner $52. AE, DC, DISC, MC, V. Dinner daily. Bus: 94 to La Cantera Pkwy. See map p 151.*

★★★ Frederick's ALAMO HEIGHTS *FRENCH/FUSION*

Blending the flavors of France with flavors from the Far East, Frederick's is a longtime favorite of locals for fine French dining in a place as unfussy and inviting as a cozy living room. Bistro Vatel (see p 153) has a hard time beating this place, for owner Frederick Costa's restaurant has been one of San Antonio's favorite fine-dining spots for more than 10 years. *7701 Broadway St.* ☎ *210/*

Dining at Fig Tree can be expensive, but it has a wonderfully romantic atmosphere.

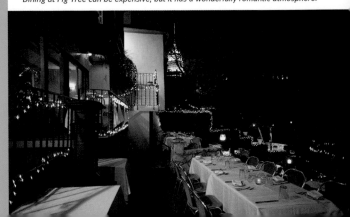

828-9050. www.frederickssa.com.
Entrees $17–$33. AE, DC, DISC, MC,
V. Lunch Mon–Fri, dinner Mon–Sat.
Bus: 9 & 209 to Broadway St. & Not-
tingham Place. See map p 151.

★★ **Grey Moss Inn** HELOTES
SOUTHWESTERN This long-revered
romantic San Antonio–area institution sits under a canopy of oak trees
off the aptly-named Scenic Loop,
northwest of San Antonio at the
edge of the Hill Country. Deer frolic
near this enchanting stone cottage
with its hardwood floors and bright
windows, as fine wines flow and dinner cooks on an outdoor mesquite-
fired stone grill. Candles, moonlight—
this place is pure magic at night.
19010 Scenic Loop Rd. ☎ 210/695-
8301. www.grey-moss-inn.com.
Entrees $17–$56. AE, DC, DISC, MC,
V. Dinner daily. No city bus service.
See map p 151.

★ **La Fogata** NORTH CENTRAL
MEXICAN/TEX-MEX Famous in
these parts for authentic Mexican
and Tex-Mex fare, La Fogata is a fabulous place to eat outside, and
enjoy a tasty margarita and a plate
of hot sizzling fajitas or enchiladas.
2427 Vance Jackson Rd. ☎ 210/340-
1337. www.lafogata.com. Entrees
$6–$25. AE, DISC, MC, V. Lunch &
dinner daily. Bus: 96 & 296 to Vance
Jackson Rd. & Lemur Dr. See map
p 151.

★ **La Fonda on Main** MONTE
VISTA *MEXICAN* I don't know if it's
the old San Antonio neighborhood,
the festive ambience of the bright
window-filled space, or the authentic
Old Mexico–style menu that I like
best. Dishes feature hot spicy season-
ings with flavors that dance on the
tongue like beautiful Spanish words.
2415 N. Main Ave. ☎ 210/733-0621.
www.lafondaonmain.com. Entrees
$10–$18. AE, DC, MC, V. Lunch & dinner daily. Bus: 90 to Woodlawn Ave.
& N. Main St. See map p 150.

*La Fogata is famous for its authentic
Mexican and Tex-Mex dishes.*

★★ **Las Canarias** RIVER WALK
AMERICAN With quite possibly the
best brunch in town—and delightful
lunch and dinner menus, too—the
AAA Four-Diamond Las Canarias
offers stylish, Spanish-villa-style dining, indoors and on the River Walk,
at the Omni La Mansion del Rio
Hotel. Casual, old-world, and inviting, Las Canarias is a treat. The prix-
fixe offerings are often outstanding.
Lavish bi-monthly wine-paring dinners showcase renowned Chef John
Brand's outstanding culinary skills
and fabulous wines. 112 College St.
☎ 210/518-1000. www.omnihotels.
com. Entrees $34–$55. AE, DC, DISC,
MC, V. Brunch, lunch & dinner daily.
Bus: 301 & 305. Streetcar: Blue line
to E. Houston & St Marys sts. See
map p 150.

★★★ **Lüke** DOWNTOWN *ALSATIAN*
I used to drive 500 miles to New
Orleans to taste food this good
at celebrity chef John Besh's Restaurant Lüke. But now Besh and part-
ner Executive Chef Steven McHugh
have opened this new restaurant on
the River Walk, adjacent to the new
Embassy Suites hotel. Besh, today's
hottest new food television star,
cookbook author, and restaurateur,
seems to have found the recipe for
success. From seafood, to hamburgers, to perfect steaks, favorite Louisiana dishes, and even Alsatian
specialties—Lüke's menu and bar

are amazing. I love it that they serve dinner till 11pm --how very European. This is the best new restaurant in town, hands-down. *125 E. Houston St. (at the Embassy Suites),* ☎ *210/227-LUKE (5853). www.luke sanantonio.com. AE, DC, DISC, MC, V. Entrees $11–$26. Lunch and dinner daily. Bus: Red streetcar. See map p 150.*

★ **Mi Tierra** EL MERCADO/MARKET SQUARE *MEXICAN* An all-night Tex-Mex fiesta all year round, this Market Square (El Mercado) Mexican food restaurant is a San Antonio tradition. *218 Produce Row.* ☎ *210/ 225-1262. www.mitierracafe.com. Entrees $8–$19. AE, MC, V. 24 hr. daily. Streetcar: Red & Yellow lines to Market Square/El Mercado, or Dolorosa & San Saba St. See map p 150.*

★★ **Osteria Il Sogno** PEARL BREWERY/MUSEUM REACH *ITALIAN* Star chef Andrew Weissmann's restaurant offers yet another good reason to check out the trendy reclaimed Pearl Brewery complex (see p 111, **9**) of shops, clubs, and hip eateries. This hot spot is known as much for its long

Las Canarias may have the best brunch in the city.

waits (no reservations) as its fine Italian fare. More affordable for lunch, but with wine it's a little more dear for dinner, this busy bistro's food lives up to its buzz. *200 E. Grayson St.* ☎ *210/212-4843. Entrees $16–$36. AE, DISC, MC, V. Breakfast Tues–Sat, lunch & dinner Tues–Sun. Closed Mon. Bus: 20 to Josephine & Isleta sts. May be reached by river taxi. See map p 150.*

★★★ **Paesano's** LINCOLN HEIGHTS *ITALIAN* Hands-down my favorite restaurant in town, Paesano's is a San Antonio institution—the shrimp *paesano* is so good it spawned a mini-empire. In Lincoln Heights, with sister properties on Loop 1604 near Stone Oak and on the River Walk, as well. *555 E. Basse Rd.* ☎ *210/828-5191; 111 W. Crockett St.* ☎ *210/ 227-2782; 3622 Paesanos Pkwy (Loop 1604)* ☎ *210/493-1604. www. paesanos.com. Entrees $10–$31. AE, DC, DISC, MC, V. Lunch & dinner daily. For Lincoln Heights location, take Bus: 505 to Treeline Park & Basse Rd. See map p 151.*

★ **Pavil** STONE OAK *FRENCH* This French brasserie, with its glimmering golden rooms and simple bistro fare, makes me feel I've landed in a favorite New York eatery. Chef Scott Cohen, who wowed us all at Las Canarias (see p 155) and at The Watermark's Pesca on the River (see p 156) restaurants, is now leading the pack of great chefs moving to Stone Oak. Of all the restaurants exploding on the scene there, this is my favorite. (Try the French onion soup.) *1818 N. Loop 1604 W.* ☎ *210/479-5000. www.brasserie pavil.com. Entrees $11–$30. AE, DISC, MC, V. Brunch Sat & Sun, lunch Mon–Fri, dinner daily. No city bus service. See map p 151.*

★ **Pesca on the River** RIVER WALK *SEAFOOD* A boutique hotel

Pesca on the River serves fresh international seafood including wild fish.

as impeccable as the Watermark requires a restaurant to match its high standards—and it has one. Rising star Chef John Brand, who is also the executive chef at the Omni La Mansion del Rio's Las Canarias restaurant (see p 155) has taken the Watermark's tourist-friendly River Walk address and left his own indelible mark at Pesca on the River, with freshly-flown-in seafood, prime steaks, and fine wines. Casual, contemporary, bright, and colorful—inside and out, Pesca is the perfect River Walk restaurant. *212 W. Crockett St.* ☎ *210/396-5817. www. watermarkhotel.com/restaurant. Entrees $25–$42. AE, DC, DISC, MC, V. Breakfast, lunch & dinner daily. Bus: 2, 3 & 5. Streetcars: Yellow & Red lines to St Marys & Commerce sts. See map p 150.*

Rosario's SOUTHTOWN *MEXICAN/ SOUTHWESTERN* This happening Southtown spot features colorful, fun art-inspired ambience and a fresh take on Tex-Mex near the Blue Star Arts district. Loud, fun, young, and hip, Rosario's rocks. *910 S. Alamo St.* ☎ *210/223-1806. www. rosariossa.com. Entrees $9.25–$17. AE, DC, DISC, MC, V. Lunch & dinner*

daily. Bus: 51 & 54 to Alamo & St Marys sts. See map p 150.*

★★★ Schilo's Delicatessen
DOWNTOWN *GERMAN* As-good-as-it-gets German fare in a fabulous old-downtown deli (pronounced "shē-low's") steps from the River Walk. They don't make coffee shops or delis like this anymore. *424 E. Commerce St.* ☎ *210/223-6692. Entrees under $10. AE, DC, DISC, MC, V. Breakfast, lunch & dinner Mon–Sat. Bus: 302. Streetcar: Yellow line to Commerce & N. Presa sts. See map p 150.*

★★ Silo Elevated Cuisine
ALAMO HEIGHTS/STONE OAK *AMER-ICAN* Farm-to-table fresh fare, clean and sleek environs, and haute cuisine made casual, Silo is often touted as one of San Antonio's best restaurants. With a new location near Stone Oak on Loop 1604, the old Austin Highway address is still my favorite. *1133 Austin Hwy.* ☎ *210/824-8686; 434 N. Loop 1604 W.* ☎ *210/483-8989. www. siloelevatedcuisine.com. Entrees $17–$45, prix fixe $25–$35. AE, DC, DISC, MC, V. Lunch & dinner daily. Bus: 214 & 509 to Austin Hwy. & Exeter Rd. See map p 151.*

San Antonio Lodging

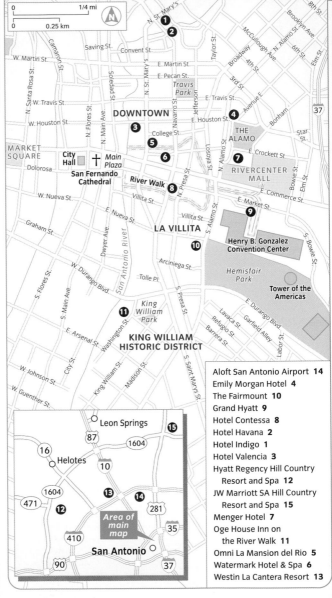

Aloft San Antonio Airport **14**
Emily Morgan Hotel **4**
The Fairmount **10**
Grand Hyatt **9**
Hotel Contessa **8**
Hotel Havana **2**
Hotel Indigo **1**
Hotel Valencia **3**
Hyatt Regency Hill Country
 Resort and Spa **12**
JW Marriott SA Hill Country
 Resort and Spa **15**
Menger Hotel **7**
Oge House Inn on
 the River Walk **11**
Omni La Mansion del Rio **5**
Watermark Hotel & Spa **6**
Westin La Cantera Resort **13**

Lodging Best Bets

Best **Airport-Area Hotel**
★ Aloft $–$$, *838 NW Loop 410 (p 160)*

Best **B&B**
★ Oge House River Walk Inn $$–$$$$, *209 Washington St. (p 162)*

Best **Budget Hotel**
★★ Hotel Indigo $$–$$$, *830 N. St Marys St. (p 161)*

Best **Old-School Charm**
★★ The Fairmount, $$–$$$, *401 S. Alamo St. (p 160)*

Best Place to **Bring the Kids**
★★★ JW Marriot SA Hill Country Resort $$$–$$$$, *1803 E. Sonterra Blvd. (p 162)*

Best Place to **Play Cowboy**
★★ The Hyatt Regency Hill Country Resort $$–$$$$$, *9800 Hyatt Resort Dr. (p 161)*

Best Place to **Play Golf**
★★★ The Westin La Cantera Resort $$$–$$$$$, *16641 La Cantera Pkwy. (p 163)*

Best Place to **Pretend You're in Old Mexico**
★★ Omni La Mansion del Rio $$$–$$$$, *112 College St. (p 162)*

Best Place to **Smoke a Cohiba on the Porch**
★★★ Hotel Havana $$, *1015 Navarro St. (p 161)*

Best **Spa**
★★★ The Watermark $$$–$$$$$, *212 W. Crockett St. (p 129)*

Best **Trendier-than-Thou Hotel**
★ Hotel Valencia $$–$$$, *150 E. Houston St. (p 161)*

Best **Value for Your Travel Dollar**
★ The Emily Morgan Hotel $$–$$$, *705 E. Houston St. (p 160)*

The Hyatt Regency Hill Country Resort and Spa evokes a classic Texan cowboy feeling.

San Antonio Hotels A to Z

★ **Aloft San Antonio Airport**
AIRPORT   What W Hotels did to shake up the staid, predictable world of downtown hotels, Starwood's new W-affiliate, Aloft, is doing at this affordable hotel just a few exits from the airport. With its contemporary design, LCD televisions, "plug-and-play" electronics charging stations, swank-looking lounge, and outdoor spaces, Aloft has a hot cutting-edge vibe young business travelers love. *838 NW Loop 410.* ☎ *210/541-8881. www.aloftsanantonioairport.com. 141 units. Doubles $92–$199. AE, DC, DISC, MC, V.*

★★ **Emily Morgan Hotel** ALAMO PLAZA/DOWNTOWN   This hotel was a pleasant surprise. My room on the 12th floor had huge arched windows and fantastic views of the city—even from the bathtub. Next door to the Alamo (see p 99), the location couldn't be better. Standard rooms are nicer than budget hotels. With good rates and a stellar location, it's a historic (and possibly haunted) hotel and a place I'd stay any time. *705 E. Houston St.* ☎ *210/225-5100. www.emilymorganhotel.com. 177 units. Doubles $159–$219. AE, DC, DISC, MC, V.*

★★★ **The Fairmount** HEMISFAIR/DOWNTOWN   This 1906 red-brick hotel made history (and the *Guinness World Records*) when, in 1985, the elegant old building was moved 5 city blocks to its current location. Today, this little independently owned property (not part of the Fairmont chain) has 37 plush rooms (each is unique, so ask to see a few first). Luke, a huge loveable lab, meets and greets guests. The hotel's Restaurant Insignia is but one of Chef Jason Dady's five popular San Antonio eateries. *401 S. Alamo St.* ☎ *210/224-8800. www.thefairmounthotel-sanantonio.com. 37 units. Doubles $189–$269. AE, DC, DISC, MC, V. See p 130,* **⑬**.

★ **Grand Hyatt** DOWNTOWN/RIVER WALK   This huge tower of hotel rooms and private residences stands on the River Walk near the Henry B. Gonzalez Convention Center. Retro-mod (with a big nod to mid-century design), it's all a bit too stark for my tastes. But if you like that look, this still-rather-new hotel is for you. A plus is its casual restaurants and bars along the river. *600 E. Market St.* ☎ *210/224-1234. http://grandsanantonio.hyatt.com. 1,003 units. Doubles $149–$474. AE, DC, DISC, MC, V.*

The Fairmount's Presidential Suite has a view of La Villita.

★ **Hotel Contessa** RIVER WALK/ DOWNTOWN   This 12-story Spanish-style hotel is a non-smoking, all-suite property in the heart of downtown on a quiet part of the River Walk, with an inviting river-level wine bar (Cork), restaurant (Las Ramblas), a rooftop pool with killer views, and a small spa—all a quick river taxi ride (or pleasant stroll) from the Arneson River Theatre (see p 102). *306 W. Market St.* ☎ *866/ 435-0900 or 210/229-9222. www.the hotelcontessa.com. 265 units. Suites $169–$309. AE, DC DISC, MC, V.*

★★★ **Hotel Havana** DOWN-TOWN   This is the best-kept secret in San Antonio and a favorite little boutique hotel. Recently resold to, and renovated by, Austin hotelier Liz Lambert (see **Hotel St. Cecilia** [p 87] and **Hotel San Jose** [p 87]), the Havana still hasn't lost its mystique. With its clandestine "forbidden fruit" Cuban vibe, this small independent hotel offers a quiet retreat from the touristy throng. The basement bar is a sublime hideaway, and the restaurant's covered river view terrace is a treat. Not on a populated part of the River Walk, but close enough that you won't mind. *1015 Navarro St.* ☎ *866/539-0036 or 210/222 2008. www.havana sanantonio.com. 27 units. Doubles $149–$189. AE, DC, DISC, MC, V.*

★ **Hotel Indigo** DOWNTOWN   From the outside, this place doesn't look promising. Inside, it's a whole other story—fresh colorful decor, down bedding, big TVs, and bright shared spaces on a quiet part of the River Walk. Many of the suite-style rooms have river views. A mile from most attractions (or a pretty 20-minute River Walk stroll), a river taxi can take you to touristy spots. Clean and so surprising—this is one of the nicest budget hotels I've found. *830 N. St Marys St.* ☎ *877/270-1389 or 210/527-1900. www.hotelindigo.*

Modern style and flare along the river at Hotel Valencia.

com. 150 units. Doubles $139–$239. AE, DC, DISC, MC, V.

★★ **Hotel Valencia** RIVER WALK/ DOWNTOWN   This hip hotel, just down popular Houston Street from the Majestic Theatre (see p 170), is big on sleek modern style, tech-friendly touches, and luxe amenities. It's young and trendy, with its swank Vbar (see p 167) and shady River Walk terraces. Here, you get not only a decent downtown location along a quiet part of the river and a chic room, but the feeling that you're one of the cool and lucky people staying at one of San Antonio's hottest, hippest hotels. *150 E. Houston St.* ☎ *866/842-0100 or 210/227-9700. www.hotelvalencia-riverwalk.com. 213 units. Doubles $179–$229. AE, DC, DISC, MC, V.*

★★ **Hyatt Regency Hill Country Resort and Spa** LEON VALLEY   This place is so cowboy cool and so Texan—walls hewn from white limestone, a mammoth lobby with roaring fireplaces, and furnishings decorated in on-hair cowhide and cushy, expensive cowboy leather. Grounds are remarkable, with their big "rambling river" inner-tube experience connecting swimming pools and the spa area, and a 27-hole golf course. The atmosphere and cuisine of the Antlers Lodge wowed me, too. Rooms are pretty standard, but the resort grounds and golf are great. *9800 Hyatt Resort Dr.* ☎ *210/647-1234. http://hillcountry.hyatt.com. 500 units. Doubles $180–$520. AE, DC, DISC, MC, V.*

JW Marriott SA Hill Country Resort and Spa STONE

OAK Boasting six restaurants (I liked the Cibolo Moon grill), on-site car rental, two TPC/PGA golf courses, an airport counter, kiddie camp, water park and "Lazy River," the largest spa in Texas, an adjacent convention center, a shopping area, bright modern rooms, and a Starbucks—this resort is resplendent with retro-mod decor and subtle Texas touches. One unpleasant surprise—they add an additional resort fee to the quoted room rate. I liked the Times Square–style spectacular TV screens in the High Velocity sports bar and fun things like nightly toasts to the sunset and fire pits by the pools. Still, the property sits far from downtown, and traffic getting there can be a nightmare. But if you're content to make the property your primary destination, this resort is sure to please. *23808 Resort Pkwy.* ☎ *866/882-4420 or 210/276-2500. 1,002 units. Doubles $275–$400. AE, DC, DISC, MC, V.*

★★★ Menger Hotel ALAMO

PLAZA/DOWNTOWN Built next to the Alamo just 23 years after its bloody siege in 1859, this historic hotel still offers an unforgettable experience. Stay in the King Ranch Suite with its awning-covered balcony overlooking Alamo Plaza. Enjoy a generous buffet in the recently renovated Colonial Room,

Omni La Mansion del Rio's Grand Spanish Colonial–style architecture evokes Old Mexico.

or have a cold one at the Menger's "Teddy Roosevelt" bar. Although the "newer" part of this hotel (and I use that term liberally here) is sadly sub-par, with rooms as small and standard as they come, the older section is charming. The Menger is said to be home to 32 different ghosts, including a chamber maid who was murdered by her husband. Next door to both the Rivercenter Mall (see p 100) and the Alamo. *204 Alamo Plaza.* ☎ *210/223-4361. www.mengerhotel.com. 316 units. Doubles $159–$199. AE, DISC, MC, V.*

★★ Oge House Inn on the River Walk KING WILLIAM DIS-

TRICT A Victorian-style Greek Revival mansion in the historic King William District, this is one of the most charming B&B properties in the city. Just a stone's throw from popular Southtown, the house rests on a quiet residential street along a serene section of the San Antonio River. *209 Washington St.* ☎ *210/223-2353. www.nobleinns.com/oge.html. 10 units. Suites $179–$349. AE, DC, DISC, MC, V.*

★★ Omni La Mansion del Rio

DOWNTOWN This hacienda-style hotel epitomizes the San Antonio experience. Grand Spanish Colonial–style architecture and furnishings offer an Old Mexico ambience, and its location is one of the finest along the River Walk. Las Canarias shares Chef John Brand with the Watermark Hotel's Pesca on the River (see p 156), and offers one of the best brunch buffets in the city, along with popular special wine dinner events that are getting a lot of good buzz from discriminating local foodies and oenophiles. *112 College St.* ☎ *210/518-1000. 338 units. Doubles $219–$379. AE, DC, DISC, MC, V.*

Watermark Hotel & Spa

DOWNTOWN   Is it the world-class spa, or the bright Pesca on the River (see p 156) restaurant (run by popular chef John Brand), or the spacious rooms with the dreamy beds that I like best? I can't decide. This little luxury hotel is sublime, and their posh, spoil-yourself-rotten spa is one of the finest in the city. Don't miss the little rooftop cafe and swimming pool area. *212 W. Crockett St.* ☎ *210/396-5800. www. watermarkhotel.com. 99 units. Doubles $279–$439. AE, DISC, MC, V.*

★★★ Westin La Cantera Resort

NORTHWEST   I could just live here at this sublime, huge, yet intimate-feeling, Starwood-property resort with its first-class accommodations, luxury amenities, fabulous restaurants, two golf courses (including an Arnold Palmer course), kids' club, spa, exercise room, Starbucks, manicured grounds, spectacular Hill Country views, 7 pools, 3 hot tubs, 3 bars, clubhouses, and fabulous restaurants—including **Francesca's at Sunset** (see p 154), known for its fine wines and Chef Ernie Estrada's innovative, fresh farm-to-table fare. This sprawling resort even has a village of private adorable *"casitas,"* or little houses, with their own swimming pool and patio areas—and rates that won't shock you. Enjoy the Hill Country, see stars at night, and feel the big Texas welcome of wide-open spaces at my all-time favorite San Antonio–area resort with easy access to downtown and to nearby SeaWorld and the Shops at La Cantera. There's even a free shuttle to the shops. *16641 La Cantera Pkwy.* ☎ *210/558-6500. www.westin lacantera.com. 508 units. Doubles $219–$459. AE, DC, DISC, MC, V.*

An evening view outside the beautiful Westin La Cantera Resort.

San Antonio Nightlife, Arts & Entertainment

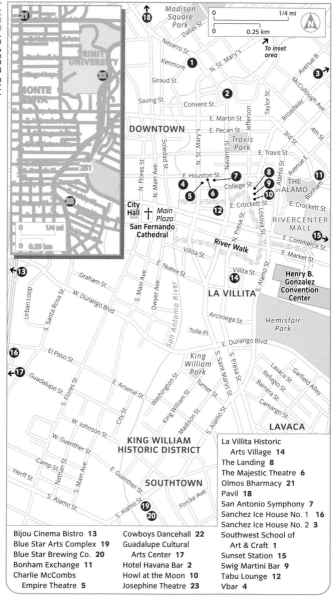

La Villita Historic
  Arts Village **14**
The Landing **8**
The Majestic Theatre **6**
Olmos Bharmacy **21**
Pavil **18**
San Antonio Symphony **7**
Sanchez Ice House No. 1 **16**
Sanchez Ice House No. 2 **3**
Southwest School of
  Art & Craft **1**
Sunset Station **15**
Swig Martini Bar **9**
Tabu Lounge **12**
Vbar **4**

Bijou Cinema Bistro **13**
Blue Star Arts Complex **19**
Blue Star Brewing Co. **20**
Bonham Exchange **11**
Charlie McCombs
  Empire Theatre **5**
Cowboys Dancehall **22**
Guadalupe Cultural
  Arts Center **17**
Hotel Havana Bar **2**
Howl at the Moon **10**
Josephine Theatre **23**

Nightlife and A&E Best Bets

Best **Dance Club**
★ Tabu Lounge, *245 E. Commerce St. (p 168)*

Best **Gay Bar**
★★ Bonham Exchange, *411 Bonham (p 167)*

Best **Brew Pub**
★ Blue Star Brewing Company, *1414 S. Alamo St. (p 166)*

Best **Martinis**
★ Swig, *111 W. Crockett St. (p 167)*

Best San Antonio **Art Stop**
★★ La Villita Historic Arts Village, *401 La Villita (p 166)*

Best **Trendy Bar Scene**
★ Vbar, *150 E. Houston St. (p 167)*

Best **Dixieland this Side of New Orleans**
★ The Landing, *123 Losoya St. (p 169)*

Best Place to **Two-Step**
★ Cowboys Dancehall, *3030 NE Loop 410 (p 168)*

Best **Performing Arts Venue**
★ The Majestic, *224 E. Houston St. (p 170)*

Best **Salsa Spot**
★★ Azuca Nuevo Latino Restaurant & Bar, *713 South Alamo St. (p 152)*

Best-Kept **Secret Bar**
★ Havana Hotel Bar, *1015 Navarro St. (p 167)*

The Majestic Theatre is San Antonio's top performing arts venue.

Nightlife and A&E A to Z

Travel Tip

San Antonio hasn't yet established an ordinance banning smoking in bars, so if you can't stand the smoke, you may want to get out of the nightclubs. Have no fear, though—many places offer outdoor patio areas where you can breathe fresh air when smoke gets in your eyes. Smoking is generally not allowed in most local theaters and sports arenas.

Art & Exhibit Spaces

★★ Blue Star Arts Complex SOUTHTOWN   This little enclave at the tail end of Southtown is a clever adaptation of historic warehouse buildings into an arts-oriented, mixed-use space with loft/studio apartments, art galleries, retail spaces, performance venues, artists' work spaces, and design studios. *1400 S. Alamo St.* ☎ *210/227-6960. www.bluestarartscomplex. com. Bus: 51, 54 & 251. Streetcar: Blue line.*

★★ La Villita Historic Arts Village DOWNTOWN   This little village of art galleries on the edge of the River Walk is considered San Antonio's first neighborhood, with some buildings dating back more than 200 years. Today, it's a vibrant arts community, home to galleries, shops, artisans at work, the fabulous little Arneson River Theatre, the Little Church (built in 1879), and nice restaurants like The Fig Tree (see p 154). *1 hr. 401 Villita St. (from the River Walk enter at the Arneson River Theatre). La Villita is located near the corner of S. Alamo and Nueva sts.).* ☎ *210/207-8610. www. lavillita.com. Daily 10am–6pm. Streetcar: Red & Blue lines to LaVillita. See p 107,* **7**.

★ Southwest School of Art & Craft DOWNTOWN   San Antonio's lovely downtown school and art exhibition space on the grounds of an old convent. *300 Augusta St.* ☎ *210/ 224-1848. www.swschool.org. Free admission. Streetcar: Blue line.*

Bars, Lounges & Cigar Bars

★ Blue Star Brewing Co. SOUTHTOWN   This brewpub boasts hand-crafted lagers (microbrews), their own original natural soft drinks, art, live music, poetry nights, theology discussions, and indoor and outdoor dining for breakfast, lunch, and dinner. It's a good (often crowded) place to end up on the first Friday night of each month during the Southtown ArtWalk. The Blue Star Arts Complex, in which this is housed, features an interesting mix of art galleries, studios, and retail spaces. *1414 S. Alamo St.* ☎ *210/212-5506. www.bluestarbrewing.com. Bus: 51, 54 & 251. Streetcar: Blue line.*

The Swig is famous for its signature martinis.

★★ **Bonham Exchange** DOWNTOWN   For 118 years, the Bonham Exchange building has stood in this central downtown spot behind the Alamo, and for almost 30 years, it has been home to a hot, flashy gay/lesbian/bi/straight nightclub. Though this three-tier, three-stage, five-bar high-tech club is a hot DJ dance spot, big-name entertainers like Tina Turner (1939–), P. Diddy (1969–), Prince (1958–), and Patrick Swayze (1952–2009) have all played (or at least danced) here. *411 Bonham.* ☎ *210/271-3811. www.bonham exchange.net. No cover before 10pm; after 10pm cover $5 Fri & Sat, $3 Sun. Bus: 22. Streetcar: Red line.*

★ **Hotel Havana Bar** DOWNTOWN/RIVER WALK   Most people don't know about this quiet little bar, and I've selfishly been okay with that, except San Antonio's best-kept secret is too delicious not to divulge. Hidden in the basement of the dreamy Hotel Havana on a part of the River Walk few ever find is a dark hideaway—terrific, tony, and clandestine. Our man in Havana won't stamp your passport, but the place will transport you to the Cuba of myth and memory, with mean *mojitos* and a subtle furtive vibe. The bar is a no-smoking zone. *1015 Navarro St.* ☎ *210/222-2008. www. havanasanantonio.com. Bus: 3, 4, 5, 8, 90 & 91.*

★ **Swig Martini Bar** DOWNTOWN   Retro-chic, trendy, and ultra-urban cool, this little cigar and martini bar overlooking the River Walk (at street level) is a great place for live jazz and Swig's tasty signature chocolate martinis. Single-barrel bourbon, single-malt scotch, and a wide selection of beer and wines make for some mean mixology—but martinis are their signature drink. This Swig was so popular it started a nationwide chain. *111 W. Crockett St.* ☎ *210/476-0005.*

The Bijou Cinema Bistro is a locally owned art-house theater.

www.swigmartini.com. No cover. Bus: 7, 301 & 304. Streetcar: Yellow line.

★ **Vbar** DOWNTOWN   Swank, sophisticated, trendy, and grown-up-friendly, this sleek and snazzy hotel bar (part of the Hotel Valencia) overlooking the River Walk hits all the right notes. Don't miss Martini Mondays and the crowded DJ-driven dance floor on the weekends. *150 E. Houston St.* ☎ *210/227-9700. www. hotelvalencia-riverwalk.com/dining/vbar.php. Bus: 301. Streetcar: Yellow line.*

Cinemas

★ **Bijou Cinema Bistro** CROSSROADS   San Antonio's only real art house theater, this locally owned cinema features not only a full food and drink menu with an attentive wait staff, but also a hallway gallery featuring the work of local artists. I like it because they show hard-to-find films (like this year's Oscar-nominated shorts), art-house fare, and mainstream movies. With seven screens, decent food, and a full bar, this theater makes going to the movies fun again. *4522 Fredericksburg Rd.* ☎ *210/734-4552. www. santikos.com/bijouex.php. General admission $9; seniors, military & matinees $7; children 11 & under not admitted. Bus: 91, 92 & 292.*

The Best of San Antonio

Dance Clubs & Texas Dance Halls

★ Cowboys Dancehall NORTHEAST This is where locals go to "kikker dance"—do the two step, Cotton-Eyed Joe, Schottische, and line dancing—with a little hip-hop thrown in just for fun. With headliner country stars most weekends, a fiddle-wielding house band, an indoor rodeo arena with bull riding events, free dance lessons, and DJs spinning country, this enormous dancehall is always teeming with rednecks, urban cowboys, and hipsters having good clean Texas fun. *3030 NE Loop 410 (at I-35).* ☎ *210/646-9378. www.cowboysdancehall.com. Cover free–$20. Bus: 505.*

★ Howl at the Moon DOWNTOWN Rock-'n-roll dueling piano players take center stage at this smoking (yes, cigarette-smoke-filled) hot spot where even the staff gets in on the show. Everybody dances and sings off-key while bartenders keep busy pouring drinks. Public humiliation and off-color jokes are part of the act, so don't stand too close to the stage unless you don't mind if the laugh's on you. *111 W Crockett St.* ☎ *210/212-4770. www.howlatthemoon.com. Cover $5 weeknights, $10 weekends. Bus: 2, 3, 4, 209, & 296. Streetcar: Yellow line.*

★ Tabu Lounge DOWNTOWN The popular Club Rive is gone, and the loud young Tabu has taken its place—expect a high-energy dance club with go-go dancers, hookahs, and a cavernous dance floor. They tout a strict dress code (no jeans, guys), but I looked around and couldn't tell. Cover charge goes up to $10 after 11pm. *245 E Commerce St.* ☎ *210/222-4700. www.tabuloungesa.com. Cover $5–$10. Bus: 17, 21, 22, 24 & 25. Streetcar: Yellow line.*

Ice Houses

★★★ Sanchez Ice House No. 1 & No. 2 CENTRAL Ice houses are an old San Antonio tradition that in recent years seems to sadly be going the way of *The Last Picture Show*. Once, these little family-friendly beer joints seemed to sit at every San Antonio corner, often housed in abandoned filling stations. These sweet little dives were often owned by Mexican American families, and here you could always find the coldest beer in town along with little snacks, like homemade tamales and tacos. One of the most authentic traditional ice houses left in San Antonio is Sanchez Ice House No. 2, located in the shadow of Interstate 35, with cheap beer and tamales. Tejano music floats in the air while

Two-stepping at Cowboys Dancehall.

kids run around the tables with cans of Big Red. *No. 1: 819 S. San Saba (at El Paso St.).* ☎ *210/223-0588. Bus: 68. No. 2: 701 Seguin St. (at Roper St.).* ☎ *210/270-7600. Bus: 21.*

Live Music/Restaurant Venues

★ **The Landing** DOWNTOWN/ RIVER WALK Founded in 1963, this is San Antonio's premier address for Dixieland and traditional jazz on the River Walk at the Hyatt (see p 160). Dixiland jazz bands perform Thurs– Sat, beginning at 8pm; Small World performs outside on Sundays, and music is also performed all other evenings on the riverside patio from 3–9pm. *123 Losoya St.* ☎ *210/223-7266. Mon–Wed 4:30–9pm; Fri & Sat 4:30pm–12:30am; Sat 11am– 1am; Sun 1–9pm (patio only). www. landing.com. Bus: 310. Streetcar: Red line.*

Orchestras

★ **San Antonio Symphony** DOWNTOWN Founded in 1939, the San Antonio Symphony is still an integral part of the arts community here. The symphony's ever-lovely home is the Majestic Theatre (see p 170), just a few blocks from the symphony's Travis Street offices. *130 E. Travis St. (box office).* ☎ *210/ 554-1010. www.sasymphony.org. Classical tickets $12–$92, pops tickets $12–$89. Bus: 77 & 277.*

Tango

★ **Olmos Bharmacy** OLMOS PARK By day a beloved old-fashioned soda fountain, by night a hot club with good nosh fare, great drinks, fab music, and even Argentinean Tango Milonga Wednesdays. This is one of my favorite late-night places to take friends. *3092 McCullough Ave.* ☎ *210/822-1188. www.olmosbharmacy.com. No cover. Bus: 5 & 509.*

The Guadalupe celebrates the cultural arts of Chicano, Latino, and Native American people.

★ **Pavil** STONE OAK Think a French brasserie is an odd place to take tango lessons? Well, maybe yes, maybe no. Beginning and intermediate classes are available for $15; private lessons, $25. *1818 N. Loop 1604 W.* ☎ *210/479-5000. www.brasseriepavil.com. No cover to enter. No city bus service.*

Theaters & Concert Venues

★ **Guadalupe Cultural Arts Center** TOBIN HILL Founded in 1980 as a nonprofit arts center located in the hip heart of San Antonio's west side, "The Guadalupe" celebrates the vibrant cultures of Chicano, Latino, and Native American people with its programming focusing on dance; literature; media arts; theater arts; visual arts; and Chicano, Tejano, and Latin American music. *1300 Guadalupe St.* ☎ *210/271-3151. www.guadalupeculturalarts.org. Tickets free–$10. Bus: 66 & 68 to Guadalupe & Brazos sts.*

★ **Josephine Theatre** TOBIN HILL This hip little non-profit community theater in a popular old neighborhood not far from downtown seats 275 and showcases an array of live talent and special performances, from Elvis-impersonator shows, to lecture-series events, to plays and live musical acts. *339 W. Josephine St.* ☎ *210/734-4646. www.josephinetheatre.org. Tickets start at $20 adults, $18 seniors & military, $12 students, $8 children 12 & under. Bus: 20 to Josephine & N. St Marys sts.*

★ **The Majestic Theatre & Charlie McCombs Empire Theatre** DOWNTOWN   Stroll past the box office or catch a show at one of these two magnificent city-owned theaters listed on the National Register of Historical Places. With touring concerts, ballet, and Broadway productions, and splendid San Antonio Symphony concerts, the glamorous Majestic, built as a movie house in 1929, is the main attraction. Elaborate balconies, tile roofs, arches, columns, statues, and a bell tower create a mystical village built into the ornate auditorium walls. The adjacent Empire Theatre, now owned by the City of San Antonio, was constructed in 1913 on the site of an 1879 opera house. Meticulously restored, this gilded theater is a bit smaller than the Majestic and offers mostly children's theater performances, music competitions, and receptions. The back of the two theater stages and a below-ground walkway connect the buildings—a secret many locals don't know. Cross the street and pass through the chandelier-lit lobby of the historic (and possibly haunted) **Sheraton Gunter Hotel,** too (see

p 111). *Majestic Theatre, 224 E. Houston St.; Empire Theatre, 226 N. St Marys St.* ☎ *210/226-3333 (box office) or 210/226-5700 (administration). www.majesticempire.com. $27–$150. Streetcar: Red line to corner of Houston & Navarro sts.*

★ **Sunset Station** ST. PAUL SQUARE   Historic Sunset Station is an arts, entertainment, and shopping destination that sprung up on the site of the Southern Pacific Depot built in 1902, snugly situated in the historic St. Paul Square district downtown. Close to both the **San Antonio Henry B. Gonzalez Convention Center** and the **Alamodome** sports and special events arena, Sunset Station is a 10-acre (4-hectare) entertainment facility featuring a restored 1884 church building, a three-story historic hotel and apartment building, and a large outdoor pavilion. Sunset Station's depot is now a stunning National Landmark with vaulted ceilings, stained glass windows, and a majestic staircase. Amtrak still runs through this area, but the big draw here is the number of popular restaurants like **Ruth's Chris Steak House** (☎ 210/227-8847) and the locally-owned Tex-Mex cafe **Aldaco's** (see p 152), along with little live-performance venues like the nearby **Cameo Theatre** (☎ 210/212-5454). *1174 E. Commerce St.* ☎ *210/222-9481. www. sunset-station.com. Streetcar: Yellow line to Hoefgen Ave. & SP Depot.* ●

A Crabtini at Sunset Station's Ruth's Chris Steakhouse.

Texas Hill Country

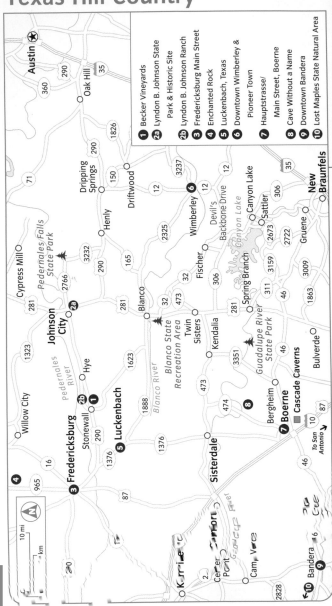

1 Becker Vineyards
2a Lyndon B. Johnson State Park & Historic Site
2b Lyndon B. Johnson Ranch
3 Fredericksburg Main Street
4 Enchanted Rock
5 Luckenbach, Texas
6 Downtown Wimberley & Pioneer Town
7 Hauptstrasse/ Main Street, Boerne
8 Cave Without a Name
9 Downtown Bandera
10 Lost Maples State Natural Area

Austin

Oak Hill

Dripping Springs

Driftwood

Henly

Wimberley

Canyon Lake

Sattler

New Braunfels

Fischer

Spring Branch

Gruene

Cypress Mill

Pedernales Falls State Park

Blanco

Blanco State Recreation Area

Twin Sisters

Kendalia

Guadalupe River State Park

Bulverde

Johnson City

Hye

Luckenbach

Willow City

Stonewall

Fredericksburg

Bergheim

Boerne

Cascade Caverns

Sisterdale

To San Antonio

Kerrville

Comfort

Camp Verde

Bandera

Pedernales River

Blanco River

Devil's Backbone Drive

Canyon Lake

290 · 360 · 35 · 1826 · 290 · 71 · 150 · 3237 · 12 · 12 · 306 · 35 · 12 · 2325 · 32 · 306 · 2673 · 2722 · 165 · 473 · 281 · 311 · 3159 · 46 · 3009 · 1863 · 281 · 2766 · 3232 · 281 · 1323 · 1623 · 473 · 3351 · 46 · 474 · 1888 · 1376 · 16 · 965 · 87 · 1376 · 2 · 6 · 2828 · 10 · 87

10 mi
km

Previous page: A shoe-shine stand in Wimberley's Pioneer Town.

Scattered like seeds of native wildflowers, beguiling little hamlets dot the scenic Texas Hill Country region. Arguably the most beautiful part of the state, the Hill Country offers the perfect excuse for a road trip. Each spring, oceans of bluebonnets, fiery bursts of red Indian paintbrush, and myriad other colorful wildflowers sweep across steep hills of limestone, cypress, and cedar. Rivers, lakes, parks, and campgrounds abound, along with charming white limestone towns that were originally old German settlements. For farmers' markets, wineries, lavender farms, cowboy beer joints, dude ranches, bed & breakfast inns, little shops—look to the hills. There is so much to see here that you'll be tempted to linger for hours at most stops. From Austin take Highway 290W; from San Antonio take Highway 281N to Highway 290W, or take Interstate 10 North.

❶ ★★ Becker Vineyards. This family-owned vineyard, winery, tasting room, shop, restaurant, bed & breakfast retreat, and lavender farm is a not-to-be-missed stop along Highway 290 in Stonewall, on the way to Fredericksburg from Austin and San Antonio. ⏱ *1 hr. 464 Becker Farms Rd., Stonewall (off of Hwy. 290-W).* ☎ *830/644-2681. www.beckervineyards.com. Mon–Thurs 10am–5pm, Fri & Sat 10am–6pm, Sun noon–6pm.*

❷ ★★ kids Lyndon B. Johnson State Park & Historic Site and the LBJ Ranch. Tour the former U.S. president's boyhood home in Johnson City, and his ranch, home ("The Texas White House"), reconstructed birthplace, and his burial site in nearby Stonewall, and explore the picturesque area where he lived along the Pedernales River. The area offers picnic and RV campsites nearby. The ranch features exhibits, films, and interesting stories of LBJ's life. Self-guided driving tours of the ranch are offered, and bus tours have recently been discontinued. While LBJ's actual boyhood home is nice, the LBJ Ranch offers much more to see. ⏱ *2 hr.* ☎ *830/868-7128 (LBJ Ranch, National Park Service). www.tpwd.state.tx.us/park/lbj or www.nps.gov/lyjo. Ranch entrance gate open 9am–4:30pm; exit gate closes at 4:30pm. No more permits are given after 4:15pm. Free driving permits for the LBJ Ranch; Texas White House indoor tours are given every 15 minutes beginning at 10am. The last tour is held at 4:45pm. Texas White House Tour admission is $2 adults, free for children 17 & under.*

❸ ★★ Fredericksburg Main Street. The Hill Country's most popular little German settlement, founded in 1846, retains a strong German influence, evident in the architecture, attitude, beer, food, music, and even speech (kids call their grandparents *Oma* and *Opa*). The city's wide Main Street is lined with antiques and collectibles shops, German bakeries and cafes, and sweet home-spun museums. Bed & breakfast and "Sunday Haus" guest lodgings, cabins, and campgrounds abound. People hold beer steins in *biergartens* or shop in the "Marketplaz" area. Most downtown shops are located between the fabulous and newly-redone **National Museum of the Pacific War** (340 E. Main St.; ☎ 830/997-8600)—which is well worth a visit—and the **Pioneer Museum/Vereins Kirche** (309 W. Main St.; ☎ 830/990-8441). Stay at **The Austin Street Retreat** (☎ 866/427-8374). Highway 290-W

Stores along Main Street in downtown Fredericksburg.

becomes Main Street as you enter Fredericksburg. 🕐 *3 hr. Visitor Information Center, 302 E. Austin St., Fredericksburg. ☎ 888/997-3600 or 830/997-6523. www.fredericksburg-texas.com. Visitors center Mon–Fri 8:30am–5pm, Sat 9am–noon & 1–5pm, Sun noon–4pm.*

The chapel at Trois Estate, near Enchanted Rock.

④ ★★ kids Enchanted Rock.
This pink granite "batholith" (underground rock formation uncovered by natural erosion) encompasses a scenic State Natural Area north of Fredericksburg and offers a not-to-be-missed adventure and a moderately easy climb to the top. A giant pink granite dome rising 425 feet (130m) above ground, the rock covers 640 acres (259 hectares) and is one of the largest batholiths in the U.S. Legends of ghost fires seen at the summit began with Tonkawa Indians who heard sounds of creaking and groaning coming from the rock (it expands and contracts as it heats up by day and cools at night). Legend tells of a Spanish conquistador who escaped from the Tonkawas by losing himself in the rock only to return reborn as one of their own. While in the area, check out the nearby **Trois Estate** (300 Trois Lane; ☎ 830/685-3415), an artisans' village with a restaurant, B&B, spa, chapel, and arresting views of Enchanted Rock. Best of all, the Trois Estate has a free **Cap Gun Museum** with what the *Guinness World Records* calls the largest collection of cap guns and vintage cap-gun memorabilia in the world. On weekends, the park often reaches capacity (in terms of parking) and frequently closes

(sometimes as early as 11am). Reopening usually occurs at 5pm. Call ahead or have alternate plans if you arrive and find the park closed. ⏱ *1½ hr. 16710 Ranch Rd. 965, Fredericksburg (7 miles/11km north of downtown Fredericksburg).* ☎ *830/685-3636. www.tpwd.state. tx.us. Day-use entrance fees $6 adults; check website for overnight camping fees. Open hours vary.*

❺ ★★★ Luckenbach, Texas. In the late '70s, Texas country music legend Jerry Jeff Walker (1942–), who wrote "Mr. Bojangles," recorded a hit album in this tiny old ghost town, and then country superstar Willie Nelson (1933–) put this hill country hamlet (population 3) on the map with the platinum hit single "Luckenbach, Texas (Back to the Basics of Love)." Almost 30 years later, country star Kenny Chesney (1968–) and rapper Kid Rock (1971–) covered the song, bringing a new wave of fame to this tiny ghost town. Today, folks still hang out at the beer joint/post office/general store and dancehall along South Grape Creek in the shade of old oak trees. Someone's always playing guitar, singing,

and telling stories around campfires, picnic tables, or by the old wood stove in the bar. They say, "Everybody's Somebody in Luckenbach," and there's something magical about finding a place locked in time like this. As a writer once said "Luckenbach is like Brigadoon: You're almost afraid to go back because it might not be there again." Take Highway 290-W to R.R. 1376 and turn right at Luckenbach Loop. ⏱ *1 hr. 412 Luckenbach Town Loop, Fredericksburg.* ☎ *888/311-8990 or 830/997-3224. www.luckenbachtexas.com. 9am–midnight.*

❻ ★ kids Downtown Wimberley & Pioneer Town. North of San Marcos on the banks of the Blanco River and Cypress Creek, Wimberley is the perfect Sunday drive destination. An artisans' village with great shops, the town is packed on the first Saturday of each month during **Market Days.** Bed & breakfasts, dude ranches, wineries, glass-blower and furniture-maker studios, an outdoor movie theater, and even an olive grove ranch—not to mention its annual **Pie Social**—are all popular attractions. Be sure

Luckenbach's post office and general store.

Lavender Fields Forever

You may equate Texas with cattle trails, but in the Hill Country, folks like to gush about the lovely lavender trail that cuts a pretty path through these hills. Not so long ago, local wine makers and farmers realized the Texas soil is much like that of the French countryside in Provence and that lavender, like grapes, grows well in the Hill Country. Today, lavender fields at farms and Texas wineries are so popular that visitors come to see and smell the pretty plants, buy fragrant soaps and other lavender products, and enjoy lavender-inspired dinners and parties and sip fine Texas wines. Each spring, local growers host a Lavender Trail festival, with special weekend events, activities, and lavender farm-to-table dinners. Texas trails never smelled so sweet!

to check out **Wimberley's Pioneer Town,** inspired by California's Knott's Berry Farm, an enchanting—and surprisingly not so kitschy—Old West village, with cabins, campsites, and lodges on the grounds of the 7A Ranch, near the banks of the Blanco River (333 Wayside Dr. ☎ 512/847-2517). The town has a

Many artisans craft and sell their work in the village of Wimberley.

barber shop, general store, saloon, ice cream parlor, log cabins, a church, opera house, and more. There's even the Remington Art Museum, featuring original bronze sculptures and art prints by famed western artist Frederick Remington. 🕐 *1 hr.* Wimberley Convention & Visitor's Bureau, 14100 R.R. 12. (at River Rd.). ☎ 512/847-2201. www. wimberley.org.

❼ ★ **Hauptstrasse/Main Street, Boerne.** Hauptstrasse is the German name for Boerne's Main Street. The little 1800s German settlement of Boerne (pronounced "Bernie") is best known for its art galleries, antique shops, bed & breakfasts, restaurants, and wine bars. Boerne is a popular day trip for locals and is a bedroom community of San Antonio, populated mostly by well-heeled ranchers and business people. On the weekend closest to Valentine's Day, Boerne hosts the big, loud, and popular Valentine's Day Massacre Motorcycle Rally. The Hauptstrasse really gets hopping during Second Saturdays Art & Wine events in galleries, shops, and bars. Market Days are also held on the second weekend of each month at the Gazebo in Main Square, with vendor booths offering antiques, arts and crafts, clothing, pottery, jewelry, and gourmet food products. 🕐 1½ hr. Boerne Convention & Visitor's Bureau, 1407 S. Main St., Boerne. ☎ 888/842-8080 or 830/249-7277; Market Days info ☎ 830/249-5530. www.visitboerne. org. Many shops closed Mon.

❽ kids Cave Without a Name. A child once said this cave outside of Boerne was too pretty to have a name, and so that's how it got this one. Discovered in the early 20th century and commercialized in 1939, this National Natural Landmark is a living cavern home to spectacular formations of stalactites, stalagmites, slender "soda straws," cave drapery, and rim stone dams. Enter six major "rooms" by way of a steep staircase, all a mild 66°F (19°C) year-round. Significant exploration of the privately owned cave didn't occur until the 1970s. Since then, it's been one of Texas's best-kept secrets, a little off the beaten path but worth the drive 11 miles (18km) northeast of Boerne. 🕐 1½ hr. (tours last 1 hr.). 325 Kreutzberg Rd., Boerne (off FM 474). ☎ 888/839-2283 or 830/537-4212. www.cavewithoutaname.com. Late May to early Sept daily 9am–6pm, early Sept to late May daily 10am–5pm. $14 adults, $12 military & seniors w/ID, $7 children 6–12, free for children 5 & under; $12 adults in groups of 12 or more. Closed Thanksgiving & Christmas Day.

❾ Downtown Bandera. Called the "Cowboy Capital of the World," Bandera is a small town known for its dude ranches and Wild West cowboy culture. Don't blink or you'll miss the kitschy frontier-style downtown with its down-home diners and "honky-tonk" saloons. The best thing about Bandera is its beautiful rolling hill country and family-friendly dude ranches, like **Rancho Cortez** (872 Hay Holler Rd., Bandera; ☎ **866/797-9339** or 830/796-9339)

A shot of the Boerne Gazebo.

bordering the **Hill Country State Natural Area** (see p 147, ❽) at the edge of this little cowboy town. 🕐 30 min. Bandera Convention & Visitor's Bureau, 1206 Hackberry St., Bandera. ☎ 800/364-3833. www. banderacowboycapital.com.

❿ ★★★ Lost Maples State Natural Area. Locals make annual pilgrimages to see the best display of colorful fall foliage to be found in the Lone Star State. Covering 2,174 scenic acres (880 hectares) north of Vanderpool on the Sabinal River, the area attracts more than 200,000 visitors each year and is a popular place for Sunday drives, hiking, biking, and camping under magnificent big-tooth maple trees. The stunning area can be jam-packed and traffic-filled in the fall (go on weekdays if you can), but nobody seems to mind—the colors are worth the hassle in order to see autumn in its full glory. Fall colors usually peak in early November, and reservations are necessary that time of year for overnight stays. 🕐 1½ hr. 37221 FM 187, Vanderpool. ☎ 830/966-3413 (info) or 512/389-8900 (reservations). www.tpwd.state.tx.us. Oct–Nov $6 adults per day, Dec–Sept $5 adults per day; see website for camping fees.

Texas Gulf Coast Beaches

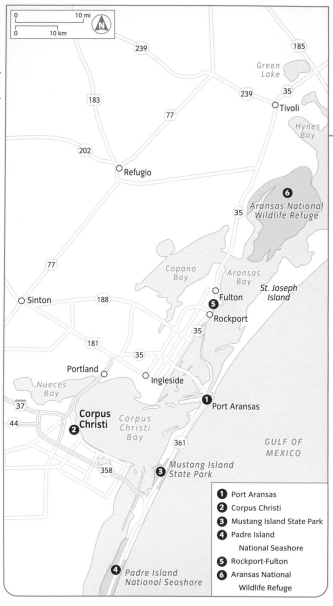

1. Port Aransas
2. Corpus Christi
3. Mustang Island State Park
4. Padre Island National Seashore
5. Rockport-Fulton
6. Aransas National Wildlife Refuge

You may be surprised to learn that both Austin and San Antonio are situated relatively close to the Texas Gulf Coast. It's only about a 2-hour drive to the nearest beach from San Antonio, and just over 3 hours from Austin. Texas beaches are not like most others—for starters, you can drive on them. The shoreline is mostly undeveloped—home to seaweed, sand dunes, and tall breeze-blown grasses. Sweet little weather-worn beach towns with great bird watching and fishing will make you fall in love with the unspoiled Texas coast. Campsites, condos, hotels, beach bars, seashell shops, and fresh Gulf seafood—it's all right there. From San Antonio, take Hwy 37. From Austin, take Hwy 35 to Hwy 37.

1 ★★★ **Port Aransas.** This is the best little beach town and one of the closest Texas Gulf Coast vacation spots to San Antonio or Austin. Port Aransas is the only established town on Mustang Island and inhabits 8 miles (13km) of this 18-mile-long (29km) barrier island. Mustang Island is located north of Padre Island, the longest barrier island in the world, and south of San Jose Island (also known as St. Joseph Island), renowned for its fabulous bird watching spots and shelling. Surrounding waters include the Corpus Christi Bay, Gulf of Mexico, Lydia Ann Ship Channel, and Corpus Christi Ship Channel. If you're making a day trip or a weekend getaway, and you want a beachy, wind-blown place where locals live barefoot and in their bathing suits almost year-round, vacationers ride beach buggies and bikes, and homes and hotels sit high on stilts, this is the place for you. With great deep-sea and bay fishing, dolphin tours, and even a casino boat cruise, Port Aransas has all the makings for a great weekend on the water. To get to the island, you must drive through Aransas Pass and take a short drive-on ferry onto Mustang Island. As you exit the ferry, you'll find yourself near the heart of Port Aransas, a tiny village with a residential population of about 3,775. Not far from "Port A" (as locals call it) is the Padre Island National Seashore. 🕐 *2 hr. Port Aransas Main Visitor's Center, 403 W. Cotter Ave., Port Aransas.* ☎ *800/45-COAST (800/452-6278) or 361/749-5919. www.portaransas.org.*

Playing on the beach of Port Aransas.

The USS Lexington aircraft carrier museum at Corpus Christi.

2 ★ kids Corpus Christi. Houston and Galveston are popular cities on the eastern part of the Texas Gulf Coast, but "Corpus" (as Texans often call it, for short) is a good-sized town not far from San Antonio (about a 2-hour drive) and offers nice hotels, good restaurants, and fabulous area attractions like the **Texas State Aquarium** (2710 N. Shoreline Blvd.; ☎ 888/477-4853 or 361/881-1200); the **USS Lexington** (2914 N. Shoreline Blvd.; ☎ 800/523-9539 or 361/888-4873), a real WWII aircraft carrier turned museum; and my favorite, the replica ships of Christopher Columbus's famous fleet that you can tour as part of the **Corpus Christi Museum of Science & History** (1900 N. Chaparral St.; ☎ 361/826-4667). Home to a small university and a U.S. naval air station, this coastal city is a pleasant place to visit if you prefer a conventional chain hotel to a little beachy fishing village. ⏱ *2 hr. Corpus Christi Visitor Information Center, 1823 N. Chaparral St. ☎ 800/766-2322. Open Tues-Sat 9am–5pm. www.visitcorpus christitx.org.*

3 Mustang Island State Park. This 3,954-acre (1,600-hectare) state park is home to about 5 miles (8km) of beach on the Gulf of Mexico in Nueces County, just south of Port Aransas. Mustang Island is a coastal barrier island with a unique and complex ecosystem, dependent upon its numerous sand dunes, some of which reach as much as 35 feet (11m) in height (15–20 ft./4.6–6.1m is average). Activities here include swimming, fishing, kayaking, camping, hiking, mountain biking, bird watching, and sunbathing. From downtown Port Aransas, take Alister Street/Highway 361 south to Mustang Island State Park. ⏱ *1 hr. 17047 State Hwy. 361, Port Aransas. ☎ 361/749-4573. Open daily year-round, 8am–10pm. www.tpwd.state.tx.us.*

4 ★ Padre Island National Seashore. With 70 miles (113km) of sandy beaches, Padre Island National Seashore on North Padre Island protects the longest undeveloped stretch of barrier island in the world. Not to be confused with South Padre Island, about 3 hours south of this park (via Highway 77), this is a quiet, undeveloped beach area and state park. It may seem odd, but here beaches are Texas public highways, so only street-legal and licensed vehicles may be driven in the park. There are sections marked by barriers near Malaquite Beach where vehicles are not permitted. All-terrain vehicles (ATVs), go-carts, golf carts, and dune buggies are prohibited, though they are allowed on non-state park beaches closer to downtown Port Aransas. Jet skis, air boats, and kite surfing are also prohibited here. Mainly, it's just a big beach where families enjoy cookouts, campfires, and water fun. From Port Aransas, take Alistair Street/Highway 361 for 18 miles (29km), turn left onto Park Road 22, and travel 3 miles (4.8km) to the Park Headquarters on the right. ⏱ *1 hr. Park Headquarters, 20301 Park Rd. 22.* ☎ *361/949-8068. www.nps.gov/pais. Vehicle entry fee (good for 7 days) $10, walking/bicycle entry fee (good for one-time entrance only) $5; for camping fees, access passes & discounted senior passes, see www.nps.gov.*

❺ ★ kids Rockport-Fulton. These twin-sister towns (separated only by a sign) are more fishing

Horseback riding at Padre Island National Seashore.

villages than beach destinations, though Rockport does boast a Blue Wave Certified beach (an environmental certification for America's cleanest beaches) with a playground for kids. Still, most consider Port Aransas beaches to be better and go to Rockport for food and fishing. Rockport's sleepy old-fashioned Main Street strip is lined with colorful weather-worn stores and wind-blown trees shaped like big haunting Bonsai trees, and Fulton is home to interesting sites like the historic **Fulton Mansion** (317 S.

A seashell shop in Rockport.

Fulton Beach Rd.; ☎ 361/729-0386) and great little fresh gulf seafood restaurants such as **The Boiling Pot** (201 South Fulton Beach Rd. ☎ 361/729-6972), **Charlotte Plummer's Seafare Restaurant** (202 N Fulton Beach Rd. ☎ 361/729-1185) and **Latitude 28° 02'** (104 N. Austin St. ☎ 361/727-9009). These towns are where San Antonio– and Austin-area fishermen may be found most weekends. For everyone else, enjoy cute art galleries, seashell shops, clothing stores, good eats, fabulous bird watching, and wildlife preserve areas. 🕐 *1 hr. Rockport-Fulton Chamber of Commerce, 404 Broadway St., Rockport.* ☎ *800/242-0071 or 361/729-6445. www.rockport-fulton.org.*

❻ ★★ Aransas National Wildlife Refuge. This 70,504-acre (28,532-hectare) wildlife refuge is situated on the Blackjack Peninsula, known for its Blackjack oaks, Red Bay thickets, live oaks, grasslands, tidal marshlands, and long narrow ponds—the perfect place to see cranes, alligators, deer, and many other species of wildlife. It's most popular from November to March, when the world's only migrating flock of over 265 whooping cranes calls the Aransas Wildlife Refuge home. Located 20 miles (32km) from downtown Rockport-Fulton, the refuge is perhaps the only place in the U.S. to see these magnificent birds up close. Established in 1937 to protect the vanishing wildlife of coastal Texas, Aransas Wildlife Reserve is ever-changing, continuously being shaped by the waters and storms of the Gulf of Mexico. The refuge has a 16-mile (26km) paved tour road, a Wildlife Interpretive Center (open daily 8:30am–4:30pm), a 40-foot (12m) observation tower, several miles of walking trails, and a picnic area. Pets must be leashed, and daily registration is required of all visitors. Wear sturdy boots or closed-toe shoes, and watch your step, as poisonous snakes may be present. No public camping is allowed. From Rockport, take IH-35 north approximately 20 miles (32km). Turn right on FM 774, go approximately 9 miles (15km) to FM 2040. Turn right and follow FM 2040 for about 7 miles (11km) to the refuge entrance. 🕐 *2 hr. FM 2040 (at Austell).* ☎ *361/286-3559. www.fws.gov.*

Aransas National Wildlife Refuge is where visitors can see different species of wildlife such as the Whooping Crane.

Texas Border Towns

If you come to Texas, you'll want to bring a passport because Austin and San Antonio are just a few short hours' drive from the border of Mexico. Good eats, pretty cathedrals, sleepy central plazas, mariachi music, margaritas, and inexpensive shops are all big draws to border towns like Nuevo Laredo and Piedras Negras. Be sure to check U.S. Travel Advisories before you go, though, as there has been a rash of drug-traffic-related violence along the Mexican side of the Texas border (though generally not in places tourists tend to go). To play it safe but still get a taste of Old Mexico, visit the lively Texas frontier towns on the U.S. side of the border and enjoy all that the blend of the two cultures can bring.

Laredo, Texas is about 2½ hours (143 miles/230km) south of San Antonio and about 3½ hours (236 miles/380km) south of Austin, and here you'll find one of Texas's most vibrant border towns. Laredo is a progressive, busy city with good restaurants and hotels like the popular, affordable **Hotel La Posada** (1000 Zaragoza St.; ☎ 956/722-1701), which underwent a $14-million renovation not so long ago. The old plaza is encircled by shops and has that familiar border-town bargain quality, where everyone is bartering and the streets are dusty—you'll think you're in Mexico. But there are also nicer areas to shop for handmade wooden furniture, metal sculptures, patio furnishings, clothing, pottery, and local art—especially along San Bernardo Avenue. With margaritas, mariachi bands, tacos, and fresh markets, Laredo is a fiesta for the senses and always leaves me dreaming in Spanish.

Just across Laredo's international bridges over the Rio Grande river is **Nuevo Laredo,** a dusty little Mexican border town with great shopping, fun bars, good restaurants, liquor stores, Mexican music, bullfights (seasonal), and quiet little plazas. For lunch, try the clean well-lighted **Cadillac Bar** (Calle Matamoros 304, at Calle Victoria; ☎ 011/52-86 77-13-15-25), with its good food, great drinks, and cold air conditioning. Shop at **Marti's** (Calle Victoria 2923, at Calle Guerrero; ☎ 011/52-86 87-12-33-37) for quality Mexican home decor, jewelry, clothing, bags, and accessories. Visit **El Mercado,** the old marketplace, with its stalls of Mexican curios and souvenirs. You can drive or walk across the bridge—I recommend parking in the Hotel La Posada's covered parking garage ($8 for the day) in Laredo and then walking across the old International Bridge No. 1. You'll need a passport to go into Mexico, even if you're walking in for just an hour or two, and you'll also pay a small exit/entrance fee (less than $2). Safety has been a concern here at night, so don't wander the streets after dark.

Best of the **Golden Corridor**

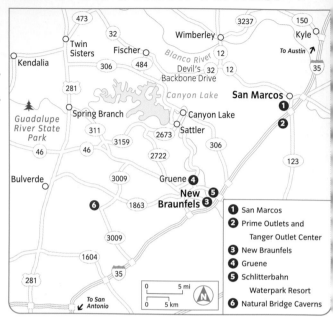

1. San Marcos
2. Prime Outlets and Tanger Outlet Center
3. New Braunfels
4. Gruene
5. Schlitterbahn Waterpark Resort
6. Natural Bridge Caverns

In the 1980s, the stretch of Interstate 35 between Austin and San Antonio was dubbed "The Golden Corridor." Since then, the area has lived up to its name—with commerce exploding along the way, linking more closely each year such booming little towns as Buda (pronounced "Byoo-dah") and Kyle, with its charming downtown. San Marcos is known as a fun college town and shopping Mecca, and New Braunfels is an old German settlement turned busy modern town known as a spot for outdoor fun on its two pretty Texas rivers. **Start on Interstate 35 S in Austin at Southpark Meadows, 9600 I-355, heading south.**

1 San Marcos. Home to Texas State University, this small town centered on an old downtown courthouse square is called "The Gateway to the Hill Country" and has a charming downtown area with great little bars like **Cheatham Street Warehouse** (119 Cheatham St.; ☎ 512/ 353-7777), where country music superstar George Strait (1952) got his start. The **San Marcos River** on the edge of campus offers a

refreshing place to float in an innertube or splash around and cool off on a hot summer day. San Marcos' **Wonder World** (1000 Prospect St., ☎ 512/392-3760) is a small, low-key amusement park featuring an ancient earthquake-made cave, high observation tower, and small petting zoo. ⏱ 1 hr. San Marcos Tourist Information Center, 617 IH 35 N., San Marcos. ☎ 512/393-5930. www. toursanmarcos.com.

Designer brands can be found at the expansive Tanger Outlet Center.

②★ Prime Outlets and Tanger Outlet Center. These two adjacent factory outlet malls comprise the third largest outlet shopping destination in the world and the largest in Texas. It looks like one big shopping center, except the Prime Outlet buildings have a Venetian theme that is attractive, if oddly out of place in Texas. Still, bargains are to be found at all the big-named chain outlets, and high-market designer brands like Lacoste, Coach, and Fendi have pricey little stores here, too. Scorching hot in the summer time and cold as can be in the bleak mid-winter, this outdoor mall is so big most people either drive their cars from one part to another or jump on the free trolleys that loop the malls. ⏱ *1 hr. 3939 IH-35S, San Marcos. Prime Outlets* ☎ *512/396-2200. Open Mon–Sat 10am–9pm; Sun 10am–7pm; closed Easter Sunday, Thanksgiving, and Christmas. www. primeoutlets.com. Tanger Outlet Center* ☎ *512/396-7446. Open Mon–Sat 9am–9pm, Sun 10am–7pm. View holidays hours online. www.tanger outlet.com.*

③ New Braunfels. This delightful German settlement along the Comal and Guadalupe rivers is booming with growth and now has a population of more than 50,000. The downtown encircles a central park and gazebo, while antiques shops, restaurants, bars, and coffee shops make this a pleasant stop. Be sure to visit **Naegelin's Bakery** (129 South Seguin Ave.; ☎ 830/625-5722), a New Braunfels tradition since 1868. If you visit in the fall, don't miss the huge **Wurstfest** celebration held late October/early November near **Landa Park** on the banks of the Comal River. Locals and visitors alike spend summer days floating in inner-tubes and rafts on the rivers, and raft and tube rentals are available at outposts along most roads near the Guadalupe and Comal rivers. ⏱ *1 hr. NB Highway Visitor's Center, 237 I-H35N., New Braunfels.* ☎ *830/625-7973. Open daily 9am–5pm. Closed Thanksgiving, Christmas Day, and New Year's Day. www.nbjcham.org.*

④★★★ Gruene. Gruene (pronounced "Green") is what Luckenbach (see p 175, ⑤) might look like now if it were located this close to Interstate 35. Once a quiet little ghost town on the banks of the Guadalupe River, today Gruene is home to lots of great restaurants, bars, shops, antiques, B&Bs, art galleries, general stores, and museums on the the edge of New Braunfels. In the shade of a water tower sits the **Gristmill** (1287 Gruene Rd.; ☎ 830/625-0684) restaurant and bar, with

A watercoaster ride at Schlitterbahn Waterpark Resort.

its great chicken-fried steaks and salads, housed in a huge, old, barn-like mill overlooking the river. Next door is the town's main attraction, **Gruene Hall** (1281 Gruene Rd.; ☎ 830/606-1281), the oldest continuously operating dancehall in Texas, appearing in numerous movies, including John Travolta's *Michael*. This is a real, old-time dancehall—it doesn't get any better (or more Texan) than this. Bungee jumping and raft trips are popular at the river just below Gruene, and "tubing" is a huge weekend tradition here all summer long. ⏱ *2 hr. 1601 Hunter Rd. (at Gruene Rd.), New Braunfels.* ☎ *830/629-5077. www. gruenetexas.com.*

⑤ ★★ kids Schlitterbahn Waterpark Resort. This monstrous water park in the town of New Braunfels is three water parks in one, with shuttles between them all. Like most theme parks, admission is pricey—but you can pack a picnic lunch, drinks, and snacks, and rent lockers to store everything while you're in the water. During November and December, Schlitterbahn is transformed into a "Hill Country Christmas" evening attraction park, with live entertainment, Dickens shows, sledding, an Alpine slide, holiday characters, food, and shopping, all under a canopy of 1.5 million glittering holiday lights. For 2-day admission prices and discounted afternoon admission (after 3pm) info, visit the website. ⏱ *3–4 hr. 381 E. Austin St., New Braunfels.* ☎ *830/625-2351. Park opens at 10am. Closes at 10pm late May–early Sept (when schools have summer breaks). www. schlitterbahn.com. 1-day general admission $40 adults; $32 children 11 & under, & seniors 55 & over.*

⑥ ★★★ kids Natural Bridge Caverns. The largest commercial caverns discovered in the state, featuring more than a mile of rooms and passages filled with stunning formations. *26495 Natural Bridge Caverns Rd.* ☎ *210/651-6101. Open daily 9am–4pm. Adults $18; children ages 3 to 11, $10. Closed Thanksgiving, Christmas Day, and New Year's Day. www.naturalbridgecaverns.com.* ●

The
Savvy Traveler

Before You Go

Government Tourist Offices

Austin Convention & Visitor's Bureau 301 Congress Ave. Suite 200, Austin, TX 78701; ☎ 800/926-ACVB (800/926-2282) or 512/474-5171.

Austin Visitor Center 209 E. 6th St., Austin, TX 78701; ☎ 866/GO-AUSTIN (866/462-8784) or 512/478-0098. www.austintexas.org.

San Antonio Convention & Visitor's Bureau 203 S. St Marys St. San Antonio, TX 78205; ☎ 800/447-3372 or 210/207-6700. www.visit sanantonio.com.

The Best Times to Go

Unless you're a sun worshiper, you may want to forget seeing San Antonio and Austin in summer—though that's when most visitors come to Texas. Triple-digit temperatures are the norm, the humidity is almost unbearably high, and restaurants and attractions are crowded. Still, San Antonio hotel rates are slightly lower then (because there are fewer conventioneers in town), and most popular outdoor attractions—such as SeaWorld, Six Flags Fiesta Texas, and Schlitterbahn—are open. Despite the sweltering heat, Austin is lovely, as rivers and the Highland Lakes offer soft Hill Country breezes and great opportunities for cool water sports. Summer is typically busy in Austin, too, and during legislative sessions (the first half of odd-numbered years) and during weekends with University of Texas's home games and graduation events, the town's lodgings can be pretty solidly booked.

Don't miss South Texas and the Hill Country in early spring when bluebonnets are in bloom. Each April, the popular Fiesta San Antonio festival ensures that hotel rooms are booked solid (and crowds, traffic, and parking are problematic), but there's not a better party in Texas—with the exception of Austin's fabulous SXSW Music Festival. Again, rooms are expensive and hard to book, and the city gets crowded, so book it all as far in advance as possible. December is a lovely time to visit San Antonio, when the River Walk drips with thousands of colored holiday lights and luminarias (candles in white paper bags filled with sand) line its pathways. And Austin loves its holidays, too, with the trail of lights and the huge holiday tree at Zilker Park.

The Weather

From mid-May through mid-October, expect regular high temperatures and often high humidity. Late fall and early spring are prime times to visit; the days are pleasantly warm, sunny, and mild. The prettiest time to visit is in late March or early April, when the heat hasn't yet hit and the wildflowers flood the nearby Hill Country and line Texas highways in a sea of glorious color. Temperate weather combined with the lively celebrations surrounding Christmas also make November and December good months to visit. Sometimes a "Blue Norther" (a blustery cold north wind) blows in, dropping daytime temperatures to between 35° and 45°F (2° and 7°C). January and February can be colder, but these months often see-saw between shirt-sleeve weather and heavy coat temperatures. Your best bet in Texas, though, is to pack for warmer weather than you'd expect, along with a back-up jacket just in case it turns cool.

Previous page: A cowboy riding horseback.

SAN ANTONIO/AUSTIN'S AVERAGE DAYTIME TEMPERATURE
& MONTHLY RAINFALL

	JAN	FEB	MAR	APR	MAY	JUNE
Avg. Temp. (°F)	51	55	62	70	76	82
Avg. Temp. (°C)	11	13	17	21	24	28
Rainfall (in.)	1.7	1.9	1.6	2.6	4.2	3.6

	JULY	AUG	SEPT	OCT	NOV	DEC
Avg. Temp. (°F)	85	85	80	71	60	53
Avg. Temp. (°C)	29	29	27	22	16	12
Rainfall (in.)	1.9	2.5	3.2	3.2	2.1	1.7

Festivals & Special Events

WINTER   A favorite Austin tradition is a visit to spin under the thousands of lights of the 165-foot (50m) **Zilker Park holiday tree** and a walk through the magnificent **Trail of Lights** (☎ 512/974-6700; www. ci.austin.tx.us/tol). The holiday lighting of Zilker's "tree" (a replica Austin moontower) is always a big event on the first Sunday in December, but the tree remains lit and activities happen underneath it nearly every night all month. The Trail of Lights, a mile-long (1.6km) display of life-sized holiday scenes, begins on the Second Sunday in December and runs through the last weekend before Christmas. A 5K run is also part of the fun. Austin also loves its big **Armadillo Christmas Bazaar** (☎ 512/447-1605; www.armadillo bazaar.com) art, craft, and gift show, held 2 weeks before Christmas at the Austin Music Hall. Come and revel in Tex-Mex food, live music, and a full bar at this high-quality shopping extravaganza.

In San Antonio, winter means lights—lots of them! Each year, the season begins with a giant **Holiday River Parade and Lighting Ceremony** on the River Walk, where trees and bridges along the San Antonio River are illuminated by more than 122,000 holiday lights.

And during the **Fiesta de las Luminarias,** starting at dusk on the first weekend in December, more than 2,500 sand-weighted white paper bags, each holding a single candle, line the banks of the river. There is no city in the U.S. quite as pretty as San Antonio at the River Walk during the holidays. Then, in mid-January, the San Antonio River is drained for cleaning and maintenance, making for great muddy fun during the **Michelob ULTRA River Walk Mud Festival.** Local royalty are elected to reign over such events as a Mud Parade and the Mud Pie Ball (for info on all these events, call ☎ 210/227-4262 or visit www.thesan antonioriverwalk.com). In February, everybody wants to be a cowboy during the **Stock Show and Rodeo** (☎ 210/225-5851; www.sarodeo. com) events at the AT&T Center. Since 1949, February has meant rodeo, with more than 2 weeks of roping and riding events, livestock judging, country bands, and carnivals—with headliner country stars (like Willie Nelson [1933–] and George Strait [1952–]) in concert.

SPRING   Two of the biggest events in South Texas take place in spring, starting with Austin's world-renowned **South by Southwest (SXSW) Music and Media Conference & Festival** (☎ 512/467-7979;

www.sxsw.com). The Austin Music Awards kick off this enormous—and enormously popular—conference (think Sundance but with a musical bent), with hundreds of concerts at dozens of venues all over town. Sign up months in advance, as the town gets crowded and it's hard to get a hotel room. It's usually held around the third week in March, often coinciding with the University of Texas at Austin's spring break.

In **San Antonio,** the whole town becomes a big party when celebrating its huge **Fiesta San Antonio** festival (☎ **877/723-4378** or 210/227-5191; www.fiesta-sa.org). Easter eggs filled with confetti are just one of the symbols of this 10-day celebration marking Texas's April 21, 1891 San Jacinto (Texas Independence Day). An elaborately costumed royal court presides over 10 days of parades, balls, food fests, sporting events, concerts, and art shows. And because Mexican and German culture are such a part of South Texas, locals celebrate the unique blend of these cultures' music (the lively button accordion and the *bajo sexto,* a 12-string Spanish guitar) during the **Tejano Conjunto Festival** (☎ **210/271-3151;** www.guadalupeculturalarts. org). This annual Guadalupe Cultural Arts Center event, held in early May, is home to some of the best *conjunto* music you'll ever hear. This is the largest event of its kind in the world.

SUMMER Juneteenth festivals are an important summer tradition in celebration of African American emancipation. Juneteenth (June 19) became a Texas state holiday in 1980, and events in Austin and San Antonio both generally include a parade, gospel singing, and family and children's events. In Austin, turn to the George Washington Carver Museum and Cultural Center

for a great line up of Juneteenth events (☎ **512/974-4926;** www. ci.austin.tx.us/carver). In San Antonio, celebrations include an outdoor jazz concert, **Gospel Fest,** parade, picnic, and more (☎ **800/447-3372** or 210/207-6700; www.visitsan antonio.com). The next month, everyone gets a big bang out of the many Fourth of July **Independence Day** celebrations. On Auditorium Shores at Lady Bird Lake, each year on July 4, the Austin Symphony Orchestra delights crowds with fireworks, cannon-fire, and a musical extravaganza, including a rousing rendition of the "1812 Overture" (☎ **888/4-MAESTRO** [888/623-7876] or 512/476-6064; www.austin symphony.org). In San Antonio, folks put out blankets on the grass at Woodland Park for the big city fireworks display. In **Luckenbach,** the big annual July 4 Family Picnic takes place (www.luckenbachtexas. com). And all of Texas seems to turn out for **Willie Nelson's Annual Fourth of July Picnic,** which changes venues each year, moving back and forth between Austin and San Antonio (www.willienelson. com). A line-up of some of Texas's favorite music stars always turns up for this all-day music fest with an Austin-meets-Woodstock quality. Then, on the last Saturday in August, the popular *Austin Chronicle* hosts its annual **Hot Sauce Festival** at Waterloo Park—the largest hot-sauce contest in the world, judged by celebrity chefs and food editors (☎ **512/454-5766;** www. austinchronicle.com). Hot bands play, too.

AUTUMN Diez y Seis ("Sixteen" in Spanish) is what locals call the 16th of September, when Mexico gained its independence from Spain, and its commemoration is feted at various venues in both Austin and San

Antonio. In Austin, at Plaza Saltillo and other sites, mariachis and folk dancers, *conjunto* and Tejano music, and great Tex-Mex fare make this a savory affair (☎ **512/974-6797** [Plaza Saltillo events] or 512/476-7502 [other events]). In San Antonio, various locations—including La Villita, the Arneson River Theatre, and Guadalupe Plaza—are filled with music and dance, a parade, and a *charreada* (rodeo) (☎ **800/447-3372** or 210/207-6700; www.visitsanantonio.com). Then, later in the month, Austin brims with visitors and locals who turn out for the hugely popular **Austin City Limits Music Festival,** held in Zilker Park. This 3-day music extravaganza kicked off in 2002 and has grown every year since with a stellar lineup of musical talent (☎ **866/GO-AUSTIN** [866/462-8784]; www.aclfestival.com). Then, one of my favorite fall events is Austin's **Texas Book Festival,** held at the Capitol (☎ **512/477-4055;** www.texasbookfestival.org). One of the largest literary events in the Southwest, this 2-day fundraiser (held in late October for Texas public libraries) draws literati from all over the U.S., though famous Texas writers and iconic locals (like *Lonesome Dove* screenwriter Bill Wittliff) are always the biggest draw.

Useful Websites

- **www.austin360.com:** The Austin *American-Statesman* newspaper website.

- **www.austintexas.org:** The Austin Convention & Visitor's Bureau website.

- **www.mysanantonio.com:** The San Antonio *Express-News'* website.

- **www.visitsanantonio.com:** The SA Convention & Visitor's Bureau website.

- **www.thesanantonioriver walk.com:** Website for the historic San Antonio *Paseo del Rio,* or River Walk.

- **www.texasmonthly.com:** Texas's hippest and most informative magazine has this helpful website featuring all that's new and happening in Texas, with reliable restaurant reviews, too.

Cell (mobile) telephones

If you're not from the U.S., you'll be appalled at the poor reach of the GSM (Global System for Mobile Communications) wireless network, which is used by much of the rest of the world. Your phone will probably work in most major U.S. cities; it definitely won't work in many rural areas. To see where GSM phones work in the U.S., check out www.t-mobile.com/coverage. And you may or may not be able to send SMS (text messaging) home.

To have the use of a cellular telephone while visiting central Texas, the easiest thing to do is buy a cheap prepaid cellphone. These are for sale in various outlets, but the best and least-expensive deal probably is offered at the local H-E-B grocery stores. Locally owned **Pocket Communications** is also in the prepaid cellphone business and has kiosks in some **H-E-B** stores. Go to www.heb.com to use the store locator.

Car Rentals

Visitors to Austin and San Antonio may want to rent a car unless they plan to stay downtown and not see things on the outskirts of town. San Antonio is probably more pedestrian-friendly than Austin, though you can get by fairly well in downtown Austin and SoCo, too. Stay near the River Walk and the Alamo in downtown San Antonio, as most attractions are nearby and those a bit farther away are easily accessible by a colorful city streetcar. In Austin, if you stay as close as you can to Congress Avenue, you'll probably be just fine. Although

Capital Metro discontinued its 'Dillo streetcar lines, downtown city buses run along a grid, so you can get where you're going without much problem. Most hotels in both cities have convenient shuttles to take you from the airport into the downtown area.

Getting **There**

By Plane

Austin and San Antonio both boast major airports not far from their respective city centers. **The Austin-Bergstrom International Airport** (airport code AUS; ☎ 512/530-ABIA [512/530-2242]; www.ci.austin.tx.us/austinairport) is the larger and newer of the two and is situated 8 miles (13km) southeast of downtown Austin on Highway 71E (Ben White Blvd.). Built in 1999 on the site of the former Bergstrom Air Force Base, this airport is big, bright, and full of live local Texana music performances and locally-owned restaurants' food. One of the perks here is that it is home to Jet-Blue and other airlines, with frequent direct flights to New York and other major U.S. cities. The **San Antonio International Airport** (airport code SAT; ☎ 210/207-3411; www.sanantonio.gov/aviation) is undergoing a renovation and enlargement, so sometimes getting in and out of the terminals can mean walking through construction sites. When the project is done, this now-small airport will serve more people and more places. Currently, one of its biggest pluses is that it's only 7 miles (11km) north of downtown—a straight shot on Highway 281. This airport is compact and well marked, and has two terminals. San Antonio

doesn't feature as many direct flights as Austin—you often have to stop in Houston or Dallas to get to San Antonio from most major cities. However, it's small enough that you won't get lost or spend a lot of time looking for your gate. When seeking a direct flight to L.A. or New York, you may want to fly in and out of Austin, instead.

Getting to and from the Airports

Rent a car and drive into the city (see "Car Rentals," above), or take a taxi or airport shuttle bus to your hotel. Hotel shuttles, city bus service, and limos are all available at both airports.

In San Antonio, taxi cabs are available at the lower level curbside at Terminal 1 and at the front curbside of Terminal 2 (both just outside baggage claim). Airport taxis will cost about $30 for downtown destinations. VIA Metropolitan Transit's bus no. 5 is the least expensive ($1.10) way to get downtown. The trip should take from 40 to 50 minutes, and you'll need exact change. Another good option in San Antonio is a shuttle; SATRANS (☎ **800/ 868-7707** or 210/281-9900; www.saairportshuttle.com), with a booth outside each of the terminals, offers shared van service from the airport to the downtown hotels for $18 per person one-way, $32 round-trip. Prices to other destinations vary; call or check the website for specifics. Vans run from about 7am until 1am; phone 24 hours in advance for van pickup from your hotel.

In Austin, taxi cabs are available at the lower level curbside, outside of the baggage claim, and the average fare downtown is $25. If you're not in a rush, SuperShuttle (☎ **800/ BLUE-VAN** [800/258-3826] or 512/ 258-3826; www.supershuttle.com) offers a less expensive alternative to cabs. Prices average $12 one-way ($22 round-trip) for trips to a downtown hotel. The downside is the shuttle service can take a long time—you are sharing your ride with others, and there's the chance you may be dropped off last. You don't have to book in advance for pickups at the airport, but you do need to phone 24 hours ahead of time to arrange for a pickup when you're leaving town. For $1, you can go from the airport to downtown or the university area on a city bus, the Airport Flyer (Route 100). It runs until about midnight. The passenger pickup is outside the arrival gates, close to the end of the concourse. Buses depart about every 40 minutes. During rush hour, traffic can really clog Highway 71. Be sure to allow extra time when you need to catch a flight.

By Car
Both Austin and San Antonio are located in South Central Texas along Interstate 35. I-35 is the north-south approach to Austin; it intersects with Highway 290, a major east-west thoroughfare, and Highway 183, which also runs roughly north-south through town. If you're staying on the west side of Austin, hook up with Loop 1, almost always called Mo-Pac

by locals, and even on signage you'll see **Mo-Pac Expressway** or even **Mopac Boulevard** after the Missouri Pacific Railroad (or "MoPac"). The original section of the highway was built in the 1970s along the right-of-way of the Missouri Pacific Railroad (now owned by Union Pacific),and trains still run on the median strip of the highway. When driving from the Austin airport, take Highway 71 going west to South Congress Avenue, where you'll exit and turn right, traveling north on Congress Avenue through SoCo and toward the State Capitol.

I-35 is also the north-south approach to San Antonio, which intersects with Highway 281. Highway 281 will take you to downtown (exit at Commerce Street). I-410 and Highway 1604, which encircle the city, are referred to as Loop 410 and Loop 1604.

By Train and Bus
The **Amtrak** (☎ 800/872-7245; www.amtrak.com) Texas Eagle makes stops in both Austin and San Antonio, and connects the two cities with a one-way fare of about $15. The Austin station is just west of downtown (250 N. Lamar Blvd.; ☎ **512/476-5684**). In San Antonio, the Amtrak station is located at St. Paul's Square between Sunset Station and the Alamodome near downtown (350 Hoefgen St.; ☎ **210/ 223-3226**). Bus service is also available to and from both cities via **Greyhound** (☎ **800/231-2222**; www. greyhound.com) with an average one-way fare of about $22 (a bit less if you book online). The Austin Greyhound terminal is located at 916 E. Koenig Lane (☎ **512/458-4463**), and the San Antonio Greyhound terminal is located at 500 N. St Marys St. (☎ **210/270-5824**).

Getting **Around**

On Foot

Visitors to San Antonio will enjoy strolling from one downtown tourist attraction to another, walking along the beautifully landscaped River Walk, or traveling on foot to historic sites along the lovely Mission Trail. Jaywalking is a ticketable offense, but it's rarely enforced. Austin was laid out in a grid in 1839, resting along the northern shore of the Colorado River (a part now called Lady Bird Lake), bounded by Shoal Creek to the west and Waller Creek to the east, so visitors will find that getting around downtown is simple. Congress Avenue runs from the State Capitol to Lady Bird Lake, and numbered streets cross the avenue, going east and west.

By Car

Many travelers coming from Dallas or Houston find that a quick trip (about an hour and 15 minutes to the Capitol City or the Alamo City is worth the relatively short drive. Austin is known for terrible traffic congestion, especially along I-35 and the Mo-Pac (Loop 1) expressway during rush hours. San Antonio has two main loops encircling the city—Loop 410 and Loop 1604—and several other highways, such as Interstate 10 and Highway 281, feed the city from these outlaying loops. San Antonio roads are said to be laid along old cattle trails, so sometimes they criss-cross and get confusing. Traffic isn't as bad in San Antonio as in Austin, except on Highway 281-North near Stone Oak, on Interstate 10 and Loop 1604, and on Loop 410 during rush hours. Interstate 10 rarely has traffic, though it does see its share of trucks. Downtown San Antonio may not seem as

traffic-crushed as Austin, which seems to be outgrowing its roadways. Both cities are trying to keep up with growth, so road construction—especially on Loop 410 in San Antonio—can also create problems.

By Taxi

The City of Austin regulates taxicab rates. These rates apply to all taxicab companies and drivers. The current meter rate is $2.55 for the first ½ mile, plus 30¢ for each additional ½ mile. Waiting time is $27 per hour.

By city ordinance, trips which originate at the airport are subject to a $1 surcharge. There is no additional charge for extra passengers. As many as four passengers may ride for the price of one passenger.

In San Antonio, all taxis charge $2 for the first ⅕ of a mile and $2.15 for each mile thereafter (plus gas surcharge, if applicable). Wait time and traffic delay is $24 per hour. There is a $1 surcharge for all trips that originate between 9pm and 5am. The minimum downtown fare is $5. The minimum airport departure fare is $11.50. Many outlying communities have minimum fares.

By Bus

Austin's public transportation system, Capital Metropolitan Transportation Authority (www.capmetro. org), operates more than 50 bus lines and features low fares. A single fare on a Cap Metro bus is $1, and a day pass costs $2. UT Shuttle bus fares are $1. There are discounts available for seniors, military with ID, and students.

San Antonio's public transportation system, VIA Metropolitan Transit Service, offers regular bus service for $1.10, with an additional 15¢ charge for transfers. You'll need exact change. Call ☎ **210/362-2020** for transit information, check the website at www.viainfo.net, or stop in one of VIA's many service centers (which you can find by checking the website). The most convenient for visitors is the downtown center, 211 W. Commerce St. (☎ **210/475-9008**), open Monday to Friday 7am to 6pm, Saturday 9am to 2pm. Downtown VIA streetcars are color-coded and provide an easy way to jump on board and head to your next downtown-area attraction. Seniors and riders with limited mobility who have valid IDs can ride the bus and use the streetcar service for just 25¢ 9am to 3pm weekdays and for free all day on weekends.

Fast **Facts**

APARTMENT RENTALS For short-term rentals, your best bet is **www.craigslist.org**. Click on the "apts/housing" link and put "Austin or San Antonio" into the search bar, and you'll likely come up with many current listings directly from the unit's owner (or the person subletting). Also check **www.sublet.com**. To find house exchanges, check out **Homelink International** (www.homelink.org), which has thousands of listings in several countries, and **Homebase Holidays** (www.homebase-hols.com).

AREA CODES Austin has a 512 area code, and San Antonio has a 210 area code.

ATM/CASH LOCATIONS There are ATMs throughout both cities, especially in the downtown areas and near city attractions. Unless you go to your bank, you'll be charged a fee from $1.50 to $3. The **Cirrus** (☎ **800/424-7787;** www.mastercard.com) and **PLUS** (☎ **800/843-7587**) networks span the globe, so look at the back of your bank card to see which network you're on, and then call or check online for ATM locations. Be sure to find out your daily withdrawal limit before you go. If you have a crisis and need to go to an American Express office about a lost or stolen card or to get cash, if you're in San Antonio go to **The Alamo Travel Group, Inc.** (9000 Wurzbach Rd.; ☎ **210/593-0084**). It's open Monday to Friday 9am to 5pm.

BUSINESS HOURS Banks are usually open Monday to Friday 9am to 4pm, Saturday 9am to 1pm. Drive-up windows are open 7am to 6pm Monday to Friday and 9am to noon on Saturday. Office hours are generally weekdays from 9am to 5pm. Shops tend to be open from 9 or 10am until 5:30 or 6pm Monday to Saturday, with shorter hours on Sunday. Most malls are open Monday to Saturday from 10am to 9pm, Sunday from noon to 6pm.

CLIMATE See "The Weather," p 188.

CREDIT CARDS Credit cards are a safe way to carry money. They provide a convenient record of all your expenses and generally offer good exchange rates. You can also withdraw cash advances from your credit cards at banks and ATMs, provided you know your PIN.

DENTISTS To find a dentist near you in San Antonio, contact the **San Antonio District Dental Society** (3355 Cherry Ridge St.; ☎ **210/732-1264**) or, in Austin, the **Capital**

Area Dental Society, (☎ 512/335-1405).

DOCTORS For a referral in San Antonio, contact the **Bexar County Medical Society** (6243 W. IH 10; ☎ 210/301-4391; www.bcms.org) Monday through Friday from 8am to 5pm, and in Austin contact the **Travis County Medical Society** (4300 North Lamar Blvd.; ☎ 512/206-1249; www.tcms.com).

DRUGSTORES Most branches of CVS and Walgreens, the major chain pharmacies in Austin and San Antonio, are open late Monday through Saturday. There's a CVS in downtown San Antonio at 211 Losoya St./River Walk (☎ 210/224-9293). In Austin, there is a downtown CVS pharmacy at 500 Congress Ave (at 5th St.) (☎ 512-478-1091). Call ☎ 800/925-4733 to find the Walgreens nearest you.

ELECTRICITY Like Canada, the United States uses 110 to 120 volts AC (60 cycles), compared to 220 to 240 volts AC (50 cycles) in most of Europe, Australia, and New Zealand. If your small appliances use 220 to 240 volts, you'll need a 110-volt transformer and a plug adapter with two flat parallel pins to operate them in Texas. Downward converters that change 220 to 240 volts to 110 to 120 volts are difficult to find in the United States, so bring one with you.

EMBASSIES/CONSULATES All embassies are located in the nation's capital, Washington, D.C. Some consulates are located in major U.S. cities, and most nations have a mission to the United Nations in New York City. If your country isn't listed below, call for directory information in Washington, D.C. (☎ 202/555-1212), or log on to **www.embassy.org/embassies**.

The embassy of **Australia** is at 1601 Massachusetts Ave. NW, Washington, DC 20036 (☎ 202/797-3000; www.usa.embassy.gov.au). There are consulates in New York, Honolulu, Houston, Los Angeles, and San Francisco.

The embassy of **Canada** is at 501 Pennsylvania Ave. NW, Washington, DC 20001 (☎ 202/682-1740; www.canadianembassy.org). Other Canadian consulates are in Buffalo (New York), Detroit, Los Angeles, New York City, and Seattle.

The embassy of **Ireland** is at 2234 Massachusetts Ave. NW, Washington, DC 20008 (☎ 202/462-3939; www.embassyofireland.org). Irish consulates are in Boston, Chicago, New York, San Francisco, and other cities. See their website for a complete listing.

The embassy of **New Zealand** is at 37 Observatory Circle, Washington, DC 20008 (☎ 202/328-4800; www.nzembassy.org). New Zealand consulates are in Los Angeles, Salt Lake City, San Francisco, and Seattle.

The embassy of the **United Kingdom** is at 3100 Massachusetts Ave. NW, Washington, DC 20008 (☎ 202/588-6500; www.britainusa.com). Other British consulates are in Atlanta, Boston, Chicago, Cleveland, Houston, Los Angeles, New York, San Francisco, and Seattle.

EMERGENCIES For police, fire, or medical emergencies, dial ☎ 911.

GASOLINE (PETROL) Gasoline cost $2.59 per gallon at press time, and taxes are already included in the printed price. One U.S. gallon equals 3.8 liters or .85 Imperial gallons.

HOLIDAYS Banks, government offices, post offices, and many stores, restaurants, and museums are closed on the following legal national holidays: January 1 (New

Year's Day), the third Monday in January (Martin Luther King, Jr., Day), the third Monday in February (Presidents' Day), the last Monday in May (Memorial Day), July 4th (Independence Day), the first Monday in September (Labor Day), the second Monday in October (Columbus Day), November 11 (Veterans' Day/Armistice Day), the fourth Thursday in November (Thanksgiving Day), and December 25 (Christmas). Also, the Tuesday following the first Monday in November is Election Day and is a federal government holiday in presidential-election years (held every 4 years, and next in 2012). Easter week (called Holy Week in San Antonio) is a big event in this largely Catholic and Mexican American community, and many businesses and schools close the Monday after Easter. Many stores are not open on Sundays.

HOSPITALS The main downtown hospital in San Antonio is **Baptist Medical Center,** 111 Dallas St. (📞 210/297-7000). **Christus Santa Rosa Health Care Corp.,** 333 N. Santa Rosa Ave. (📞 **210/704-2011**), is also downtown. Contact the **San Antonio Medical Foundation** (📞 210/614-3724) for information about other medical facilities in the city. In Austin, **Brackenridge Hospital** is the closest downtown facility, located at 601 E. 15th St. (📞 512/324-7000).

LIBRARIES San Antonio's magnificent main library is located downtown at 600 Soledad Plaza (📞 **210/207-2500**). Austin's **Faulk Central Library** is located downtown at 800 Guadalupe St. (📞 **512/974-7400**).

LIQUOR LAWS The legal drinking age in Texas is 21. Under-age drinkers can legally imbibe, as long as they stay within sight of their legal-age parents or spouses, but they need to be prepared to show proof of the relationship. Open containers are prohibited in public and in vehicles. Liquor laws are strictly enforced, and the rules are sometimes confusing. There are many dry communities in Texas where buying and even transporting alcohol is not legal. If you're concerned, check www.tabc.state.tx.us for the entire Texas alcoholic beverage code. Bars close at 2am on Saturdays, and many close as early as midnight on all other nights of the week. Liquor stores do not stay open late, and they cannot be open on Sundays. See p 19 for more information.

MAIL At press time, domestic postage rates were 28¢ for a postcard and 44¢ for a letter. For international mail, a first-class letter of up to 1 ounce costs 98¢ (75¢ to Canada, 79¢ to Mexico); a first-class postcard costs the same. For more information, go to **www.usps.com** and click on "Calculate Postage."

NEWSPAPERS & MAGAZINES The *San Antonio Express-News* (www. mysanantonio.com) and the *Austin American-Statesman* (www.statesman.com) are the only mainstream sources of news in these cities.

PASSPORTS For Residents of Australia: You can pick up an application from your local post office or any branch of Passports Australia, but you must schedule an interview at the passport office to present your application materials. Call the **Australian Passport Information Service** at 📞 **131-232** or visit the government website at www. passports.gov.au.

For Residents of Canada: Passport applications are available at travel agencies throughout Canada or from the central **Passport Office,** Department of Foreign Affairs and International Trade,

Gatineau, QC K1A 0G3 (☎ 800/567-6868; www.ppt.gc.ca). Canadian children who travel must have their own passports.

For Residents of Ireland: You can apply for a 10-year passport at the **Passport Office,** Setanta Centre, Molesworth Street, Dublin 2 (☎ 01/671-1633; **www.foreign affairs.gov.ie)**. Those under age 18 and over age 65 must apply for a 3-year passport. You can also apply at 1A South Mall, Cork (☎ 021/494-4700) or at most main post offices.

For Residents of New Zealand: You can pick up a passport application at any New Zealand Passports Office or download it from their website. Contact the **Passports Office** at ☎ 0800/225-050 in New Zealand or 04/474-8100, or log on to **www.dia.govt.nz.**

For Residents of the United Kingdom: To pick up an application for a standard 10-year passport (5-yr. passport for children under age 16), visit your nearest passport office, major post office, or travel agency, or contact the **United Kingdom Passport Service** (☎ 0300/222-0000, **www.ips. gov.uk)**.

POLICE Call ☎ 911 in an emergency. For non-emergency calls, dial ☎ 311.

POST OFFICE In San Antonio, the most convenient post office for visitors is at 615 E Houston St (☎ 210/212-8046), at North Alamo Street, in the San Antonio Federal Building. In Austin, the main post office is located at 8225 Cross Park Dr. (☎ 512/342-1259); more convenient for visitors are the Capitol Station (111 E. 17th St., in the LBJ Building) and the Downtown Station (510 Guadalupe St.). For information on other locations, phone ☎ 800/275-8777.

SAFETY The crime rates in both Austin and San Antonio have not risen substantially in recent years, and there's a strong police presence downtown; muggings, pickpocketings, and purse snatchings are rare. Still, use common sense as you would anywhere else: Walk only in well-lit, well-populated streets. In San Antonio, it's generally not a good idea to stroll south of Durango Avenue after dark, and in Austin, it is best not to stroll in areas of East Austin (east of I-35) after dark.

SMOKING In San Antonio, smoking is prohibited in all public buildings and common public areas (that includes hotel lobbies, museums, enclosed malls, and so on). However, it is permitted in bars or specific enclosed areas of restaurants, on designated restaurant patios, and in smoking sections of restaurants that comply with city codes, bus stops, bingo halls, comedy clubs, and other specially-designated places. In Austin, the smoking ban is more stringent: It is prohibited in all public buildings and common public areas (that includes hotel lobbies, museums, enclosed malls, and so on), but it's also prohibited in enclosed bars or enclosed bar areas of restaurants. However, smoking is permitted in open-air bar areas.

TAXES The sales tax in Texas is 6.25%; however, Texas cities, counties, transit authorities, and special purpose districts have the option of imposing an additional local sales tax for a combined total of state and local taxes of 8.25%. In San Antonio, the hotel/motel bed occupancy tax rate is 9% of net receipts, and the City also collects 1.75% for Bexar County—a total of a whopping

16.25%. In Austin, the state and local hotel/motel bed occupancy taxes total 15%.

TAXIS Call Yellow Cab in Austin (☎ 512/452-9999) and San Antonio (☎ 210/222-2222).

TELEPHONES For directory assistance, dial ☎ 411.

TIME San Antonio and Austin (and all of the rest of Texas, except for the El Paso area) are in the Central Time Zone. The continental United States is divided into **four time zones:** Eastern Standard Time (EST), Central Standard Time (CST), Mountain Standard Time (MST), and Pacific Standard Time (PST). Alaska and Hawaii have their own zones. For example, noon in New York City (EST) is 11am in Chicago (CST), 10am in Denver (MST), 9am in Los Angeles (PST), 8am in Anchorage (AST), and 7am in Honolulu (HST).

Daylight saving time is in effect from 2am on the second Sunday in March through 2am on the first Sunday in November, except in Arizona, Hawaii, the U.S. Virgin Islands, and Puerto Rico. Daylight saving time moves the clock 1 hour ahead of standard time.

TIPPING Tips are an important part of many workers' incomes, and gratuities are the standard way of showing appreciation for services provided. (Tipping is certainly not compulsory if the service is poor!) In hotels, tip **bellhops** at least $1 per bag ($2–$3 per bag if you have a lot of luggage) and tip the **chamber staff** $1 to $2 per day (more if you've left a disaster area for him or her to clean up). Tip the **doorman** or **concierge** only if he or she has provided you with some specific

service (for example, calling a cab for you or obtaining difficult-to-get theater tickets). Tip the **valet-parking attendant** $1 to $2 every time you get your car.

In restaurants, bars, and nightclubs, tip **service staff** 15% to 20% of the check, tip **bartenders** 10% to 15%, tip **checkroom attendants** $1 per garment, and tip **valet-parking attendants** $1 per vehicle.

As for other service personnel, tip **cab drivers** 15% of the fare; tip **skycaps** at airports at least $1 per bag ($2–$3 per bag if you have a lot of luggage); and tip **hairdressers** and **barbers** 15% to 20%.

TOILETS You won't find public toilets or "restrooms" on the streets in most U.S. cities, but they can be found in hotel lobbies, bars, restaurants, museums, department stores, railway and bus stations, and service stations. Large hotels and fast-food restaurants are probably the best bet for good, clean facilities. If possible, avoid the toilets at parks and beaches, which tend to be dirty; some may be unsafe. Restaurants and bars in resorts or heavily visited areas may reserve their restrooms for patrons. Some establishments display a notice indicating this. You can ignore this sign or, better yet, avoid arguments by paying for a cup of coffee or a soft drink, which will qualify you as a patron.

USEFUL PHONE NUMBERS For transit information in San Antonio, call ☎ 210/362-2020; call ☎ 210/226-3232 for time and temperature. In Austin, get the time and temperature by dialing ☎ 512/476-7744.

VISAS For information about U.S. visas, go to http://travel.state.gov and click on "Visas."

Airline, Hotel & Car Rental Websites

Major Airlines

AEROMEXICO
www.aeromexico.com
AIR CANADA
www.aircanada.com
AIR FRANCE
www.airfrance.com
AIR NEW ZEALAND
www.airnewzealand.com
AMERICAN AIRLINES
www.aa.com
BRITISH AIRWAYS
www.british-airways.com
CONTINENTAL AIRLINES
www.continental.com
DELTA AIR LINES
www.delta.com
JETBLUE
www.jetblue.com
LUFTHANSA
www.lufthansa.com
NORTHWEST AIRLINES
www.flynaa.com
QANTAS AIRWAYS
www.quantas.com
UNITED AIRLINES
www.united.com

US AIRWAYS
www.usairways.com
WEST JET
www.westjet.com

Car Rental Agencies

ALAMO
www.alamo.com
AVIS
www.avis.com
BUDGET
www.budget.com
DOLLAR
www.dollar.com
ENTERPRISE
www.enterprise.com
HERTZ
www.hertz.com

Major Hotel & Motel Chains

BEST WESTERN INTERNATIONAL
www.bestwestern.com
FOUR SEASONS
www.fourseasons.com

HILTON HOTELS
www.hilton.com
HOLIDAY INN
www.holidayinn.com
HYATT
www.hyatt.com
INTERCONTINENTAL HOTELS & RESORTS
www.ichotelsgroup.com
MARRIOTT
www.marriott.com
RADISSON HOTELS & RESORTS
www.radisson.com
RAMADA WORLDWIDE
www.ramada.com
SHERATON HOTELS & RESORTS
www.starwoodhotels. com/sheraton
WESTIN HOTELS & RESORTS
www.starwoodhotels. com/westin

Index

See also Accommodations and Restaurant indexes, below.

Photo **Credits**

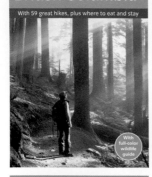
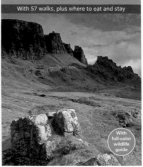